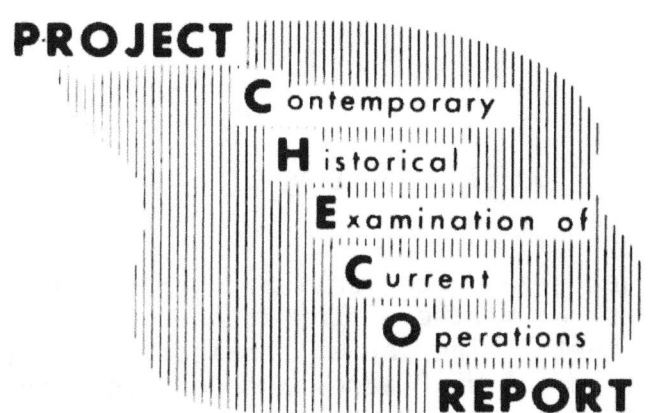

PROJECT CHECO REPORT

VNAF IMPROVEMENT AND MODERNIZATION PROGRAM, JULY 1971 - DECEMBER 1973 (U)

1 JANUARY 1975

CHECO/CORONA HARVEST DIVISION
OPERATIONS ANALYSIS OFFICE
HQ PACAF

Prepared by:
Captain Thomas D. DesBrisay
Project CHECO 7th AF

PROJECT CHECO REPORTS

The counterinsurgency and unconventional warfare environment of Southeast Asia has resulted in the employment of USAF airpower to meet a multitude of requirements. The varied applications of airpower have involved the full spectrum of USAF aerospace vehicles, support equipment, and manpower. As a result, there has been an accumulation of operational data and experiences that, as a priority, must be collected, documented, and analyzed as to current and future impact upon USAF policies, concepts, and doctrine.

Fortunately, the value of collecting and documenting our SEA experiences was recognized at an early date. In 1962, Hq USAF directed CINCPACAF to establish an activity that would be primarily responsive to Air Staff requirements and direction, and would provide timely and analycal studies of USAF combat operations in SEA.

Project CHECO, an acronym for Contemporary Historical Examination o Current Operations, was established to meet this Air Staff requirement. Managed by Hq PACAF, with elements at Hq 7AF and 7/13AF, Project CHECO provides a scholarly, "on-going" historical examination, documentation, and reporting on USAF policies, concepts, and doctrine in PACOM. This CHECO report is part of the overall documentation and examination which is being accomplished. It is an authentic source for an assessment of the effectiveness of USAF airpower in PACOM when used in proper context. The reader must view the study in relation to the events and circumstance at the time of its preparation--recognizing that it was prepared on a contemporary basis which restricted perspective and that the author's research was limited to records available within his local headquarters area.

ROBERT E. HILLER
Director of Operations Analysis
DCS/Operations

DEPARTMENT OF THE AIR FORCE
HEADQUARTERS PACIFIC AIR FORCES
APO SAN FRANCISCO 96553

REPLY TO
ATTN OF: XOAD

15 July 1975

SUBJECT: Project CHECO Report, "VNAF Improvement and Modernization Program, July 1970 - December 1973 (U)"

TO: SEE DISTRIBUTION PAGE

1. Attached is a TOP SECRET document. It should be transported, stored, safeguarded, and accounted for in accordance with applicable security directives. Retain or destroy in accordance with AFR 205-1. Do not return.

2. This letter does not contain classified information and may be declassified if attachment is removed.

FOR THE COMMANDER IN CHIEF

V. H. Gallacher

V. H. GALLACHER, Lt Col, USAF
Chief, CHECO/CORONA HARVEST Division
Directorate of Operations Analysis

1 Atch
(TS) Project CHECO Report, "VNAF Improvement and Modernization Program, July 1971 - December 1973, 1 January 1975

DISTRIBUTION LIST

1. SECRETARY OF THE AIR FORCE

    a. SAFAA 1 (1)
    b. SAFLL 1 (2)
    c. SAFOI 2 (3-4)
    d. SAFUS 1 (5)

2. HEADQUARTERS USAF

    a. AFNB 1 (6)
    b. AFCCS
        (1) AFCCN 1 (7)
        (2) AFCVC 1 (8)
        (3) AFCHOS 2 (9-10)
    c. AFCSA
        (1) AF/SAG 1 (11)
        (2) AF/SAMI 1 (12)
    d. AFIGO
        (1) AFOSI/IVOA 3 (13-15)
        (2) IGS 1 (16)
    e. AFIS
        (1) INDOC 1 (17)
        (2) INZA 1 (18)
        (3) INTX 1 (19)
        (4) INAKB 1 (20)
        (5) INYXA 1 (21)
    f. AFODC
        (1) AFPRC 1 (22)
        (2) AFPRE 1 (23)
        (3) AFPRM 1 (24)
    g. AFDP 1 (25)
    h. AFRD
        (1) AFRDP 1 (26)
        (2) AFRDQ 1 (27)
        (3) AFRDQPC........... 1 (28)
        (4) AFRDR 1 (29)
        (5) AFRDQL 1 (30)

    i. AFSDC
        (1) AFLGX 1 (31)
        (2) AFLGF 1 (32)
        (3) AFLGT 1 (33)
        (4) AFLGY 1 (34)
    j. AFXO
        (1) AFXOD 1 (35)
        (2) AFXODC 1 (36)
        (3) AFXODD 1 (37)
        (4) AFXODL 1 (38)
        (5) AFXOOG 1 (39)
        (6) AFXOSL 1 (40)
        (7) AFXOOSN 1 (41)
        (8) AFXOOSS 1 (42)
        (9) AFXOOSR 1 (43)
        (10) AFXOOSW 1 (44)
        (11) AFXOOSZ 1 (45)
        (12) AFXOXAA 6 (46-51)

3. MAJOR COMMAND

    a. TAC
        (1) HEADQUARTERS
            (a) XPSY 1 (52)
            (b) DOC 1 (53)
            (c) DREA 1 (54)
            (d) IN 1 (55)
        (2) AIR FORCES
            (a) 12AF
                1. DOO 1 (56)
                2. IN 1 (57)
            (b) USAFSOF(DO) ... 1 (58)
        (3) WINGS
            (a) 1SOW(DOI) 1 (59)
            (b) 23TFW(DOI).... 1 (60)
            (c) 27TRW(DOI).... 1 (61)
            (d) 33TFW(DOI).... 1 (62)
            (e) 35TFW(DOI).... 1 (63)
            (f) 366TFW(DOI)... 1 (64)

iv

(g)	67TRW(DOI)	1 (65)
(h)	316TAW(DOX)....	1 (66)
(i)	317TAW(DOI)....	1 (67)
(j)	474TFW(DOI)....	1 (68)
(k)	463TAW(DOX)....	1 (69)
(l)	58TAC FTR TNG WG	1 (70)
(m)	354TFW(DOI)....	1 (71)

    (4) TAC CENTERS, SCHOOLS
        (a) USAFTAWC(IN)... 1 (72)
        (b) USAFTFWC(DR)... 1 (73)
        (c) USAFAGOS(EDA).. 1 (74)

b. SAC

    (1) HEADQUARTERS
        (a) XPX........... 1 (75)
        (b) LG 1 (76)
        (c) IN 1 (77)
        (d) NR 1 (78)
        (e) HO 1 (79)

    (2) AIR FORCES
        (a) 2AF(IN) 1 (80)
        (b) 8AF(DOA) 2 (81-82)
        (c) 15AF(INCE).... 1 (83)

c. MAC

    (1) HEADQUARTERS
        (a) DOI 1 (84)
        (b) DOO 1 (85)
        (c) CSEH 1 (86)
        (d) 60MAWG(DOI)... 1 (87)

    (2) MAC SERVICES
        (a) ARRS(XP) 1 (88)

d. ADC

    (1) HEADQUARTERS
        (a) DOA 1 (89)
        (b) DOT 1 (90)

    (2) AIR DIVISIONS
        (a) 25AD(DOI) 1 (91)

e. ATC
    (1) DOSPI 1 (92)

f. AFSC

    (1) HEADQUARTERS
        (a) XRP 1 (93)
        (b) SDA 1 (94)
        (c) HO 1 (95)
        (d) ASD(RWST) 1 (96)
        (e) RADC(DOT) 1 (97)
        (f) ADTC(CCN) 1 (98)
        (g) ADTC(DLOSL) .. 1 (99)
        (h) ESD(YWA) 1 (100)
        (i) AFATL(DL) 1 (101)

g. USAFSS

    (1) HEADQUARTERS
        (a) AFSCC(SUR) ... 2 (102-103)

h. USAFSOS

    (1) HEADQUARTERS
        (a) ESD 1 (104)

i. PACAF

    (1) HEADQUARTERS
        (a) IN 1 (105)
        (b) XOEA......... 2 (106-107)
        (c) CSH 1 (108)
        (d) DC 1 (109)
        (e) LG 1 (110)
        (f) XOAD......... 6 (111-116)

    (2) AIR FORCES
        (a) 5AF
            <u>1</u>. CSH 1 (117)
            <u>2</u>. XP 1 (118)
            <u>3</u>. DO 1 (119)
        (b) 13AF(CSH)..... 1 (120)

    (3) AIR DIVISIONS
        (a) 313AD(DOI) ... 1 (121)
        (b) 314AD(XP) 1 (122)
        (c) 327AD(IN) 1 (123)

    (4) WINGS
        (a) 8TFW(DON) 1 (124)
        (b) 56SOW(WHD) ... 1 (125)
        (c) 388TFW(DO) ... 1 (126)
        (d) 405TFW(DOI).... 1 (127)
        (e) 432TRW(DOI)... 1 (128)

j. CINCUSAFE

    (1) HEADQUARTERS
        (a) DOA 1 (129)
        (b) DOLO 1 (130)
        (c) DOOW 1 (131)
        (d) XP 1 (132)

    (2) AIR FORCES
        (a) 3AF(DO) 1 (133)
        (b) 16AF(DO) 1 (134)

    (3) WINGS
        (a) 401TFW(DCOI) 1 (135)
        (b) 513TAW(DOI) 1 (136)

4. SEPARATE OPERATING AGENCIES

    a. DMAAC/PR 1 (137)

    b. 3825 Acad Svs Gp
       (1) AUL/LSE-69-108 .... 2 (138-139)
       (2) HOA 2 (140-141)

    c. Analytic Svs, Inc 1 (142)

    d. AFAG(THAILAND) 1 (143)

TABLE OF CONTENTS (U)

	Page
LIST OF TABLES	ix
ABOUT THE AUTHOR	x
OVERVIEW	xi

CHAPTER

I. INTRODUCTION 1

    Background 1
    VNAF Status--July 1971 5
        Fighter Capabilities 6
        Fixed-wing Gunship Capabilities 9
        Airlift Capabilities 9
        Helicopter Capabilities 11
        Reconnaissance Capabilities 13
        Air Logistics Capabilities 13
        Training Capabilities 14
        Facilities and Base Support Capabilities 15
    The Role of Advisors in the I&M Program 16

II. EVOLUTION OF THE I&M PROGRAM, JULY 1971-SEPTEMBER 1973 22

    Project 981/982 22
    FSR-73 23
    Project Enhance 31
    Project Enhance Plus 34
    Post-Cease-Fire Developments 45

III. VNAF OPERATIONAL CAPABILITIES 56

    Introduction--Command and Control Considerations 56
    Fighters 60
        Evolution of the Fighter Force 62
        Final Preparations for Receipt of F-5Es 69
        Fighter Limitations 70
    Fixed-wing Gunships 76
    Airlift 81
    Helicopters 91
    Reconnaissance 95
        Visual Reconnaissance/FACs 95
        Photo Reconnaissance 100
        Electronic Surveillance 101
        Coastal Surveillance 103
    VNAF Intelligence 106
    Proposed Improvements to VNAF Combat Capabilities 107

	Page
IV. SUPPORT FUNCTIONS	113
Training	113
Pre-Enhance Plus	113
Post-Enhance Plus	117
Post-Cease-Fire	119
Vietnamese Capacity for Training	123
Logistics (Supply and Maintenance)	125
Mid-1971 Through Late 1972	126
Enhance Plus and Its Aftermath	127
Air Logistics Command Computerization Problems	133
Base Capabilities Versus Depot Capabilities	137
Progress Toward Logistics Self-Sufficiency	141
Facilities	146
Facilities Transfer	146
Civil Engineering	150
Communications-Electronics (C-E)	155
V. FACTORS AFFECTING VIETNAMIZATION	164
U.S. Advisors	164
Transition to DAO	170
VNAF Morale	174
VI. POST-CEASE-FIRE ASSESSMENT	181
Military Activity and the Enemy Threat	181
RVNAF and VNAF Capabilities	184
Assessment of Progress and Outlook for the Future	186
APPENDIX--VNAF Squadron Activations and Disposition	190
FOOTNOTES	197
GLOSSARY	220

LIST OF TABLES (U)

Table	Title	Page
1	VNAF Fighter Squadrons--July 1971 vs July 1973	61
2	VNAF Gunship Squadrons--July 1971 vs July 1973	77
3	VNAF Transport Squadrons--July 1971 vs July 1973	82
4	VNAF Helicopter Squadrons--July 1971 vs July 1973	92
5	VNAF Reconnaissance Squadrons--July 1971 vs July 1973	96
6	VNAF Liaison Squadrons--July 1971 vs July 1973	97
7	VNAF CROC/ROC Status	109
8	Transfer of U.S. Facilities to the VNAF	151
9	By Service Transfer of U.S. Facilities to the VNAF-- 1 November 1972 Through 28 January 1973	152
10	NAVAIDs/AC&W Site Status as of November 1973	161

ABOUT THE AUTHOR (U)

(U) Captain Thomas D. Des Brisay entered active military duty in August 1965 as a Distinguished Air Force ROTC Graduate. Following CONUS tours as an AFIT student and an Operations Research Officer, he served in 1968 and 1969 as an Operations Research Officer at Seventh Air Force, Tan Son Nhut AB, Republic of Vietnam, and as a Staff Scientist at Task Force Alpha, Nakhon Phanom RTAFB, Thailand. During the period 1969 through 1973, Captain Des Brisay served at Headquarters PACAF where he wrote a series of studies on Air Force combat operations in Laos and North Vietnam, and co-authored a CHECO report on F-111 Operations in SEA. Between July 1973 and June 1974, he was editor for Project CHECO's Udorn Detachment. Captain Des Brisay holds a Bachelor of Science degree in Mathematics from the University of Portland, and a Master's of Computing Science degree from Texas A&M University. He has completed Squadron Officer School and is currently enrolled in the Air Command and Staff College Non-resident Seminar Program.

OVERVIEW (U)*

(S) The period from July 1971 through the end of 1973 was a time of transition, growth, and profound challenge for the Vietnamese Air Force (VNAF). As U.S. personnel continued to withdraw from South Vietnam (SVN), the VNAF was faced with growing combat requirements and demanding force expansions. Then, following a massive Communist offensive in the Spring of 1972, VNAF personnel, support, and operational capabilities were pushed to the limit to respond to intensified combat needs, force structure increases, and accelerated squadron activation schedules. These difficulties were overshadowed in late 1972 when, in anticipation of a cease-fire and an accompanying total withdrawal of U.S. forces from Vietnam, there was an unprecedented infusion of aircraft and equipment into South Vietnam, and a massive transfer of remaining U.S. facilities to the South Vietnamese. Once more the VNAF force structure was expanded and activation schedules were accelerated. Shortly thereafter, on 27 January 1973, the Agreement to End the War and Restore Peace in Vietnam was signed, and during the next 60 days U.S. forces and advisors were withdrawn from Vietnam. Unfortunately, the "cease-fire" did not bring with it a period of peace and stability, thus necessitating continuing VNAF combat requirements in addition to its monumental transition, expansion, and training tasks. The combination of these factors--marked

---

*This volume parallels a study which the author subsequently wrote for another Air Force project examining recent events in Southeast Asia; both volumes are based largely upon the same research materials, hence the similarity.

VNAF growth, continuing combat requirements, and withdrawal of U.S. forces and advisors--presented the VNAF with its greatest challenge of the conflict.

(S) Following the cease-fire, U.S. in-country support for the VNAF was acutely limited. The number of U.S. personnel allowed in Vietnam was small and tightly controlled. The type of support was limited to technical assistance--advisors, per se, were not permitted. The time allowed for assistance was restricted to one year after the cease-fire (although this self-imposed constraint was eventually relaxed). Finally, the extent of U.S. financial support was carefully limited and was under increasing scrutiny for reduction.

(C) Under these circumstances, it was remarkable that continuing progress toward self-sufficiency* was realized in the year following the cease-fire. In fact, on the basis of attitudes and opinions reflected in correspondence between "improvement and modernization" planners during 1972, it was the consensus that the VNAF would not be able to survive an expansion and acceleration of the magnitude which later actually occurred. The fact that a VNAF collapse did not result is less a condemnation of the predictions of planners than it is a testimonial to their efforts, and those of the Vietnamese Air Force, to derive order and progress from an overwhelmingly difficult situation.

---

*Discussion of the term "self-sufficiency" is provided on pages 132 and 133.

(U) This report examines the events which occurred, the goals pursued, the problems encountered, and the achievements attained in the program to improve and modernize the Vietnamese Air Force between July 1971 and December 1973. It also addresses the limitations which, as of the end of 1973, remained to be overcome on the road toward VNAF self-sufficiency.

CHAPTER I

INTRODUCTION (U)

Background (U)

(S) By July 1971,* through the Consolidated Republic of Vietnam Armed Forces Improvement and Modernization Plan (CRIMP), the VNAF had attained a size of 37 squadrons and 36,000 personnel,[1] which represented a doubling in size during the preceding three-year period. Thus, by mid-1971, the VNAF was well on its way toward the goal of a 50-squadron force structure, which was essentially programmed** for completion by the end of 1972.[2] Early 1971 marked a crossroads for the VNAF, and for the Republic of Vietnam Armed Forces (RVNAF) as well. In May 1971, for the first time since the beginning of U.S. involvement, the number of combat sorties flown in South Vietnam by the VNAF exceeded those flown by U.S. forces.[3] Furthermore, by mid-1971 more than half of the U.S. forces stationed in South Vietnam had already been withdrawn, and combat activity was at a relatively low level. At the same time, however, the future was clouded by the prospect of accelerating U.S. withdrawals and uncertainty surrounding enemy military intentions and capabilities.

---

*(S) The evolution, through June 1971, of the program to expand, improve, and modernize the South Vietnamese Air Force has been detailed in previous CHECO reports. See Project CHECO Reports <u>Vietnamization of the Air War, 1970-1971</u>, 8 Oct 71, Secret; <u>The VNAF Air Divisions Reports on Improvement and Modernization Program</u>, 23 Nov 71, Secret; <u>VNAF Improvement and Modernization Program</u>, 5 Feb 70, Secret; <u>Organization, Missions, and Growth of the Vietnamese Air Force</u>, 8 Oct 68, Secret.

*The 50th Squadron, an F-5E Air Defense Squadron, was to be activated in mid-1973.

(S) The rate of U.S. withdrawals, and the level of combat activity, were vitally important to the success of Vietnamization. Although the VNAF had achieved noteworthy progress in attaining programmed levels of equipment and personnel, it was clear that continued explosive growth, coupled with accelerated U.S. withdrawals, would severely tax the VNAF's capability to absorb its new equipment and train its new personnel while at the same time meeting operational requirements. With key personnel already stretched thin, thousands of untrained recruits were filling the lower end of the VNAF ranks. Simultaneously, expanding quantities and types of equipment burdened VNAF logistics capabilities which were already strained. The maintenance of a degree of stability was essential to the success of the Vietnamization program: the VNAF required time and stability to train its new personnel, develop the capability to support and maintain new equipment, and to employ that equipment in existing or new roles.[4] Central to conditions of stability were (1) avoidance of drastic changes to programmed U.S. withdrawal and VNAF expansion plans, since acceleration of either would force the VNAF to absorb equipment and missions prematurely, and (2) continuance of low levels of combat activity in South Vietnam, which would allow the VNAF to concentrate on training and expansion rather than operational requirements. Unknown to Improvement and Modernization (I&M) planners, however, the VNAF, as well as the RVNAF, was entering a period not of stability, but of unprecedented turmoil. Within the next 18 months, South Vietnamese forces would face their sternest test of the war: continued and, in fact, expanded growth in the face of an all-out invasion by North Vietnam (NVN), a massive influx of military supplies and equipment, and a total withdrawal of U.S. military forces.

(S) The progress of the VNAF toward self-sufficiency, as of mid-1971, could be assessed on the basis of two distinct criteria: (1) achievement of programmed CRIMP schedules, or (2) ability to cope with the threat. With regard to the attainment of CRIMP schedules, the I&M program was quite successful. Yet, viewed from the standpoint of ability to meet an intensifying enemy threat, the VNAF was clearly inadequate.

(TS) On the one hand, the VNAF's status could be viewed strictly on the basis of adherence to unit activation schedules, personnel force levels, and facility transfers as dictated in the CRIMP. After all, the improvement and modernization of the VNAF was designed to give the VNAF "a specific set of capabilities. Parity with combined RVNAF/U.S./Free World Military Armed Forces capabilities required to counter NVN aggression supported by the Soviet Union, People's Republic of China, and Soviet bloc was not the goal."[5] Thus, an assessment of VNAF progression toward CRIMP goals led to the conclusion that the I&M program had been quite successful.

(S) The basic problem in such an evaluation of the I&M program was that the assumptions and goals of the program were not static. Initially, the goal had been to foster a self-sufficient VNAF capable of operating within SVN, in an insurgency environment, in support of RVNAF ground operations. At the outset, these were envisioned as the conditions which would follow a negotiated settlement and U.S. withdrawal. It was believed that many of the roles and missions previously accomplished by the USAF would not be required on the same scale after a negotiated settlement, and that missions beyond VNAF capability, such as air defense and interdiction, could be performed by USAF resources in Southeast Asia (SEA) should the need arise. By design, therefore, the VNAF was to have capabilities which would fall far short of the combined Allied capabilities in SEA at the height of the conflict.[6]

(S) As time passed, however, it became increasingly clear that some of the basic assumptions underlying the I&M program were no longer valid. A protracted presence of U.S. forces in Vietnam, even in Southeast Asia, was no longer a certainty, and the arrival of the day when the RVNAF would have to bear the entire burden of combat operations was a prospect that demanded attention. Also, since the option of reintroducing U.S. forces into SEA was increasingly uncertain, it could no longer be comfortably assumed that the level of combat activities in South Vietnam would continue to decline. CRIMP planners were compelled to evaluate the VNAF, and the RVNAF, on the basis of their ability to meet the growing threat. These planners faced a dilemma: the CRIMP had been "accelerated to the maximum feasible limits," yet an alternative to U.S. support might have to be found,[7] in which case RVNAF forces, already strained to the limit, would have to be expanded even more.

(U) The following paragraphs outline the status of the VNAF, as of July 1971. First, the overall status of the I&M program, including unit activations, personnel levels, and general progress and problems are presented. Second, VNAF operational and support capabilities and limitations will be summarized.

(S) __VNAF Status--July 1971 (U)__. As of July 1971, the VNAF had reached a 37-squadron strength. Squadron activations were on or ahead of schedule; by the end of 1971 they were programmed to reach a 39-squadron strength, which as late as 1970 had been the end strength programmed for the VNAF. CRIMP called for the activation of an additional 11 (net gain of 10) squadrons during 1972.[8] While this was a demanding goal, CRIMP planners were confident that it was attainable, assuming that drastic changes in the CRIMP were avoided and a degree of stability could be attained in the level of combat in South Vietnam. This confidence also applied to the VNAF personnel force structure, which was to increase from the 36,000 July 1971 level, to nearly 50,000 by the end of 1972.[9]

(S) Despite their basic optimism regarding the attainability of CRIMP goals, planners hastened to point out that the VNAF faced formidable obstacles in the quest for self-sufficiency. The attainment of a given level of aircraft, squadrons, and personnel, while it might look good on paper, did not necessarily reflect the operational capabilities envisioned in CRIMP planning. Perhaps the most striking example of disparity between attainment of force structure goals versus desired capabilities is provided by the VNAF personnel situation. From a level of 17,000 personnel in 1968, the VNAF was programmed to expand to the 50,000 mark by late 1972, a tripling in size in four years. The impact of this expansion on middle management was staggering. It would take years to provide the new recruits with the training and experience required to take over middle management positions. Yet these VNAF personnel were expected to support and operate an increasingly sophisticated and modernized Air Force, an essential element in a credible South Vietnamese military force. As reflected by the personnel situation, the VNAF faced formidable tasks in the months and years ahead.

(S) Fighter Capabilities (U). As of July 1971, the VNAF fighter force consisted of a total of 195 aircraft organized into three A-1 squadrons, five A-37 squadrons, and one F-5/RF-5 squadron. While the South Vietnamese fighter pilots were regarded as excellent in the accurate delivery of ordnance in daylight, good weather conditions, the fighter force suffered from a shortage of combat-ready crews. Eight of the nine squadrons were operationally ready (OR), but the pilot manning for these OR squadrons varied from 37 to 96 percent.[10]

(S) The shortage of qualified pilots was a symptom of the growing pains from which the VNAF was suffering. There had been an increase in the number of fighter aircraft and squadrons without a corresponding increase in the training of new fighter pilots. During the 18 months preceding July 1971, over 1,100 South Vietnamese went through helicopter pilot training, while only about 70 completed fighter training.[11] The South Vietnamese could provide a finite number of candidates for pilot training, and the priority for helicopter pilot training was high at that time. While this problem could eventually be resolved by shifting the priority back to training of fighter pilots, that approach would also take time since pilot training was a relatively long-lead-time item.

(S) The shortage of pilots was the most serious, but by no means the only personnel problem limiting the operational capabilities of VNAF fighter squadrons. Personnel shortages in supply, maintenance, and other support functions were also having an inevitable impact on capabilities.[12] Opinions on the extent of that impact, however, varied substantially. In one message, for example, the Air Force Advisory Group (AFGP), addressing the failure of the VNAF to attain programmed projections for fighter sorties, denied that maintenance capabilities had substantially restricted the generation of fighter sorties. While recognizing the impact of the shortage of qualified pilots, the message attributed the low sortie rate primarily to a dissimilarity between American and South Vietnamese management philosophies:[13]

> (S) . . . The VNAF has not been fragged to its capacity. Within the VNAF, measurement of achievement and effective management is based upon meeting the primary mission tasks and maintaining aircrew proficiency to meet those tasks. The generation of flying sorties merely to satisfy flying hour allocations is neither acceptable nor indicative of effective utilization of assets.

(While the applicability to VNAF sortie rates of these Advisory Group comments may be uncertain, they are worth noting if only because they follow a vein which permeates the VNAF I&M program; namely, the impact upon the Vietnamization program of the divergence between American and South Vietnamese viewpoints. This topic repeatedly surfaces throughout this report.)

(S) While the VNAF fighter force was capable in daytime, Visual Meteorological Conditions (VMC) air support operations, in a low-threat environment, it suffered from limitations in a number of areas, including all-weather bombing and night operations. The VNAF did not have a night strike program and conducted all-weather strikes only occasionally, despite the fact that the A-1/A-37 force was capable of night delivery of ordnance, VNAF fighter pilots were night- and weather-qualified, and the VNAF had a continuation night-training program. There were a number of reasons for this. First, the RVNAF had "neither an overall air targeting program nor an integrated air/ground interdiction program."[14] Since there was little development of night preplanned targets, there was no requirement for preplanned night airstrikes. Nighttime targets were usually the result of hamlet attacks or troops-in-contact (TIC), which were covered by gunships. Second, rules of engagement specified that the delivery of ordnance by fighters be controlled by Forward Air Controllers (FACs). VNAF FAC aircraft were not equipped for instrument or night operations. A Combat Required Operational Capability (CROC) had been prepared to correct that deficiency. Finally, VNAF squadrons were fully committed to daytime sorties. Any night sorties, therefore, could be conducted only at the expense of day sorties.[15]

(S) Another difficulty faced by the VNAF fighter force was the need for a viable air defense capability. As of July 1971, the VNAF had only one squadron of F-5 aircraft, and they were beginning to train for VMC air defense. The VNAF was programmed to activate three more F-5 squadrons beginning in FY 74, but until then they would possess only a very nominal VMC air defense capability, and no all-weather air defense capability at all.[16]

(S) Fixed-wing Gunship Capabilities (U). As of 1 July 1971, the VNAF had only one fixed-wing gunship squadron. The squadron, composed of 16 AC-47 gunships based at Tan Son Nhut Air Base (AB), flew missions in all four South Vietnamese military regions and portions of Cambodia. While considered effective, the primary limitation of the gunship force was its size. In September 1971, however, activation of an AC-119G squadron was scheduled. In addition to doubling the size of the VNAF gunship fleet, this action promised improved capabilities by virtue of the AC-119's superior flight and operational characteristics.[17]

(S) In preparation for the AC-119 squadron activation, VNAF crews were integrated into the USAF's 17th Special Operations Squadron, which was the source of the aircraft for the projected September transfer. This training approach was considered quite successful. Additionally, maintenance of the new gunships promised to present no unusual problems since the VNAF had a base of experience by virtue of their C-119 airlift aircraft. Thus, the VNAF gunship force appeared to be headed toward rapid completion of CRIMP goals.[18]

(S) Airlift Capabilities (U). July 1971 was a time of flux and transition for the VNAF airlift fleet. A squadron of C-47s had just been activated during the previous month, and another C-47 squadron was scheduled for activation that very month. Activation of the latter squadron would give the VNAF four airlift squadrons (two C-119 and two C-47 squadrons), and a total of 64 airlift aircraft. In addition, two squadrons of C-7s were scheduled for activation by June 1972. Thus, in the course of a single year, VNAF airlift resources would triple from a two-squadron, 32-aircraft force to a six-squadron, 112-aircraft force. The aircraft possessed would also increase in both type and sophistication-- from two systems (AC-119 and AC-47), to four systems (C-123 and C-7 added).[19]

(S) The explosive growth of the airlift force had its inevitable problems, the most serious of which, again, were related to the training of personnel to operate and support the aircraft. Availability of aircrews was particularly critical, and each new squadron activation further diluted the aircrew strength of established squadrons. The VNAF supplied aircrews to the new squadrons by borrowing from the aircrews of established squadrons, and by relying on pilot training programs to fill the vacant spaces. Unfortunately, there simply were not enough pilots to go around, and pilot trainees were not graduating at a rate adequate to satisfy rapidly expanding needs. The shortage of experienced support personnel, especially in the maintenance area, was also serious, and was further exacerbated by the proliferation of aircraft types, increasing sophistication, and the sharp rise in aircraft numbers. To promote the development of the needed maintenance capabilities, training teams were dispatched to South Vietnam to conduct maintenance training for C-123 and C-7 maintenance personnel. Highly qualified Vietnamese teams, once trained, in turn trained other Vietnamese personnel. Training was facilitated by integrating Vietnamese personnel into USAF C-123 and C-7 units.[20]

(S) With the activation of new units, despite the personnel shortages, the VNAF airlift capability was steadily increasing. During July 1971, VNAF airlift accounted for two-thirds of the cargo carried for RVNAF forces. The vast majority of this support was provided during the day. Night airlift missions were flown when absolutely necessary, but were normally avoided. (Although VNAF airlift crews were night/weather qualified, many airfields were not adequately lighted, approach and departure routes at many fields were not secure at night, and limited ground handling support precluded 24 hour operations.) While facing formidable expansion problems, by July 1971 the VNAF was well on its way toward satisfying CRIMP airlift goals.[21]

(S) <u>Helicopter Capabilities (U)</u>. Unlike their U.S. counterparts, the RVNAF placed all helicopters under VNAF management. Tactical mobility was critical to the RVNAF, yet it was not possible for them to continue to enjoy the level of support provided by the U.S. helicopter armada.[22] Considering the limited helicopter resources available to the RVNAF, it would have been impractical to assign helicopters to the various Army of the Republic of Vietnam (ARVN) units. The central management of helicopters by the VNAF was accomplished in accordance with Joint General Staff (JGS) Directive 310-19, which outlined mission priorities and general management and maintenance guidelines. The directive was designed to insure the maximum utilization of limited helicopter resources. It "was aimed at resolving the conflict between the ARVN and the VNAF and it did so on VNAF terms."[23]

(S) Improvement and modernization of the VNAF helicopter fleet provided a good example of the magnitude of the tasks facing the VNAF, and of the inevitability of "shortfalls" in VNAF resources when compared with the resources available while U.S. forces were in Vietnam. In the 18 months preceding July 1971, VNAF helicopter resources had nearly quadrupled (from 112 to 413 aircraft) on the way to the 532 helicopters specified in the CRIMP.* Even that end CRIMP strength represented only one-tenth the number of helicopters used by the U.S. Army in South Vietnam.[24]

(S) As in the fighter, gunship, and airlift operational areas, the expanding helicopter force faced demanding personnel, training, and experience problems. However, as of July 1971, training of pilots and support personnel was keeping pace with CRIMP schedules and was considered successful. The VNAF helicopter force was flying 12 percent of the helicopter missions being flown in South Vietnam, as compared to only 1 percent two years earlier. Failure of helicopters to perform night missions was a problem area, but night and instrument training were underway to help provide a night capability. As recently graduated aircrews gained experience, night/instrument capabilities were expected to improve. The VNAF helicopter force appeared well on its way toward completion of CRIMP goals.[25]

---

*(S) In CRIMP planning, helicopters were to represent over 40 percent of all VNAF airframes.

(S) Reconnaissance Capabilities (U). VNAF reconnaissance capabilities, as of July 1971, were limited. After six RF-5s had been added to the VNAF's three RC-47s in 1970, no further additions were scheduled until 1972 when 20 EC-47s and nine more RC-47s were to be transferred. The VNAF RF-5 force averaged about 60 missions a month, but their effectiveness was severely limited by inadequacies in the camera system used in the aircraft. The RC-47s were employed both for inland photo reconnaissance and for visual reconnaissance over coastal waters, but their limited number (three) was an overriding constraint on effectiveness. In general, reconnaissance was a relatively low priority mission in comparison with the other operational requirements already discussed. Progress toward CRIMP objectives was slow, and was primarily scheduled to occur in 1972.[26]

(S) Air Logistics Capabilities (U). The importance of VNAF logistical support and maintenance of VNAF aircraft and equipment was expressed in a semi-annual I&M conference in the following manner: "The heart of whether the VNAF will survive as a fighter force is dependent on their ability to maintain their aircraft and equipment."[27] Considering that the number and type of VNAF aircraft were proliferating at a rate exceeding the ability of VNAF personnel to keep pace, both in number and experience, this was one of the most complex and difficult tasks facing the VNAF I&M program. To centralize VNAF supply and repair capabilities, and thus to make maximum use of thinly stretched VNAF personnel, an Air Logistics Command (ALC) was established at Bien Hoa AB in early 1971. The ALC was to provide depot-level maintenance and logistics support for the entire VNAF structure, thereby reducing supply and maintenance requirements at the individual bases. Emphasis was on training to build up the level of manning and experience required at such a facility. While it was obvious that time and stability would be required to bring the VNAF maintenance and supply capabilities to the point that they could support the programmed VNAF force, the consensus was that the VNAF was on the road to self-sufficiency in this area.[28]

(S) <u>Training Capabilities (U)</u>. The role of training in the VNAF I&M program was aptly summarized in a previous CHECO Report, Vietnamization of the Air War, 1970-1971:[29] (U)

> (S) Training was the key to VNAF self-sufficiency; and more than anything else, CRIMP--the largest Military Assistance Program (MAP) in United States history--was a training program. Training had to meet two essential objectives for the VNAF to become self-sufficient: (1) personnel had to be trained to meet the immediate needs of expansion, and (2) the VNAF had to develop the capability to train replacements for personnel lost through attrition.

(S) As of July 1971, the VNAF had made steady progress toward self-sufficiency in training. The VNAF Air Training Command (ATC) was becoming self-sufficient in maintenance training, English language training, and training of their technical personnel. At the same time, management, leadership, and professional training capabilities were being expanded.[30] A wide variety of training programs were used to help the VNAF meet its staggering training needs. Maintenance training programs were established in South Vietnam, using (1) Vietnamese instructors trained in the United

States in conjunction with (2) USAF training teams deployed to South Vietnam. Based on the success of these programs, more training teams were deployed to cover a variety of other specialties. Further, integration of VNAF personnel into USAF units provided on-the-job training (OJT) experience for newly trained VNAF personnel with USAF units; VNAF OJT was also utilized. Finally, training of Vietnamese personnel in the Continental U.S. (CONUS) was reduced, but did continue as a supplement to in-country programs.[31]

(S) The most notable trend in training programs, as of July 1971, was not the number of personnel being processed (which was formidable in itself), but rather the philosophy being used in training them. There had been a dramatic and irreversible shift from training in the U.S. to training in South Vietnam. This was significant not only in that it promised eventual VNAF self-sufficiency in training, but it also represented the first time the USAF was "exporting the training rather than importing the students"[32] in a Military Assistance Program.

(S) <u>Facilities and Base Support Capabilities (U)</u>. As of July 1971, transfer of U.S. facilities in South Vietnam to the VNAF was not keeping pace with the CRIMP schedule (because of continuing U.S. requirements for those facilities), and VNAF base support capabilities at transferred facilities were weak. To complicate matters, some VNAF units were activating early, while some USAF units were retaining combat missions beyond the scheduled dates. In general, the delays in facility transfers had not reached the point that scheduled activation of VNAF operational capabilities had been impaired. In some cases, however, such as at the overcrowded Tan Son Nhut AB, the situation threatened to become more critical and to slow the attainment of operational readiness status by VNAF units. U.S. command emphasis was applied to overcome the natural tendency to devote total attention to the activation and improvement of operationally oriented capabilities at the expense of base support capabilities. It was obvious, however, that the transfer of facilities, and particularly the support and maintenance of these facilities, had been somewhat neglected in deference to higher priority capabilities; increasing emphasis would be required in these neglected areas if VNAF self-sufficiency was to be realized.[33]

The Role of Advisors in the I&M Program (U)

(C) In July 1971, General Lucius D. Clay, Commander in Chief, Pacific Air Forces, directed a reevaluation of the progress of Vietnamization. Responding to this directive, Brigadier General Otis C. Moore, the Chief of Staff, Seventh Air Force (7AF), made the following remarks in a letter to 7AF working-level personnel:[34] (U)

> (C) The Improvement and Modernization Program for the
> Vietnamese Air Force has been reviewed and measured by
> so many interested agencies that it is difficult to
> identify any aspect of the program, or the product,
> that has not been examined in detail. However, General
> Clay is concerned about our evaluation of the VNAF and
> its ability to take over the air war after we leave.
> He thinks that our normal measurements may be incom-
> plete, or even biased by our optimistic conviction that
> Vietnamization must be successful. For these reasons
> he has asked me to solicit your help in assessing our
> progress in Vietnamization at the working level. . . .
> We would like you to review the questions listed in the
> Attachments. . . .

The responses to Brigadier General Moore's survey provide unique insights into the Vietnamization process and represent an ideal backdrop for interpreting the VNAF I&M-related events occurring in the two years following the survey. Highlights from the responses to the survey are provided below:[35] (U)

> (C) Oriental thought . . . it must be recognized that the thought processes which permeate all of Southeast Asia have been formed under a dominant Chinese influence.
> The great thinkers of China--Confucius, Mencius, and Mo Tzu--distinctly different but with much in common, preached the virtue of contentment--and most orientals have practiced it to a remarkable degree.
> China, possessing a well developed culture predating Christianity, viewed herself as the "Center of the Universe"--contentment, filial piety, and family honor served as the essence of the thought base . . . much of what is Vietnam existed in this cultural influence of centuries. Chinese philosophy has influenced every facet of Vietnamese life and custom. . . .
> Thus it's not too difficult to understand that Vietnamese who follow Confucius, Mencius and Mo Tzu or who subscribe to Taoism, Buddhism or other religions of the Far East, can be depended upon to view life in a much less aggressive fashion than a technologically attuned "US Advisor." The influences which caused him to be what he is are rooted in antiquity and a few years of Western influence, even when applied directly, can only mold the moment. For the future the thought process we have attempted to implant in Southeast Asia will be challenged by a tropical environment, a national affinity for contentment, and a natural skepticism concerning Western intrusions. The catalyst will be understanding and patience.
>
> [Specific survey questions and selected responses follow.]
> ARE WE OVER-ADVISING?
> -Perhaps we are simply because we expect too much of the Vietnamese. If we really want them to meet our standards we are not over-advising, but we need better trained and more understanding advisors. In addition to being technically qualified, advisors should have (Vietnamese) language training and should be schooled in Vietnamese history and culture. . . .

17

Judging from personal observation for more than four years in Vietnam, my answer to this question must be yes. It is necessary to qualify this by saying that many of the individuals who are assigned as advisors appear not to be properly qualified or prepared. More specifically, many of them seem to know very little about Vietnamese culture, have little or no knowledge of the language and have come to Vietnam for the first time. Any one of these should be considered to be detrimental to effectively functioning in an advisory capacity, but unfortunately, all three categories seem to apply to a large portion of our advisors. By the time he learns many of the things that will allow him to adequately communicate with his counterparts, it is unlikely that he will become the instructor/advisor as he has been the student too long. The criteria for determining the effectiveness of an advisor does not vary directly according to the individual's technical proficiency, but rather to factors such as those previously referenced as well as to the individual's personal motivation, personality and to his leadership abilities. Therefore, if it is not possible to assign qualified and motivated individuals then we are most assuredly over-advising and diluting our effort. . . .

DO THE THINGS WE DO CAUSE THE VNAF TO HOLD BACK AND NOT USE THEIR INITIATIVE?

-Unfortunately, in many cases, operational requirements force the USAF instructor to step in and do the job himself. . . . This of course frustrates VNAF initiative and encourages their malingering. . . .

-Although there are exceptions, dependent on the mutual respect and rapport established between USAF and VNAF individuals, the general feeling is that as long as we indicate we will continue to afford help in certain areas, the VNAF will continue to take full advantage of our resources and assistance. In this sense, we are holding them back and contribute to their lack of initiative. . . .

DOES THE VNAF REALLY UNDERSTAND THAT WE WANT THEM TO MAKE THEIR OWN DECISIONS?

-The VNAF do understand that we want them to make their own decisions. One problem is that we may not accept their decisions unless they coincide with ours. . . .

-The answer to this question is generally yes. Perhaps an anecdote related by Brig Gen Lee, Deputy Chief of Staff for Operations, Republic of Korea Air Force (ROKAF), best explains the ROKAF as well as the VNAF approach to this problem. Gen Lee stated that it was useless for him to

attempt to make decisions because he was like a beggar looking at a menu. It was alright to look, but he would eat what was given. That is, he would do what the United States directed because he had no choice. . . . It must be understood, however, that the decisions will be based on Oriental logic and in many instances we will not agree with the decision unless we also approach the problem with an understanding of the Orientals' perspective. . . .
-We are encouraging the VNAF to use their initiative. However, this encouragement is not effective unless we have earned their respect and demonstrated knowledge and appreciation of their cultural differences and clearly understand that in applying this encouragement it must be done tactfully and diplomatically. One of our (USAF's) greatest failings is that we are not adequately schooled in the oriental psychological reaction to our encouragement. We just cannot take the direct-hardline approach and obtain desired results. . . .
HOW CAN WE ENCOURAGE THEM TO USE THEIR INITIATIVE?
-The apparent reluctance of VNAF Headquarters to delegate decision making authority to the lower echelons tends to stifle a subordinate's enthusiasm about using his initiative. The solution to this problem should come from the USAF higher echelons of command. The higher echelons of the VNAF should be encouraged to allow and encourage their subordinates to use more initiative and they should delegate more authority to them. . . .
-The best method would be to get out of their way and force them to take the initiative. While initially the operational capability might be seriously jeopardized, it would teach the VNAF what is required and illuminate its shortcomings while there would still be a USAF in-country capability ready to go in and help out when the VNAF requested assistance. . . .
(MAINTENANCE) - First we must be aware that the VNAF's standards and overall capability are not ours and not likely to be as high as ours. Thus, it follows that there will be a decrement in the customer service provided by VNAF owned, operated and maintained facilities. Our job is to minimize that decrement. We can best do that and encourage VNAF initiative by insuring that the quality and level of training they receive is of the highest caliber. Next we must be steadfast in our efforts to advise and cooperate with the VNAF. We must not be too eager to bail them out of bad situations; instead we should give them the opportunity to resolve the problems.

ARE WE PROVIDING PROPER GUIDANCE TO HELP THEM BUILD A DECISION MAKING CAPABILITY?
-The guidance that the USAF is providing is more than adequate to help them build a decision making capability. Appropriate VNAF officers are invited to be members and observers of decision making boards and councils. But is this guidance being assimilated and then used by the VNAF? I don't think so, not that the Vietnamese are rejecting our guidance but because of their customs. The American people have always been noted for taking the initiative, . . . while the Vietnamese culture and social background is geared to a much slower pace. . . .
DO YOU SEE ANY STUMBLING BLOCKS TO PROGRESS?
-The language barrier of course is a major stumbling block. Those USAF individuals assigned directly to Air Force Advisory Teams should be required to under-go [sic] minimum formal language training in the United States. A continuation of language study and study of Vietnamese cultural and social structure after arrival in-country should be mandatory. We place the burden of overcoming the language barrier on the Vietnamese and generally there is little effort on our part to learn the Vietnamese language or their customs. . . .
-Low VNAF priorities for manpower distribution in the support area accounts for many of the delays and problems that pose stumbling blocks to progress. Political or economic power of individual personalities often dictate the order of priorities to units. As long as political influence and the oriental social structure continue to override mission priority, this problem will exist. We are deficient in that we are impatient and lack understanding of the importance to the Vietnamese of observing their time honored customs with which we do not agree or understand. The Vietnamese are still capable of establishing a logistics system that will satisfy their needs. It will be years before the Vietnamese will be capable of accepting and fully utilizing our logistics system. We must modify our logistics training to a program system that is compatible with their capability and resources. . . .
-The pressure of the U.S. Government to fulfill phase-down time tables and get the job done as quickly as possible is going to adversely effect [sic] or degrade progress in the entire I&M Program. As we follow our national policy we must all accept this degradation, adjust to our own political decisions and still maintain the flexibility to keep programs going in spite of the

> knowledge that we are not going to accomplish our tasks
> with the degree of proficiency and high standards we
> have strived for in the past. . . .

(U) Many of the remarks made in the mid-1971 survey continued to exhibit striking applicability during the following two years. The sweeping evolution of events during 1972 and 1973, rather than rendering the survey obsolete, only served to underscore and heighten the significance of the observations it contained.

CHAPTER II

EVOLUTION OF THE I&M PROGRAM
JULY 1971-SEPTEMBER 1973 (U)

Project 981/982 (U)

(S) In August 1971, the Chief of Staff of the Air Force (CSAF) implemented a two-pronged logistics project to support and accelerate selected aspects of the VNAF portion of the CRIMP. Essentially, the purpose of Project 981/982 was to compress the delivery of all aircraft previously scheduled for transfer by July 1973. This also included the transfer of attrition aircraft as well as the munitions, fuel, and Aerospace Ground Equipment (AGE) required for their support. Under 981/982, the aircraft and equipment were delivered by 1 November 1971.[36] Project 981 dealt with principal items such as aircraft, vehicles, and ammunition, while Project 982 dealt with secondary items such as spares and repair equipment/capabilities. The extent of the activity under Project 981/982 is reflected by a listing and brief description of the various "pacer" programs which were established by the Air Force Logistics Command (AFLC) in support of the project:

<ul style="list-style: none;">
<li>Pacer Bits — Control of VNAF depot-level maintenance support.</li>
<li>Pacer Cactus — Expedite delivery of the T-53 engine tools on requisition.</li>
<li>Pacer Jig — Expedite delivery of UH-1H airframe jigs.</li>
<li>Pacer Link — Utility package for project Pacer Power and Pacer Plate.</li>
<li>Pacer Memory — Reconfigure the VNAF UNIVAC 1050-II computer, complete the satellite program, and rewarehouse and inventory the VNAF supply accounts.</li>
</ul>

Pacer Plate - Equip the VNAF electroplating facility.
Pacer Power - Equip the jet engine overhaul shop, Precision Measuring Equipment/Non-Operational Inspection Lab, and accessory backshops.
Pacer Spare - Fill authorized T-53/T-55 engine levels in VNAF Army stockage; establish a T-55 overhaul capability at the ALC.
Pacer Stock - Control and development of VNAF depot level reparable stock for USAF-type aircraft.
Pacer Swift - Transfer Consolidated Engine Maintenance sites and establish depot level repair programs.
Pacer Tool - Identify tools/equipment required for installation and maintenance of shop equipment.
Pacer Wheels - Equip contract vehicle repair facility.

Additional Pacer projects were established at later dates to speed the delivery of selected assets in support of Force Structure Review (FSR)-73 and Project Enhance, described below.

FSR-73 (U)

(S) The Force Structure Review consisted of an annual examination and reapportionment of the RVNAF manpower ceiling to accommodate priority force structure changes.* The FSR for fiscal year (FY) 1973 began in October 1971. In a 23 October message, the Commander in Chief, Pacific Command (CINCPAC) directed that the CRIMP be reevaluated to insure that the RVNAF had the capability of assuming increasingly greater responsibility as U.S. redeployments continued. Specific RVNAF capabilities and requirements to be reviewed included, but were not limited to:

---

*(S) Each FSR was initially accomplished as a joint effort by the Military Assistance Command, Vietnam (MACV), the Air Force Advisory Group (AFGP), and RVNAF representatives. The results were forwarded through channels to the Joint Chiefs of Staff (JCS) and the Secretary of Defense (SECDEF) for review, modification, and approval.

a. Improved interdiction capabilities including an expanded sensor/radar capability, the mini-gunship concept, sensor delivery/ readout capability, additional AC-119 aircraft, and the modification of A-37 for interdiction.

b. Increasing medium-lift helicopter support.

c. Air Cavalry capability.

d. Improvement in Market Time (coastal surveillance and interdiction) capabilities, including VNAF air support.

e. Logistic improvements: supply, maintenance, and transportation functions.

f. Level of leadership and morale.

g. Improved quality and scope of RVNAF individual and unit training.

h. Accelerated activation of units.[38]

(S) The significance and impact of FSR-73 lie in its digression from authorized CRIMP, which was the formal, existing plan for the expansion of the VNAF. During FY 72 the VNAF was scheduled, under CRIMP, to expand to a personnel level of 47,000 (from its July 1971 level of 36,000). That expansion was proceeding as scheduled when FSR-73 planning began. FSR-73 authorized raising the FY 72 goal by an additional 2,000, bringing the projected VNAF force to more than 49,000.[39] In addition to this immediate expansion, FSR-73 proposed that 12,300 spaces be added to VNAF manning during FY 73, increasing projected personnel strength to over 61,000.[40]

(S) There were a number of reasons behind the drastic expansion of the VNAF proposed by FSR-73 planners. Essentially, however, the plans for expansion under FSR-73 reflected a growing realization that as U.S. redeployments accelerated, and continued U.S. presence in SEA became less certain, it became increasingly important to structure a VNAF capable of shouldering a greater portion of RVNAF air support requirements. Although the shift toward that philosophy was inherent in the large increases proposed in FSR-73, it was not complete--the VNAF force structure was still based on the assumption that the level of hostilities would remain relatively low, and that the bulk of certain capabilities, such as air defense, would continue to be provided by U.S. forces for the foreseeable future. Nevertheless, there had been a concerted effort to reduce the areas, such as interdiction, in which continuing U.S. support would be required, and to increase the depth and scope of VNAF capabilities.

(S) Support for FSR-73, and optimism concerning the ability of the VNAF to absorb such a dramatically increased expansion, was anything but unanimous. Indeed, the FSR-73 proposal itself noted the need for caution in accelerating the activation of units, and recommended that activations programmed for FY 72 not be accelerated. These positions were based upon several conclusions stated in the proposal, viz:[41]

> (S) (a) That the ability to accelerate the activation of units depends primarily on recruiting and training manpower.
>
> (b) That any accelerated activation of units not already programmed in FY 72 could not be supported without an increase in the logistic base.

(c) That trained technicians are not available to support any unprogrammed accelerated activation of units.

(d) That further accelerated activation of units would lead to dissipation of available manpower and adversely affect combat readiness of units already in existence.

In turn, these conclusions led FSR-73 planners to recommend:

That no further accelerated activations be considered until additional manpower is provided and the availability of required equipment is determined.

(S) The issue, however, went deeper than the ability to accelerate the activation of currently planned units. The more basic question was whether or not the VNAF could survive an expansion of the magnitude being planned. In February 1972, the Air Force Advisory Group outlined the impact of the proposed FSR-73 expansion:[42]

(S) Currently, the VNAF is meeting and surpassing the schedule of unit activations planned under the . . . CRIMP. . . . In the period from Nov 71 through Dec 72, the VNAF is scheduled to activate eleven new squadrons and convert one squadron to new equipment. In FY 4/73, a conversion to AC-119K gunships is planned. The schedule of almost one activation/conversion per month constitutes a formidable task especially when considered in the light of other complicating factors.

(S) The RVNAF Force Structure Review (FSR-73), as it is presently constituted, provides for new missions in addition to those of the CRIMP and for a substantial upgrading of the logistical support base for the VNAF through FY 73. The major changes include the assumption of the air role now being performed by the U.S. Navy for Market Time and the introduction of five 32 UE [Unit Equipment] STOL [Short Take-off and Landing] squadrons. As outlined in the 8 Oct 71 SECDEF memo pertaining to RVNAF interdiction, there is an urgent requirement to attain these capabilities in the same period as the scheduled CRIMP activations/conversion. . . .

(S) The FSR-73 provides for these and other actions to enhance VNAF capabilities. It also tentatively authorizes an increase in VNAF manpower strength, 2,138 for FY 72 add-on, and 12,257 for FY 73. This represents an increase from the present 47,058 to 61,453 by end FY 73.

(S) The key to achieving any measure of success in assimilating the FY 73 tasks is the availability of personnel. We are seeking Vietnamese Joint General Staff agreement to authorize recruiting in sufficient quantities to keep the basic training pipeline filled; however, it should be realized that with a maximum effort on the part of the VNAF, it will take approximately two years to train out the 14,000 personnel required. . . .

(S) Middle management and pilot shortages are also considerations. Of the 47,000 personnel currently assigned, 27,000 have entered the VNAF since 1 Jan 69. Of 40,000 enlisted personnel, only 12,000 have a five or higher skill level. Currently, pilot availability is only 70 percent of the pre-FSR-73 requirement.

(S) In summation, we believe that achieving the goals established for FY 73 will severely test the VNAF. As new organizations are formed or new missions undertaken we expect some degradation in operational capability as experienced personnel are spread thin among existing units. . . . In view of these circumstances, any further acceleration of tasks or further assignment of tasks in FY 73 should be discouraged.

(S) The finalized MACV FSR-73 was completed in January 1972 and forwarded, through CINCPAC, to the JCS. Major items identified in the document included the personnel necessary to operate Phu Cat and Phan Rang Air Bases, provide the Air Logistics Command with a 90 percent repair capability, increase UH-1H flying hours, provide base support after U.S. withdrawal, convert a C-47 squadron to AC-119Ks, and increase the Maritime Air Patrol squadron strength. Other items, while involving smaller numbers of personnel, were significant. They included the Beacon Only Bombing System, improving the Air Liaison Officer (ALO)/FAC system, improving the airlift control system, improving the food distribution system, and establishing an Intelligence Targets Branch.

(S) It should be noted that of the overall increase of 14,500 VNAF personnel in FSR-73, 4,100 spaces were earmarked for the introduction of five squadrons of STOL aircraft into Vietnam, and activation of an air base for their beddown. The STOL aircraft concept had been given high-level support as an alternative to U.S. interdiction capabilities, and the aircraft and other aspects of the concept were to be tested under the program known as Credible Chase. The 4,100 spaces earmarked for support of the Credible Chase concept were included in the MACV proposal only after a directive message from the JCS. Inclusion of the spaces was contingent on the successful completion of the Credible Chase evaluation as a prerequisite to filling the spaces.*

(S) In the meantime, while FSR-73 was in the preparation stage in late 1971 and early 1972, advanced recruitment authority was sought from the RVNAF JGS by the Advisory Group, 7AF, and MACV. While FSR-73 had yet to be formally approved, it was evident that a sizeable increase in VNAF

---

*(S) Ultimately, however, the STOL "mini-gunship" aircraft and armament envisioned in the concept did not prove adaptable to a combat environment, and the concept itself was dismissed as impractical. It is nevertheless a fact that as a result of high-level interest and support at a crucial phase in the Vietnamization program, a great deal of time and effort were expended on the project, which was vigorously opposed by field commanders and lacked support among South Vietnamese military leaders.[43]

manning would occur, and that this would severely strain VNAF training capabilities. Thus the advanced recruitment authority was sought to spread the impact of the expansion over a long period of time.[44] Yet the JGS steadfastly refused to permit early recruitment to help fill FY 73 manning levels until FSR-73 had been formally approved by the Department of Defense (DOD). The following comments, made in an end-of-tour report by the Director of Plans and Programs, AFGP, shed light not only on the attitudes of the JGS, but on those of U.S. planners as well:[45]

> (S) The factors which place constraints upon the VNAF . . . preventing them from taking timely and complete programming actions stem from . . . the apparent lack of appreciation in both the U.S. and RVNAF channels of the long lead times required for activation and attainment of operational readiness of flying units. An example of the U.S. unawareness is exemplified by the "Vietnamization of Interdiction" program in which it was an expressed desire that the VNAF activate five STOL squadrons for participation in the 72-73 dry season operations. Fortunately, delays in the testing of the aircraft and other events led to an indefinite postponement of the STOL operation, but had the program proceeded on schedule, the VNAF would have been required to enter a crash training program and redirect personnel from existing units. No consideration was given to the impact of this type action on the mission of the remaining force. While this is the most graphic, there are examples of similar U.S. unilateral planning. For the RVNAF, the unawareness is exemplified by their almost rigid insistence that no action can be taken prior to final approval of a plan regardless of the circumstances involved. In the case of the RVNAF Force Structure Review for FY 73 the MACV-approved proposal indicated that an increase of over 14,000 personnel for the VNAF in FY 73 was appropriate. Despite pleas for permission to recruit some of these proposed 14,000 in advance of DOD final approval to soften the impact of up to two years of training lead time (aircrews), the Joint General Staff insisted no action could be taken until final approval

of FSR-73 by DOD. It required two letters from COMUSMACV [Commander, U.S. MACV] to the Chairman of JGS and vigorous prompting through MACV staff channels before JGS acceded to recruitment of some 2,000 personnel in advance of FY 73. This recruitment authority was effective on 1 May 72 which was in reality a small concession. As a result of this type action, the attainment of the VNAF end-FY 73 program objectives will not be realized until late FY 74.

(S) The JGS review of FSR-73 resulted in tentative approval of the STOL spaces, and the supporting air base, pending the results of Credible Chase tests. At the same time, however, the JGS strongly recommended that MACV reconsider FY 73 activation of a number of squadrons and implementation of new capabilities which MACV had proposed for FY 74. The units/capabilities recommended for FY 73 consideration included two additional F-5E squadrons, one additional C-47 squadron, a greater expansion of the maritime air patrol capability, and an improved Undergraduate Pilot Training (UPT) program. These capabilities were not to be included in FSR 73, however, until higher headquarters received further information from the field, and until a source of manpower space trade-offs could be found: that source ultimately proved to be the spaces allotted to the defunct Credible Chase project. In the meantime, the rest of FSR-73 was approved,[46] with final, formal approval by SECDEF coming on 14 May 1972. The VNAF was in for a period of unprecedented growth, which would come during an equally unprecedented period of turmoil and combat ushered in by the North Vietnamese 1972 Spring Offensive in South Vietnam.

Project Enhance (U)

(S) The North Vietnamese 30 March 1972 invasion of South Vietnam was by far the most severe and sustained military test faced by the RVNAF to that time. The implications of this invasion for the Vietnamization program were far-reaching and traumatic. As has been already shown, the invasion came at a time when the I&M program was already facing its sternest challenge to date: increased and accelerated expansion of personnel and unit force levels; broadening of mission requirements; and increased logistical and training demands on an undermanned and undertrained force heavily weighted with inexperienced recruits.

(TS) The U.S. response to the invasion, in the RVNAF I&M context, was Project Enhance. Actually, Project Enhance had been in the planning stages prior to the invasion. It had initially been conceived as a minor action, an extension to and a revitalization of Project 981/982,[47] but the invasion altered and expanded its focus. The reaction of the Air Force Advisory Group to the prospect of yet another burden on the VNAF I&M program, however, was cautious:[48]

> (TS) New weapons considered for VNAF should be handled as separate projects. Long lead time for training and weapons systems procurement is not adaptable to 981/982 procedures.
>
> (TS) VNAF manning is insufficient and will continue to be the limiting constraint in [the] foreseeable future for support of additional quantities of aircraft. Manning limitations also preclude an acceleration of existing activations schedules. AFGP has already requested replacement [of] attrition aircraft and will continue to do so as losses occur. . . . All programs, i.e., transfer of equipment, spares, and new activations are progressing as rapidly as possible considering VNAF manning. . . .

(S) Project Enhance was initiated on 23 May 1972. Its scope was broader than that of 981/982, and its impact more far-reaching. Project Enhance applied to various elements of RVNAF forces, but by far the greatest emphasis was placed on the VNAF. With regard to the VNAF, the project had three objectives: replace VNAF combat losses, fill I&M shortfalls, and enhance the VNAF capability to counter the North Vietnamese Army (NVA) offensive in light of USAF withdrawals. The project was given high-level support, assigned a high priority, and designated for completion in some 60 days, by 1 August 1972.[49] The enormity of the task at hand was evident in the Project Enhance directive, in which the JCS specified the various actions to be taken:[50]

    (S) A. Replace combat losses and reconstitute RVNAF stocks to currently authorized levels.

    (S) B. Provide essential equipment needed for immediate improvement of RVNAF combat capability.

        (1) An additional 32 UH-1 assault helicopters.
        (2) 30 STOL aircraft. . . .

    (S) C. Provide additional equipment to Enhance RVNAF immediate combat capability.

        (1) 5 additional F-5A aircraft.
        (2) 48 additional A-37 aircraft. . . .

    (S) D. Provide additional essential equipment to give RVNAF an enhanced capability over the longer term. It is recognized that RVNAF may not have current capability to crew and operate the additional equipment, some of which will have to be placed in storage.

        (1) Accelerate delivery of 14 RC-47 aircraft (reconnaissance aircraft).
        (2) Accelerate delivery of 23 AC-119K aircraft (fixed wing gunships).

    (3) Accelerate delivery of 23 EC-47 (intelligence collection aircraft).
    (4) Accelerate delivery of 2 RC-119s (coastal patrol and naval gunfire support ships).
    (5) Provide 12 C-119G aircraft for maritime patrols.

  (S) E. Provide a further increase of essential equipment to enhance RVNAF capability over the longer term.

    (1) Accelerate delivery of 28 C-7 aircraft (transport aircraft). . . . In order to achieve the maximum impact on and benefit to ongoing actions, it has been directed that equipment and supplies . . . be accelerated so as to arrive in RVN [the Republic of Vietnam] as quickly as possible.

(S) Associated with these delivery actions, there was a concomitant requirement to furnish equipment, maintenance, and supply items for the identified aircraft, and to provide the capability to support the aircraft and equipment once it was delivered to South Vietnam.* The situation was greatly complicated by the inability of the VNAF to provide the needed personnel, much less trained personnel, to support the accelerated or previously unscheduled systems being delivered. To overcome this problem, Annex U employed the concept of contractor augmentation to support the VNAF. The intent was to use contractors to replace withdrawing USAF personnel by establishing those technical and support functions beyond immediate VNAF capabilities. Once this was accomplished, contractors were to train VNAF personnel, gradually phasing out in conjunction with

---

*(C) The plan for implementing the actions necessary to meet the Project Enhance directive was titled the "USAF Logistics Plan for Vietnam Air Force, Annex U-Project Enhance Directive," more commonly known as Annex U, V-Log (i.e., Annex U, Vietnamization-Logistics).

the growth of VNAF manning and skills. Augmentation had high priority in the Enhance actions, since it would be of greatest assistance to the VNAF in carrying out their war effort and opposing the enemy offensive then raging throughout South Vietnam.[51] Annex U summarized the task, and stressed the importance of contractor assistance:[52]

> (S) This directive primarily concerns actions required to move material into Vietnam by the target date, complete definitization of in-country transfer actions, and establishment of firm demands on the USAF logistic system for follow-on support requirements. The major constraint in implementation of the project within the established time frame is the lack of VNAF capability to receive, store, maintain and operate the materials/equipment being provided. Therefore, the directed actions require expansion of existing augmentation contracts or initiation of new contracts to meet support shortfalls caused by these VNAF personnel/capability constraints. Other contract support may be required to insure movement and processing of required materials.
>
> (S) USAF advisory effort is assumed to continue as currently programmed for the purposes of implementing this project. Extensive augmentation, however, may be required to receive, maintain, and process material inputs. Contractor augmentation as well as AFLC [Rapid Area Maintenance/Rapid Area Supply] teams will be used to meet increased requirements.

Project Enhance Plus (U)

(S) As the combined result of Project Enhance and final revision of FSR-73 in the summer of 1972, the squadron strength projected for the VNAF for the end of FY 73 had again been increased, from 52 to 58 squadrons.[53] By October 1972, the VNAF had activated 51 squadrons, and the remaining seven were programmed for activation over the next 18 months. At that time, VNAF manning stood at 52,400 personnel, heading toward the

61,800 FSR-73 goal. In late October, however, Project Enhance Plus was directed. That project dictated yet another expansion and acceleration. It increased the VNAF inventory by 20 percent, and would lead to a projected VNAF force structure of 66 squadrons (65 to be activated by July 1973).[54] The VNAF manning ceiling would increase by 3,000, resulting in a projected total of 64,500.[55]

(S) As had been the case for previous expansions and accelerations of the Vietnamization program, Enhance Plus planners faced two valid but opposing requirements: (1) the need to create a flexible and strong VNAF capable of meeting the threat as USAF forces withdrew from the conflict, and (2) the critical need for stability and orderly growth in a VNAF which was already stretched gravely thin. Each requirement was indisputable, yet the two were mutually exclusive. In the case of the most recent expansion prior to Enhance Plus, Project Enhance, a decisive factor had arisen, forcing planners to override the need for stability in favor of accelerated VNAF improvement and modernization. That factor had been the North Vietnamese invasion. Again, in the case of Enhance Plus, a decisive factor had arisen: the possibility of an imminent, negotiated cease-fire and total withdrawal of U.S. forces from Vietnam.

(S) At issue, then, was how the U.S. could promote the growth of a strong and flexible RVNAF, while at the same time withdrawing all U.S. military personnel from Vietnam and limiting future support to a one-for-one replacement. The U.S. response to the challenge was Project Enhance Plus. Enhance Plus was to place in the hands of the South Vietnamese, on or before 10 November 1972,* all of the aircraft and supporting equipment needed to meet RVNAF's projected end strength together with one year's supply of war materiel, including spares to serve as Not Operationally Accountable (NOA) and attrition aircraft. As such, the initial phase of Enhance Plus, delivery of the aircraft and materiel to Vietnam, represented the most intense logistical exercise of the SEA conflict. It was a classic hard-core logistical exercise of a "rapid deployment of material to meet an urgent requirement in a short compressed timeframe."[56]

(S) The magnitude of the operation was reflected by the massive amount of equipment and materiel identified in the Enhance Plus execute message. The VNAF portion of Enhance Plus requirements is outlined below:[57]

> (S) The objective of this program is to maximize the amount of equipment in the hands of the RVNAF by 20 Nov 72 [later changed to 10 Nov 72]. . . . This will include delivery of 981/982, CRIMP and Project Enhance remaining requirements, plus expedited delivery of additionally identified aircraft, AGE, support equipment and spares. . . .
>
> (S) The quantity and types of Air Force primary items over and above CRIMP/Enhance requirements are as follows:
>
> | | |
> |---|---|
> | aircraft A-1 | 19 |
> | aircraft AC-119K | 22 (within CRIMP) |
> | aircraft A-37B | 90 |
> | aircraft C-130A | 32 |
> | aircraft F-5A | 126 |
> | aircraft UH-1 | 277 |
> | vehicles | 855 |

*   *   *   *   *   *   *

---

*(S) Enhance Plus was first directed on 20 October 1972, but was cancelled two days later. It was reactivated on 25 October 1972, with the CSAF directive message disseminating to USAF units on 26 October 1972.

> (S) Short deadline and the importance of this action will necessitate withdrawal or diversion as required from active and reserve components and other worldwide sources with subsequent replacement from production resources or AF redistribution actions. . . .
>
> (S) Necessary arrangements will be made for Vietnamization of the on-going VNAF support included in existing US contracts. Actions must be taken to insure that contract augmentation of the VNAF is sufficient to continue essential logistics services without US military presence. Contract support will be provided as soon as possible to assure adequate levels of receipt, care, preservation, storage, and security.

(S) In effect, the Enhance Plus program consisted of two distinct stages. The first related to the immediate task of delivering all the aircraft, equipment, and materiel specified in the directive. As such, the first phase was purely a logistical exercise, and in fact represented the most intense logistics operation of the SEA conflict. The second phase of Enhance Plus was the more difficult, more demanding, and ultimately the more critical task. That phase consisted of the host of actions required to help the VNAF absorb the massive influx of military equipment and materiel which Enhance Plus provided. Complicating the matter was the possibility that the cease-fire agreement might very well specify that no military personnel would be allowed in SVN to assist in the task.

(S) The 26 October Enhance Plus directive specified a project deadline of 10 November. The problems and complexities involved in meeting that deadline are a story in themselves, and are much too extensive to include in detail in this report. To provide a feel for the difficulties experienced, however, a few of the major problems encountered are included below. The time deadline necessitated air transportation of virtually all Project Enhance aircraft and supporting equipment, thus placing a heavy strain on U.S. airlift capabilities. Many of the aircraft specified for delivery were not immediately available in sufficient quantity from U.S. resources, and delicate negotiations had to be rapidly pursued and concluded with foreign countries to obtain the aircraft (32 F-5s were obtained from Iran, 48 from Taiwan, and 36 from Korea). Negotiations also had to be pursued to allow U.S. aircraft to transit or land in a number of foreign countries. Many of the aircraft themselves had to be shipped by C-5 cargo aircraft, and thus required partial disassembly, crating, loading, and shipping--all by the 10 November deadline (66 A-37 aircraft were in this category). Some of the aircraft were from Reserve and National Guard units, and ferrying them to Vietnam in time required mobilizing their crews, bringing them on active duty, and safely making the long trip. Finally, some of the aircraft involved were old and slow, and required augmented crews and the deployment of repair teams and materiel in order for the aircraft to close on schedule (6 C-119s were in this category). Despite these and other obstacles encountered, the more than 250 aircraft identified for air-delivery to Vietnam met the 10 November deadline.[58] All told, the Enhance Plus deliveries and in-country turnovers totaled 625 aircraft, including 19 A-1s, 24 AC-119s, 66 A-37s, 32 C-130As, 116 F-5As, and 9 UH-1 helicopters, all air-delivered into SVN; and 24 A-37s, 4 C-7As, 23 EC-47s, and 307 UH-1 helicopters (30 for the International Commission of Control and Supervision), transferred from U.S. resources within Vietnam. Besides these aircraft, 5,000 tons of support equipment were air-delivered and transferred. (At Bien Hoa Air Base alone, 2,500 tons of materiel were unloaded.) Additionally, by the 10 November deadline, nearly 100,000 tons of RVNAF equipment and materiel were delivered or en route to SVN by sea.[59]

(S) During Enhance Plus planning and execution, planners in Washington envisioned that much of the equipment would initially be placed in storage, and would only gradually be placed in operation as VNAF unit activations proceeded under the CRIMP.[60] Original Enhance Plus guidance to the field, however, "gave no indication of intention for disposition of assets."[61] The Chief of the AFGP, Major General James J. Jumper, reiterated this point in his end-of-tour report:[62]

> (S) . . . The question of what to do with these 600 plus aircraft was not addressed by any explicit instructions or guidance from higher (PACAF-CSAF)[*] headquarters. Some aircraft . . . could be absorbed into existing units, but beyond that point either the aircraft would have to be put in permanent storage and reclaimed at some future time by a civilian contractor, or, new units activated, additional manpower authorized and a major transition program undertaken.

(S) Thus, the field commanders in fact had no approved plans for the disposition of the equipment and material once it arrived in SVN. This planning was finalized after the fact, beginning in November 1972. The approach taken in Vietnam by Vietnamese and U.S. planners was to use Enhance Plus aircraft and equipment to activate new squadrons immediately rather than placing Enhance Plus equipment in storage. This was largely

---

*PACAF--Pacific Air Forces.

a South Vietnamese decision, and one which would be steadfastly pursued despite considerable opposition by high-level U.S. I&M planners.[63] That the South Vietnamese insisted on placing Enhance Plus resources into newly activated, albeit severely undermanned, units attested to the importance the RVNAF had come to place on airpower, and to their determination and confidence in initiating such an undertaking. An Advisory Group message summarized the VNAF attitude as follows:[64]

> (S) When Enhance Plus assets began arriving in October, it was believed that all assets would have to be in-country by X[*] + 60. . . . The estimated continuation of the North Vietnamese threat and the prospect of a rapid USAF withdrawal from SEA caused the VNAF and JGS to exert extra effort toward building the strongest possible air order of battle in the shortest possible time. The VNAF embraced the logic of immediate transition training into the Enhance Plus aircraft immediately and to the maximum extent possible while Blue Suit USAF personnel were still in-country to support, assist, and train.

(S) The South Vietnamese decision to opt for the formation of active squadrons, rather than storing Enhance Plus aircraft and equipment, resulted in the need for a revision of the CRIMP force structure. This revision, if U.S. support and approval were to be obtained, would have to be coordinated through the chain of command to the JCS, and approved by the Office of the SECDEF (OSD). On 1 December, AFGP forwarded an informal, 66-squadron force structure proposal for initial review. As of that date, final JGS and VNAF approval of the plan was still pending, but--as noted by the AFGP--the plan did represent the combined labors of the AFGP and VNAF staffs:[65]

---

*X - date of the cease-fire implementation.

(S) AFGP/VNAF staffs commenced slowly and cautiously in considering training/transition programs for the various weapons systems due to the uncertainty of when X day would occur with a [concomitant] reduction of the daily operational airlift, close air support and air defense sortie requirements making aircraft and maintenance/aircrews available for a transition program. Continuing exploration by AFGP/VNAF staffs has enabled a transition program to begin which will, in 60 days, see two C-130A squadrons activated and qualified, and a transition program for each of the other weapons systems well underway toward achieving aircrew and maintenance qualification. Outstanding support for this VNAF program has been received from 7AF, MACV, PACAF, CSAF, AFLC, the depots and many other agencies and at this point, while much remains to be accomplished, the program is entirely feasible in every respect. . . . The VNAF Have taken a very positive approach to planning and executing the transition program in order to strengthen their AOB [Air Order of Battle] as much and as quickly as possible.

(S) The same AFGP message went on to outline the method by which an already undermanned VNAF intended to pursue the newly planned activations:[66]

(S) In summary, the above force structure proposal is the result of an reevaluation of the VNAF crew manning in light of the urgent need to absorb added assets into [the] active inventory and modernize the force. The activation schedule can be realized only by reducing the crew ratio from the wartime level to one compatible with a cease-fire transition period. A redistribution of VNAF pilot assets by the VNAF staff, with a view to minimum manning until more UPT graduates are received, has enabled the VNAF to man the revised force structure on a near term phase basis. In general the C-130A pilots were taken from two C-123 squadrons to be deactivated. F-5 cockpits will be filled by A-37 pilots, the resulting A-37 shortfall will be filled by excess C-123, C-119 and C-47 transport pilots, plus some upgrading of A-1 and O-1 pilots. In addition, the monthly utilization rates were reduced to match projected capability during the eighteen months needed to fill out and train the revised force. . . . The AFGP computed force structure proposal requires 4,000 less manpower spaces than that requested by the VNAF for the program. Coordination with the VNAF is continuing and should be resolved soon.

> (S) Logistics considerations: One hundred eighty-eight USAF augmentees from CONUS are being utilized at TSN AB [Tan Son Nhut AB) on the C-130A acft. . . . One hundred sixty-three USAF blue suit augmentees were resourced . . . for AC-119K training program at Da Nang AB. . . . The shortfall in VNAF maintenance will be compensated for by contract maintenance until VNAF training is completed. Seventy contract maintenance personnel are presently employed on Enhance Plus assets and an additional 671 have been requested. . . .
>
> (S) We recognize that planning has out-distanced program authorization in some instances, but time has been of the essence. It has been intended that a complete and coordinated revised VNAF FY 1973-74 force structure be submitted . . . through MACV, CINCPAC to JCS in order to get early OSD approval.

(S) The point made in the previous quote concerning VNAF coordination, and requested manning levels, reflected a somewhat uncharacteristic enthusiasm and eagerness displayed by the South Vietnamese concerning their ability to absorb and grow into the proposed expanded force structure. During the coordination stages for the new force structure proposal, the ambitious level of aircraft (the VNAF requested keeping some of the C-119s being replaced by C-130s) and manning being sought by the VNAF prompted the following note of caution in a letter from Major General J. J. Jumper to Lieutenant General Tran Van Minh, Commander, VNAF:[67]

> (S) A concern of some importance . . . is that the rapid expansion of VNAF since 1969, which has been even more compressed with introduction of Project Enhance Plus assets, has over-extended VNAF maintenance and aircrew assets to the degree that retaining any excess aircraft will result in drawing off maintenance and aircrew assets from the C-130, F-5A and A-37 force. A major training effort and considerable time will be required for VNAF to reach the experience level needed to operate most effectively equipment now in the inventory. Manpower, budgetary considerations, training time and training

facilities are all critical factors. The VNAF manpower and experience level problem will be further compounded if there is a reduction of RVNAF after a cease-fire agreement. . . .

(S) I believe the strongest consideration should be given at this time to structuring the VNAF along austere lines with a maximum number of combat type aircraft assigned that VNAF can support, on a minimum number of bases consistent with prudent base loading, and with a minimum number of non-combat administrative support type aircraft.

(S) On 13 December 1972, AFGP forwarded a complete VNAF force structure proposal, informally coordinated at the working level with MACV, the JGS, and the VNAF, comprising 66 squadrons, including 19 tactical fighter squadrons, and containing a 64,500 manning level.[68] On 18 December the CSAF provided AFGP, through PACAF, a modified force structure as a preferred alternative. The modified plan proposed a 61-squadron force, representing a reduced UE of 164 aircraft. The UE reduction was proposed to provide for NOA and attrition aircraft within existing VNAF inventories, since many of the aircraft delivered during Enhance Plus had been programmed for that purpose. The AFGP response, forwarded in a 22 December message to PACAF, stated the case for the 66-squadron force:[69]

(S) Subject force structure was developed to incorporate Enhance Plus assets into the active VNAF inventory in order to meet the seriousness of the North Vietnamese threat. The rationale for this structure was based on the following premises:

(A) Under terms of the cease-fire agreement, no increase to authorized strength would be allowed.

(B) Aircraft losses would be replaced on a timely one for one basis. The revised force structure [AFGP's 66-squadron proposal] is a minimal force when compared to the Free World Military Force in being for the past several years. It is structured to provide the VNAF with potential to develop a trained force capable of meeting the threat for the foreseeable future. A reduction of authorized strength is not advisable from a threat oriented operational viewpoint.

(S) On 28 December, in a message to CSAF, PACAF underscored their strong support of the AFGP position. Additional rationale for supporting the 66-squadron proposal was also provided:[70]

> (S) The AFGP-proposed final revised VNAF force structure reflects the results of considerable negotiations between and approval by the AFGP, VNAF, 7AF, COMUSMACV, and RVNAF JGS. That these staffs concurred in and authorized an increase in VNAF manpower is considerable indication of resolve within VNAF/RVNAF JGS. Previous efforts to obtain RVNAF/JGS approval for VNAF strength increases have been obtained only after overcoming strong opposition. Force structure was designed to meet the North Vietnamese threat and represents an approach to the 69 squadron position as previously forwarded in Air Appendix of MACV-Mid Range Plan [through FY 78]. . . . This may be our final opportunity to establish a viable VNAF force structure and take advantage of VNAF trade-off spaces to accommodate VNAF manpower increases. It also indicates JGS recognition of the importance of airpower and as such sould be supported.

> (S) Based on the above, request your support for the 66 squadron force level in the joint arena. However, support for the 66 sqdn force structure does not preclude later modification to allow for NOA, attrition, or reduce overhead. A continuing review of force structure requirements will be made as VNAF training, personnel recruitment, and squadron activations occur. Final terms of a cease-fire agreement, decision on headroom ceilings, and evidences of enemy intentions during cease-fire period may also allow for modifications in force structure. Thus, as the force structure develops, it may become appropriate to make modifications.

(S) On 3 January 1973, CINCPAC also added his support to the 66-squadron proposal, adding that substitution of the F-5As delivered during Enhance Plus was a matter of expediency only. The F-5As were not considered a permanent substitute, but were to be replaced by F-5Es as they became available. As did AFGP and PACAF, CINCPAC also noted his continuing support for the MACV Mid-Range force structure proposal which would increase the VNAF squadron level to 69 by FY 78 (this was to include 20 tactical fighter squadrons). Based on these recommendations, the JCS supported a VNAF force structure of 66 squadrons (to be reached by the end of FY 74), and approved, for planning purposes, a 20 tactical fighter squadron force (8 F-5E and 12 A-37 squadrons, to be operational by FY 78).[71]

Post-Cease-Fire Developments (U)

(S) The official date of the "cease-fire" in Vietnam was 27 January 1973. Following the cease-fire, the VNAF faced the task of absorbing the massive amount of equipment and materiel delivered during Enhance Plus, manning and operating the facilities transferred from U.S. forces, and growing into the expanded operational, maintenance, and support requirements acquired during the previous year. In retrospect, the impact of Enhance Plus on the VNAF was staggering. Its effects would continue to be felt in the months subsequent to the cease-fire as the VNAF, with U.S. contractor and Defense Attache Office (DAO) assistance, would try to gain a logistic, personnel, and training equilibrium.*

---

*(S) In the opinion of key U.S. personnel who remained in Vietnam to guide DAO and contractor efforts,[72] one of the lessons the Air Force learned was that, at the last hour in the Vietnam conflict, the U.S. "poured too much, too fast, down the Vietnamese throat."[73] It was also the consensus that the recovery of the VNAF from the impact of Enhance
(Continued)

(S) To assist the VNAF in their expansion to a self-sufficient, 66-squadron force, very limited levels of U.S. personnel would be available. As specified in the cease-fire agreement, only 50 U.S. military personnel would be allowed in Vietnam. Further, self-imposed U.S. constraints placed a ceiling of 1,200 DOD civilians, and 5,000 U.S. contractor personnel for in-country assistance. A further constraint, initially imposed but eventually relaxed, was a one-year time limit on U.S. contractor assistance to the South Vietnamese. MACV and the AFGP, the organizations through which U.S. assistance to the RVNAF had previously been channeled, were to be phased out within 60 days of the cease-fire, by which time all U.S. military personnel (except the 50 specified above) would be withdrawn from the RVN. The DAO was established in-country and assumed responsibility for carrying out all of those in-country military matters within the purview of the United States Support Activities Group (USSAG)/7AF, and CINCPAC.[74]

(S) Within the DAO, assistance to the VNAF was managed by the Air Force Division. Essentially, the Air Force Division was the agency which filled the void left by the departing AFGP. It inherited the latter's responsibilities in pursuit of VNAF improvement and modernization, with its ultimate goal of self-sufficiency.[75] The tasks confronting the Air

---

(Continued)
Plus, and the continuing growth, training, and maturing of the VNAF required two healing factors: time and conditions of reasonable stability. Yet, in view of the limited success of the cease-fire agreement in halting combat, VNAF progress would have to be accomplished concurrently with continuing combat requirements.

Force Division were monumental. On the road toward their goal, the VNAF faced immediate obstacles in the areas of personnel, combat crew and maintenance training, logistics support, construction, and modification programs (CROCs). In addition, they faced serious long-term problems in the logistics support areas which had long received lesser emphasis than the high-priority operational areas. The weakness of VNAF support capabilities was only heightened by the impact of Enhance Plus. The "VNAF Logistics Guidance" plan, published in March 1973, underscored this point:[76]

> (S) Previous planning envisioned VNAF logistics development through the 1975 time frame using required advisors (military, [DOD] civilian, and/or contractor) in achieving a high degree of self-sufficiency. Increased hostilities, opening of new VNAF bases, and the recent peace agreement required a new direction in many areas of logistics planning to compensate for dilution of VNAF skill, VNAF manning deficiencies, one year tenure of DOD civilians and expedited completion of facility modification. Logistics planning during the initial phases of Enhance Plus did not provide for the increased force structure of the VNAF to their objective 66 squadrons. Planning was for storage of the majority of these aircraft and when decision was reversed to activate new squadrons, the VNAF were not equipped logistically to do so.

(S) The magnitude of the logistics problems facing the VNAF prompted early recognition that VNAF self-sufficiency in supporting a 66-squadron force would not be attainable within the one-year time constraint initially imposed on U.S. contractor support.[77] Remarking on the progress of the RVNAF toward self-sufficiency, a DAO, Air Force Division paper pointed out:[78]

> (S) The South Vietnamese Armed Forces have made remarkable strides in logistical and administrative support operations from the viewpoint of management and technical capability. They have moved from an environment in which most decisions and technical operations were performed by military advisors to one in which no military advisors are provided and only limited technical assistance is provided by a small number of contractors or U.S. Government civilians. However, in some technical areas, they continue to have a major personnel shortfall in the middle management levels. . . .
>
> (S) The VNAF has had by far the most difficult task in developing logistics self-sufficiency. The increase in the number of squadrons and complexity of aircraft have created a requirement for technology and management which cannot be fully met in the limited time available. Therefore, the VNAF will continue to require technical assistance to a greater extent and longer than the other services.

(TS) Clearly, the major factor constraining the VNAF in their efforts to attain self-sufficiency in the support of their 66-squadron, 64,500-man force, was the lack of trained, experienced personnel resulting from the rapid expansion of the VNAF. This basic constraint manifested itself by a host of problems in operational, maintenance, supply, and facilities capabilities. A July 1973 DAO report substantiated this assessment, stating that "the impact of Enhance Plus has put the VNAF in the position of having to grow into operations, maintenance, supply, personnel, and facilities. Training and lack of supply and maintenance support impose the most severe limitations."[79] To provide the background for the problems which faced the VNAF during the post-cease-fire period, a 15 December 1972 USAF planning document outlined the personnel problems projected for the coming months:[80]

(TS) Current over-all VNAF authorization manning ceiling is 61,760, with approximately 52,600 currently assigned, for an 84% ratio. . . . Also, approximately 8,000 VNAF personnel are currently involved in various stages of training which reduced the VNAF current productive manpower force to about 44,000 personnel of their 61,760 authorized personnel. Long training lead times are often involved for highly technical skill. The new VNAF personnel requirement, as a result of Enhance Plus, and considering tradeoffs, yields a new ceiling requirement of 64,500 or an additional 2,740 personnel. These additional personnel represent an additional training requirement. Training is recognized as a primary constraint in Vietnamizing Logistics.

(S) In the words of the Director of the Air Force Division, DAO, it was "amazing" that the Vietnamese were able to absorb the massive expansion resulting from CRIMP, Enhance, and Enhance Plus. "We've force-fed them more than I think anybody could stand, but they have been able to absorb it."[81] A look at the situation from the Vietnamese viewpoint provides additional insight and adds further weight to the Director's remarks. A letter, written by Lt Gen Tran Van Minh, the VNAF Commander, nearly 10 months after the initiation of Enhance Plus, summarized:[82]

(S) . . . To fully understand our problems so as to adequately solve them . . . we think it helpful to put these problems within the framework of the VNAF when the Project "Enhance Plus" came into being and to review developments concerning the carrying out of this project so far:

(S) On Oct. 21, 1972, while [the] war in Vietnam was at its most critical stage, the VNAF was having to bring all its efforts to bear upon the fighting, and at the same time the Paris peace talks were entering the final phase, we were notified of the project known as "Enhance Plus" which provided for the turn-over of 615 [sic] airplanes to the VNAF. A few days later, the first airplanes under the said project began to arrive in Vietnam, and around Nov. 20, 1972, the last one reached Vietnam, not including a number of helicopters already available in Vietnam which were gradually turned-over to the VNAF prior to the withdrawal of U.S. forces.

(S) Immediately after being notified of the "Enhance Plus" Project Oct. 21, 1972, the VNAF Command, on the one hand set out to prepare for the receipt of the planes, and, on the other, studied a new force structure for the VNAF, drew up plans of expanding and utilizing forces of fighter, transport, helicopter, reconnaissance planes so as to be abreast of the new juncture, and prepared TO & E [Table of Organization & Equipment] for newly established unit, etc.

(S) On Dec. 1, 1972, the first squadron under the "Enhance Plus" Project was activated, and on June 1, 1973, the last squadrons of the aforementioned project were formed (with the exception of the Cruiser Squadron 720, that has not yet been established pending your concurrence).

(S) Thus, after 40 days of preparation and planning, and in a short space of 6 months, the VNAF has completed the establishment of:

- 8 Fighter Squadrons
- 2 Transport Squadrons
- 1 Armed Transport Squadron
- 6 Squadrons and 8 Flights of Helicopters
- 1 Training Squadron
- and reinforced Reconnaissance Squadrons with 35 O-2 planes.

(S) That made a total of 18 squadrons and 8 flights. In addition, UH-1 Helicopter Squadrons' quota increased from 33 to 38 planes.

(S) To meet the requirement for crews necessitated by newly-activated squadrons, the VNAF has proceeded with:
- Cross-training 59 A-37 pilots for F-5s (completed).
- Cross-training 49 O-1 pilots for A-37s (completed).
- Cross-training 144 C-123 and C-119 crew members for C-130 (completed).
- Cross-training 190 AC-119G crew members to AC-119Ks (completed).
- Cross-training 52 C-123 crew members to RC-119Gs for the Cruiser Squadron 720 (completed).

-Cross-training 36 O-1 pilots for O-2s (completed).
-Training of 420 helicopter pilots (first course started on July 1, 1972).

(S) Previously all the above training was carried out in the United States with longer period of time and much expense.

(S) The VNAF has recruited more personnel to increase its strength from 53,926 to 61,660 (it will increase to 64,909 in the future). The training of specialists have [sic] been pushed forward to replenish newly-activated units.

(S) In order to form 18 squadrons and eight flights in the record time of six months with only 40 days of preparation many problems have been solved.

(S) . . . We must admit however, that there are still many shortcomings that need be overcome. Most of them are not caused by any organ but it is due to the quick expansion of the VNAF to deal with new threats and new developments of the situation. Thus, it takes time to correct them.

(S) Thus, much progress had been made in pursuing the goal of VNAF self-sufficiency. Nevertheless, the VNAF I&M program continued to present difficult and challenging problems which would demand continuing U.S. assistance and vigorous pursuit by VNAF personnel. Perhaps the most urgent requirement in pursuit of VNAF self-sufficiency was the development of an efficient VNAF logistics system. The VNAF had the aircraft, and had enough crews to man them (although crew strength was not at maximum authorization, the crews available could fly at rates exceeding the maintenance capability): their greatest weakness lay in maintaining the aircraft, and providing the supplies needed to keep them flying. As the Director of the Air Force Division put it, logistics "is what this whole show is about now; we're trying to develop their capability to maintain their aircraft themselves. Believe me, they've got the best pilots in the world . . . some pilots with 10,000 hours of combat time. Their biggest deficiency is logistics in maintaining their aircraft."[83] Accordingly, the September 1973 V-Log Plan presented the revised tasks facing the VNAF in developing its logistics system, and outlined the approach and objectives of U.S. assistance during the final quarter of the first year following the cease-fire in South Vietnam:[84]

CONCEPT

(S) The VNAF's combat capability will continue to be maintained and supported concurrently with expansion of its logistics base. Priority of effort will be directed toward establishing effective maintenance and supply systems to support assigned weapon systems, mission essential equipment, and essential facilities. The ultimate objective is to achieve a viable logistics management system which provides VNAF self-sufficiency consistent with cost and time constraints.

* * * * * * *

GENERAL

(S) The Vietnamese program continues to be one of the priority efforts of the U.S. Air Force. Significant progress has been made during the past months with the major delivery programs completed, the VNAF force structure expanding from 52 to a programmed 66 squadrons (activation of RC-119L pending JCS approval), and sortie rate accomplishments reaching new highs. Responsibility for base management has been assumed by the VNAF, with their units being required to maintain capabilities in a high threat environment.

(S) With the transition to the DAO structure completed and the original force beddown posture virtually achieved, the priority of V-Log efforts requires strengthening the VNAF's capabilities to operate effectively with reduced levels of U.S. support. In accomplishing this, the primary considerations are correcting deficiencies, completing necessary training programs, and establishing programs to fulfill specific follow-on objectives.

OBJECTIVES

(S) . . . a. <u>Increase the maintenance capability for aircraft, engines, equipment and facilities. Correct identified deficiencies as indicated below:</u>

(1) The August 1973 V-Log review revealed that the VNAF lack sufficient skilled personnel to maintain all assigned aircraft, engines, AGE, vehicles, and facilities. Programs must be established to return these resources to a serviceable condition. Actions should then be taken to identify items which will reflect adequate utilization, maintenance, redistribution and storage, as appropriate.

*　　*　　*　　*　　*　　*　　*

b. <u>Train VNAF in required logistics skills:</u>

(1) The VNAF have made significant and rapid progress in their overall manning, with over 95% of authorized personnel now assigned or in training pipeline. This rapid expansion of the labor force has, however, caused the following additive problems:

(a) Saturation of VNAF training capability.

(b) Majority of assigned personnel are three level.

(c) Dilution of overall skill level of the total VNAF work force. At present, nearly 10,000 airmen are in initial training while the majority of airmen assigned to the active units are at the apprentice level. This situation requires continuing action and necessary visibility to insure all available training resources are being utilized to improve this situation.

*　　*　　*　　*　　*　　*　　*

c. <u>Improve accountability and control over supplies and equipment; increase the efficiency and responsiveness of the VNAF supply system.</u>

(1) The massive transfers of supplies and equipment during 1972 resulted in significant backlogs in the various VNAF supply receiving functions with a corresponding reduction in inventory accuracy. Weapon systems and equipment transfers (USAF/U.S. Army to VNAF) accomplished in conjunction with accelerated unit activations resulted in degradation of accountability in many instances.

(2) Actions taken to date have eliminated backlogs and improved accountability, but additional emphasis is required.

*   *   *   *   *   *   *

d. Complete ALC Expansion. There is an established program to provide the VNAF with an extensive depot maintenance capability at the ALC. Expeditious completion of this program is essential as it provides the basic capabilities to allow the VNAF to achieve the programmed level of logistics self-sufficiency. While progress is being made in all areas, some slippages have delayed completion. Revised schedules must now be met and completion must be accomplished to insure program support to the VNAF.

e. Fulfill other established USAF program objectives. Other V-Log objectives are outlined as separate actions in this plan. These include resolution of issues, such as F-5 program and the RC-119L requirement, expanding the VNAF computer system, and establishment of an off-shore support organization.

f. Phase down the DAO organization and reduce the U.S. contractor presence as other objectives are achieved. Plans have been made to reduce DAO civilian manning either on an incremental basis or as rapidly as possible. Additionally, U.S. contractor support will be terminated as training and augmentation requirements are completed. Continuing action is necessary to assure that the DAO phase down is accomplished only as training programs and logistics actions are completed and other goals are achieved. Follow-on contract support requirements . . . must be established.

(U) The evolution of the I&M program between mid-1971 and mid-1973 had been hectic, in response to major and often unexpected events; dramatic, in the scope of the changes wrought in the I&M program; and far-reaching, in terms of the VNAF's capability to absorb equipment, train personnel, and support its increasingly sophisticated and diverse weapons systems. The growth and state of VNAF mission capabilities during this period are presented in the following chapter.

CHAPTER III

VNAF OPERATIONAL CAPABILITIES (U)

Introduction--Command and Control Considerations (U)

(U) RVNAF command and control relationships strongly influenced the employment and effectiveness of VNAF operational capabilities in support of RVNAF forces. A discussion of these considerations is therefore presented here as an introduction to VNAF operational capabilities.

(C) The VNAF, Vietnamese Navy (VNN), and ARVN were formally under the command of the Joint General Staff. In practice, however, the JGS was concerned almost exclusively with day-to-day management only of ground forces, and both the VNAF and VNN maintained separate and distinct headquarters and staffs which were physically apart from the JGS compound and functioned almost entirely independently. In short, the JGS did not exercise day-to-day command and control over the VNAF and VNN; the JGS allocated resources, established and monitored policies, and published directives--their involvement in operational matters, however, was normally after-the-fact. When significant command matters arose among the services, they were personally, and most often verbally, resolved by the Military Region (MR), VNAF, and VNN Commanders, and by South Vietnamese political officials at the highest levels. The Military Region Commanders exercised the most direct command and control over VNAF strike aircraft and helicopters, while VNAF headquarters served more as a monitoring agency, and the Air Divisions as suppliers.[85] An October 1973 DAO assessment outlined these relationships, and underscored the enormous power wielded by the MR Commanders:[86]

> (C) To describe the function of the VNAF in the total RVNAF military capability, a general analogy can be made with the U.S. concept of Unified and Component Commands. Each of the MRs act as a Unified Command. As the component command, the VNAF is responsible for training and equipping the air arm of the Military Region. Virtually all operational concept and doctrine is established and implemented by the MR Commander. The Air Force combat resources in each MR respond only to requests made by the MR Commander or his operation [s] staff. The MR Commander has absolute authority over his available forces and therefore determines the extent of joint operations as well as establishing the interfaces between the component services within his region. The usefulness of the "Unified Command" analogy ceases at the concept of joint staff employment. MR staffs are dominated by ARVN personnel. The DASC [Direct Air Support Center] Commander (normally a COL or LTC*) is responsive to the MR G-3 [collectively, the Operations Staff; individually, chief of that staff]. Informal relationships exist between the MR Commander and the Air Division Commanders in each region.

> * * * * * * *

> (C) VNAF Headquarters does not command or control the Air Force resources. . . . Command and control of strike aircraft and helicopters rests with the ARVN Corps [MR] Commander. The monitoring of air operations by VNAF Headquarters personnel is tempered by the quantity, quality and timeliness of data reported. . . . Like the other component commands and the JGS itself, the VNAF Headquarters staff gets the information the Military Region Commander wants them to have, when he wants them to have it.

(C) Thus, the VNAF did not exercise centralized command and control over its strike and helicopter resrouces. In reality, command and control was decentralized and in the hands of the MR Commanders. The daily role played by the VNAF Tactical Air Control System (TACS) strongly

---
*COL--Colonel; LTC--Lieutenant Colonel.

reflected the command and control realities outlined by the DAO, above. Basically, the VNAF TACS consisted of a Tactical Air Control Center (TACC); four Direct Air Support Centers, one for each Military Region; and Tactical Air Control Parties, assigned at each province, regiment, and MR, and normally consisting of Air Liaison Officers, Forward Air Controllers, and radio operators.[87] When a given ARVN battalion required air support, it forwarded a request to its regimental Tactical Operations Center (TOC), which reviewed and consolidated requests from the various battalions, and forwarded those deemed appropriate to the MR TOC. Theoretically, the ALO assigned to each Regimental TOC was to provide expertise on the employment of airpower, and was to advise the MR DASC of the actions taken by the Regimental TOC. The MR TOC reviewed and consolidated requests from the various Regimental TOCs, established air support requirements, and notified the MR DASC. The ALO assigned to the MR TOC was to provide expertise in matters related to air support. The DASC contacted the appropriate Air Division to ascertain the ability to generate the required number of sorties. Subsequently, the DASC informed the TACC, which in turn published the frag.[88]

(C) Notably, daily sortie schedules within each MR were stable. The number of sorties fragged was a function of overall operational requirements, maintenance capabilities, and unit training, rather than day-to-day operational needs. Once established, the number of <u>fragged</u> sorties was rarely changed. The number of sorties actually <u>flown</u> in a given MR on a given day, however, varied widely, and it was this actual number flown which reflected operational needs. The MR commanders established the policy that fragged missions would not be flown unless required.[89]

(C) A crucial element in the link between the VNAF TACS and the ground commanders were the ALOs. The ALO represented the practical point of contact between the supplier and the user. Ideally, ALOs should have been assigned down to the battalion level, but personnel limitations precluded that approach. Instead, at the battalion level, liaison in air operations matters was to be provided by a designated ARVN officer who had attended a one-month course on the employment of aircraft, strike request procedures, and so forth. At the regimental level, ALOs were assigned to provide expertise and advice related to the employment of airpower. In practice, however, most ALOs were inexperienced, low-ranking pilot washouts or non-rated observers. Consequently, they were ignored by ARVN commanders. This problem, which would have to be solved if effective employment of air support were to be realized, had been recognized by U.S. advisors for years. Earlier AFGP and VNAF efforts to assign more qualified, higher-ranking ALO personnel were frustrated by the shortage of qualified officers and pilots, and by VNAF assignment priorities which reflected the prevalent attitude that the ALO's job was less esteemed and respected than that of a pilot assigned to an operational squadron. Enhance Plus had the effect of further prompting the transfer of qualified pilots to newly activating squadrons.[90] The DAO assessment cited above summarized the ALO situation as of October 1973.[91]

> (C) The ALO/FAC* system in the VNAF is the victim of personnel shortages due to the pilot requirements created by the Enhance Plus Program. . . . The ALOs . . .

---

*VNAF FACs are discussed in the Visual Reconnaissance section, p. 99.

are young inexperienced officers. Only one MR ALO is a rated pilot. The rest of the ALOs are officers who have received some training as observers. The result of this situation is that the [Vietnamese] Air Force representative, upon whom the ground commander is to depend for advice, is relatively inexperienced and considerably junior in military rank to the man he is to advise. In practice, any joint use of air power is entirely dependent upon the background, qualification and attitudes of the ground commander.

(S) Near the end of 1973, VNAF headquarters once again proposed assigning fighter pilots as ALOs. If that action were pursued, it would have a positive, upgrading influence on the level of expertise of ALOs and would undoubtedly increase their esteem in the eyes of the ground commanders. However, it was believed that further improvement in the ALO situation, and ultimately in the manner in which air support was employed, would also require the assignment of higher-ranking officers who would be on an equal level with the ARVN officers they were advising.[92] Even then, the flexibility and responsiveness of the VNAF in support of ground forces would continue to be limited by a more basic constraint: the decentralized control of air resources under the MR Commanders.

Fighters (U)

(S) The VNAF fighter force (see Table 1) was at the heart of the CRIMP; the development of that force, and the mission capabilities it was to provide, were basic goals of the VNAF I&M program. Of the traditional combat tasks facing the VNAF--close air support, interdiction, and air defense--greatest emphasis had been placed on close air support, for reasons of practicality, economics, estimated threat, and VNAF ability to absorb new missions. The VNAF fighter force, as of late 1971, was still programmed

TABLE 1: VNAF FIGHTER SQUADRONS
July 1971 vs July 1973 (U)

	1 July 1971			1 July 1973		Qtr of CY* for
Sqdn	A/C UE**	Base	Sqdn	A/C UE	Base	New Activation
516	A-37/18	Da Nang	NC***	NC/24	NC	-
520	A-37/18	Binh Thuy	NC	NC/24	NC	-
524	A-37/18	Nha Trang	NC	NC/24	NC	-
526	A-37/18	Binh Thuy	NC	NC/24	NC	-
528	A-37/18	Da Nang	NC	NC/24	NC	-
514	A-1/24	Bien Hoa	NC	NC/NC	NC	-
518	A-1/18	Bien Hoa	NC	NC/24	NC	-
530	A-1/18	Pleiku	NC	NC/24	NC	-
522	F-5A/B/18	Bien Hoa	NC	NC/23	NC	-
	RF-5A/6	Bien Hoa	NC	NC/7	NC	-
Total Squadrons	Total UE		532	A-37/24	Phu Cat	4/72
9	174		534	A-37/24	Phan Rang	4/72
			546	A-37/24	Binh Thuy	2/73
			548	A-37/24	Phan Rang	2/73
			550	A-37/24	Da Nang	2/73
			536	F-5A/17	Bien Hoa	4/72
			538	F-5A/14	Da Nang	1/73
			540	F-5A/17	Bien Hoa	1/73
			542	F-5A/17	Bien Hoa	2/73
			544	F-5A/17	Bien Hoa	2/73
			Total Squadrons	Total UE		
			19	427		

* CY -- Calendar Year
** A/C -- Aircraft
*** NC -- No Change

Source for Tables 1-6, (S) CHECO Report, Vietnamization of the Air War, 1970-1971 (U), 8 Oct 71 (S). AFGP, "Military Assistance Progress Report (U)," for the quarterly periods between Jul 71 and Dec 72 (S). U.S. DAO, Saigon, "DAO Quarterly Assessment Report (U)," Jul and Oct 73 (S).

primarily to provide close air support in a low threat, counterinsurgency environment. By that time, however, the prospect of continuing, and potentially complete, U.S. withdrawal from Vietnam and, indeed, from Southeast Asia, was having an impact on I&M planners.[93] In late 1971, well before the spring 1972 NVA invasion, planners were exploring in detail the possible ways of improving VNAF capabilities in close air support, and of establishing credible VNAF capabilities in the interdiction and air defense roles. The enemy invasion, especially when coupled with later cease-fire negotiations, served to underscore the need for improved VNAF capabilities in a conventional war, high-threat environment. Further, it intensified the awareness of shortfalls in the programmed I&M structure, and increased the urgency of providing the VNAF with the potential to assume broadened mission capabilities.

(TS) <u>Evolution of the Fighter Force</u> (U). The need to overcome shortfalls in the air defense and interdiction missions had a forceful influence in the evolution of the fighter force. The first major plan to provide the VNAF with an interdiction capability, however, did not propose fighter resources. Credible Chase, the program to equip the VNAF with STOL "mini-gunship" squadrons, received high-level interest and support in late 1971 and early 1972. While the program was eventually abandoned for a variety of practical reasons, the high-level support it enjoyed reflected the awareness among U.S. leaders that the withdrawal of U.S. air forces would leave the VNAF with serious shortfalls, especially in interdiction and air defense capabilities. It was widely recognized that it was beyond both the RVN's capability and fiscal reality to attempt to provide, and support, the massive level of resources applied by U.S. forces in interdiction operations in SEA. Nevertheless, support and operation of a limited interdiction capability in critical border areas was felt to be within the scope of VNAF mission capabilities if proper equipment were provided.[94] Similarly, the modest VNAF F-5 air defense capability programmed under CRIMP could be improved if the appropriate number and type of aircraft were provided. An April 1972 message from the AFGP summarized the status of the VNAF's interdiction and air defense potentials as viewed at that time, and proposed a number of actions to upgrade VNAF capabilities:[95]

> (S) Air defense is currently being performed by the U.S. Air Force supplemented with two F-5A aircraft. The NVAF [North Vietnamese Air Force] has the primary mission of air defense, however, a capability for offensive operations exists. Consisting of 250-275 aircraft, the NVAF have the capability to strike most of the installations in South Vietnam. . . . The minimal AAA [antiaircraft artillery] capability developed for the ARVN could be a significant deficiency. Primary emphasis has been placed on VNAF for future AD [air defense] and the acquisition of three 18 UE F-5E interceptor squadrons has been programmed and approved for activation in 1974. These fighter squadrons should provide an operational air defense capability in FY 75. . . . Continued support by U.S. forces will be mandatory until at least one VNAF F-5E squadron is operationally ready.
>
> *   *   *   *   *   *   *
>
> (S) In the air interdiction role, the capability of the VNAF is limited to eleven planned fighter attack squadrons, one AC-47 squadron and one AC-119G squadron. The fighters (A-1s and A-37s) required U.S. assistance when operating in high threat areas, to counter the heavy air defenses which the NVN possess and have shown they can move with their forces. Similarly, the gunships

required escort protection when operating in the same environment. FAC aircraft further limit most fighter strikes to day VFR [Visual Flight Rules] conditions although some added capability is being developed. There are some actions being taken to enhance VNAF interdiction capability within the next eighteen months or more but they are not of a nature that would significantly change the current capabilities. (Some of these actions are the forthcoming introduction of the AC-119K with 20mm [millimeter] cannon and sophisticated detection devices, modification of the A-37 for carriage of a 20mm gun pod. . .). In view of these limitations, it would appear that if the VNAF is to have a true air interdiction capability, some consideration must be given to providing it with suitable equipment. If U.S. airpower and the air superiority which it provided is withdrawn, the VNAF should be modernized to offset the high threat environment presented by NVN AAA and the likely use of the now relatively inactive NVN Air Force. . . . To provide the VNAF with a capability to concentrate on the RVN border infiltration routes while providing a suitable degree of survivability, we recommend that the following be considered:

(A) Substitute a more capable attack aircraft such as the F-4 or A-7 for the aging A-1.

(B) Provide longer range and more capable FAC aircraft to replace the O-1 and U-17.

(C) Modernize the AC-119G gunship with 20mm cannon to provide a greater truck killing capability.

(TS) The requirement to introduce more sophisticated aircraft into the VNAF, however, had to be weighed against the inevitable impact on other VNAF capabilities. An April 1972 CINCPAC message echoed the Advisory Group's concern by stating that "the increased threat posed by NVA gun and missile anti-aircraft capabilities as well as possible shortfalls in A-1 and A-37 aircraft availability all favor considering the upgrading of a portion of the VNAF TACAIR [Tactical Aircraft] fleet with more modern and capable aircraft."[96] The same message noted, however, that the addition of such aircraft had to be "carefully weighed against the availability of qualified manpower to meet the operational and logistic requirements that such additions would engender." I&M planners, weighing both the requirement for more capable aircraft and the need to avoid the introduction of still another weapon system into the VNAF, proposed the following long-range solution: replacement of the aging A-1 with additional A-37 squadrons, to provide improved close air support and interdiction capabilities, and provision of additional F-5E squadrons capable in both the interdiction and air defense roles.[97] An October 1972 memorandum from Brig Gen Richard G. Cross, Chief of the Air Operations Division, MACV, further explained the rationale behind these force structure changes, which were proposed for the 1975 to 1978 time period:[98]

> (TS) The proposed VNAF force structure is the result of a hard reappraisal of the shortfall that will exist in the VNAF air mission responsibility. . . . DOD guidance directs our planning toward the total withdrawal of U.S. air support in the post FY 75 time period. The withdrawal of U.S. air assets will uncover a shortfall in the VNAF capability to support the CAS [Close Air Support], INT [Interdiction], and air defense missions. The driving constraint on the proper structuring of the VNAF is the shortage of trained pilots and maintenance personnel caused by the rapid buildup of the force during the last three years. Any precipitous insertion of a new weapons system into the VNAF force structure would cause an unacceptable degradation of their existing operational capability. E.g., it would take the pilot resources of two A-37 squadrons to train one squadron of F-4C's. Therefore, the approach used by the planners for the VNAF force structure makes every attempt to maximize existing VNAF capabilities and more fully exploit programmed aircraft. The additional A-37 squadrons have the least impact on the VNAF manpower, training, and logistical problem areas. The F-5E, originally dedicated to the air defense role, is now proposed as a dual-purpose aircraft; air defense and ground attack. . . . The end FY 78 fighter structure proposed 8 squadrons of F-5E dually certified and 12 squadrons of A-37s bringing

> the fighter force to twenty squadrons. This force. . . .
> provides nominal CAS and INT support of near border
> areas, and a limited air defense capability for South
> Vietnam.

(S) This approach was supported by the JCS who formally stated, in an October 1972 memorandum for the SECDEF, that there was no short-term solution to increasing the capability of the VNAF, due to the long lead time required to train pilots and maintenance personnel. They pointed out, however, that the proposed A-37 and F-5E squadrons would cause the least logistical impact on the VNAF and, by exploiting the ground attack capability of the F-5E, would enhance VNAF close air support and interdiction capabilities as well as increasing the air defense potential.[99]

(S) Later that same month, the thinking which was prevalent in the Mid-Range Force structure Review was reflected in the list of attack aircraft specified for delivery under Enhance Plus. Additional A-37 aircraft were to be provided to the VNAF, as were a large number of F-5A aircraft which were intended as on-hand substitutes until F-5Es became available. It was obvious after the cease-fire, however, that it would be many months, if not several years, before the aircraft and equipment poured into SVN during Enhance Plus would be absorbed and their operational potential fully exploited.[100] Nowhere was this more true than in the exploitation of the F-5.

(S) Prior to Enhance Plus, VNAF F-5A resources consisted of a single squadron located at Bien Hoa, with a detachment of six aircraft stationed at Da Nang for air defense purposes. The first involvement of the VNAF in the air defense role had begun in January 1972, when the VNAF deployed

those six F-5A aircraft and associated crews from Bien Hoa AB to Da Nang
AB to begin training in air defense alert tactics with the USAF. Shortly
thereafter, two F-5s began standing five-minute alert. These aircraft
were initially fragged for training sorties, but by April 1972 they began
flying daylight operational sorties. Total VNAF assumption of the RVN air
defense mission, however, was not scheduled to commence until the VNAF's
first squadron of F-5Es became operationally ready in mid-1974,[101] following the scheduled arrival in SVN of the first F-5Es in early 1974.
This arrival date could not be accelerated due to both aircraft production
schedules and long training lead times for aircrews and ground crews.[102]
Thus, the VNAF would not have a "sophisticated Air Defense system to repel
the North Vietnamese upon U.S. withdrawal,"[103] and some U.S. aircraft
would be required to remain in the area as a deterrent.[104]

(S) During Enhance Plus, however, large numbers of F-5As were delivered to the VNAF. As a result, the VNAF activated five more squadrons
of F-5As in late 1972 and early 1973. By June 1973, the VNAF had three
squadrons designated for employment in the close air support and interdiction roles (stationed at Bien Hoa), while three other squadrons (at
Bien Hoa, Da Nang, and Phu Cat, respectively) were being trained and
equipped for the air defense mission.[105]

(S) As of mid-1973, at Da Nang, the VNAF maintained two F-5s on
five-minute alert, two on 15-minute alert, and two more on backup. An
additional four aircraft were maintained on alert at Bien Hoa. As
expected, however, the embryonic F-5A air defense force had very limited

capabilities, and at best was an interim measure until the F-5E squadrons could be formed. A July 1973 DAO assessment noted:[106]

> (S) The Air Superiority/Air Defense potential of the VNAF is marginal. In the Air Defense role, the VNAF is handicapped by aircraft which have no capability (because of available weapons) in the front intercept environment. In addition, (again because of weapons) they are constrained to a clear air mass situation and stern attack geometry. Geographical shape and radar masking give VNAF very little early warning. The command and control system, although responsive, is still not quick enough to take advantage of early warning. In the air superiority role, the VNAF faces more experienced pilots flying equipment that is similar in capability. This will result in a serious disadvantage during the learning curve until the VNAF pilots gain experience in air-to-air combat. [Neither] training resources nor supervisory incentive are . . . sufficient to overcome these deficiencies in the near future.

(C) It should be noted that some, but not all, of the F-5A's equipment limitations would be overcome with the introduction of the F-5E. A DAO comparison of the two aircraft indicated:[107]

> (C) The F-5E is faster and vastly more maneuverable than the F-5A. . . .
>
> (C) The F-5E has greater range or bomb load than the F-5A. . . .
>
> (C) The F-5A is restricted to clear air mass (engines ice up), utilizes "Kentucky windage" for air-to-air attack with guns, and eyeball to determine when in range to launch the Infrared AIM-9B Missile.
>
> (C) The F-5E has a lead computing sight, search and track radar and a missile in-range computer.
>
> (C) Neither the F-5A or the F-5E is an all-weather interceptor since the AIM-9B/E is a clear air, infrared homing missile which can't be successfully launched in clouds.

(C) Because of thrust to weight ratio, wing loading and extreme flight stability, the F-5E will, pilots being equal, more than match the MIG-21 in the standard maneuvering combat arena. Its area of potential superiority is much greater than the MIG-21 and gives the F-5E the upper hand whereas the F-5A is a match for the MIG-21 in a very restricted environment.

(S) <u>Final Preparations for Receipt of F-5Es (U)</u>. In late 1973, VNAF personnel were being withdrawn from F-5A squadrons for training in preparation for the F-5Es, which were to begin arriving in January 1974. This placed another burden on the already severely strained F-5A squadron maintenance capability, and prompted the DAO to seek further contractor support for the F-5 squadrons. An 11 October 1973 DAO message stated:[108]

> (S) The current threat and forthcoming dry season . . . indicates that every effort be taken to generate the maximum number of operational[ly] ready aircraft. Especially the F-5.
>
> (S) The thirty percent O/R for F-5A aircraft cannot be improved with the existing VNAF manning and low skill level within the 3 AD [3d Air Division]. We have just gone through the experience of withdrawing ALC personnel from 3 AD facilities into ALC operations. In addition, 126 VNAF personnel will soon be entered into F-5E training, further diluting their capability and compounding the F-5A maintenance capability/situation.
>
> (S) Therefore, it is imperative that within 30 days means be provided to augment the 3 AD [with] skilled additional personnel to replace the diverted O&I [Operations & Inspection] skills into ALC depot operations and F-5E trainees and also bring the F-5 force up to an acceptable O/R status.

(C) VNAF F-5 maintenance and manning problems notwithstanding, the final preparations for the arrival of the first F-5Es in RVN promised to usher in the long-awaited day when the VNAF would boast an operationally ready F-5E force. This giant step toward VNAF self-sufficiency was near, and while there was obviously a great deal of work and training yet to be accomplished, the VNAF was being provided with the potential to expand their air-to-ground attack capabilities and to develop an Air Defense force capable of responding to the North Vietnamese threat.

(S) <u>Fighter Limitations (U)</u>. In daytime, clear weather conditions, VNAF fighter pilots were considered to be among the best in the world. Some pilots had as much as 10 years of combat experience. This experience not only facilitated accurate ordnance delivery, but also resulted in familiarity with terrain and enhanced the ability to identify well-concealed targets.[109] On the other hand, VNAF TACAIR (except A-1s) suffered from continuing lack of significant night/all-weather capability. Inadequate all-weather delivery equipment, very limited initial and continuation night/all-weather training for A-37 and F-5 crews, and little emphasis by operations supervisors resulted in a fighter force with minimal night/all-weather delivery capability.[110] (Fortunately, the gunship fleet provided significant support to RVNAF forces at night, ameliorating the seriousness of the TACAIR night deficiency.) The need for an all-weather bombing capability had long been recognized by I&M planners, and progress had been made in selecting and providing the necessary delivery equipment. SEEK POINT, chosen under CROC-64-70 was designed to equip the VNAF with a ground-based, radar-directed bombing system which was unsophisticated, easily maintained, and inexpensive.[111]

The SEEK POINT system consisted of a ground radar site which, by means of an on-board beacon, guided the VNAF aircraft to the approximate release point. By the time of the cease-fire, three of five planned SEEK POINT systems had been shipped to SVN, and two Combat Skyspot MSQ-77 radars were left there by departing U.S. forces to provide in-place equipment which could be replaced by the two remaining SEEK POINT systems at a later date. Following the cease-fire, emphasis was placed on using contractor support to attain an operational status as soon as possible, while at the same time training the Vietnamese to maintain and support the systems. As of late 1973, a fourth SEEK POINT system had been shipped to Vietnam.[112] The systems were suffering from maintenance and supply support problems, but progress was being made in correcting those deficiencies. A larger problem was developing the VNAF capability and inclination to operate and support the system, and to remedy a general lack of emphasis on instrument training and operations.

(S) The lack of emphasis which VNAF management had historically placed on night/instrument operations was reinforced by a shift of ground combat activity from nighttime to daytime following the cease-fire. Combined with these factors, A-1 flight instrument problems, caused by spares, shortages, and cannibalization, all but prevented A-1 night combat operations, and the low F-5 sortie rate, caused by maintenance problems and a shortage of fully trained and qualified crews, argued against the F-5's use for all but the most essential missions.[113] Some A-1 and F-5 night training sorties occurred, but night combat flights were seldom flown. In short, areas which VNAF managers viewed as essential were pursued with vigor, but areas considered to be of secondary importance were neglected -- and the VNAF considered night training and night combat sorties to be of secondary importance. Coloring the VNAF attitude toward night operations was the general philosophy prevalent throughout the RVNAF leadership, i.e., that air resources should be used as sparingly as possible, and saved until they were needed most during an expected Communist offensive. That philosophy was reflected not only by the low emphasis placed on night operations, but also by the standing policy, issued by all four of the MR commanders, that daily fragged sorties would not normally be flown unless ground combat activities dictated their use. Thus, while daily fragged sortie rates remained essentially constant, actual sorties flown from day to day fluctuated widely, seldom reaching the fragged level.[114]

(S) The same philosophy of economy of air resources which manifested itself in day and night sortie rates, also came into play in the conduct of daily combat missions. Perhaps the most serious limitation of the VNAF fighter (and fixed-wing gunship) force was its high vulnerability when operating in heavily defended areas. Clearly, the VNAF had been designed basically for a low threat, insurgency environment. The anti-aircraft guns and missiles introduced en masse into SVN during the 1972 North Vietnamese Spring Offensive in effect closed many areas to A-1s and A-37s, which constituted all but one of the VNAF's fighter squadrons. Accordingly, locations believed to contain a high AAA/surface-to-air Missile (SAM) threat were nearly always avoided.* Enemy defenses in remaining areas, particularly the SA-7 STRELLA SAM, prompted the VNAF to release its ordnance from above 6,000 feet, and frequently from above 10,000 feet. It was the judgment of DAO personnel and military observers that in the event of a major Communist offensive, however, VNAF pilots, who had proven their skill and bravery on numerous past occasions, would lower their bombing altitudes despite the risk from enemy defenses. (This subjective assessment tended to be substantiated on occasions when VNAF pilots "pressed" their attacks to lower altitudes to support ground forces in serious combat situations.) Even if that proved true, however, it was conceded that such actions would result in high attrition rates which could be sustained for only a short period of time.[115]

(S/NFD) The impact of enemy defenses on VNAF delivery altitudes, tactics, and attrition, and ultimately on the VNAF's ability to perform effectively during an enemy offensive, although clearly far-reaching, was difficult to define. Even harder to assess was the subtle interplay between VNAF bombing tactics and accuracy, the selection of targets and definition of air support requirements, the acceptance and role of the VNAF in the eyes of the ground commander, and the impact of air support on the ground situation. For example, the degree of accuracy which could be expected

---

*(S) This factor, in conjunction with the control of air resources by MR commanders and the concentration of intelligence information in areas near friendly forces (see pp. 97, 106), resulted in an overwhelming emphasis on employment of VNAF air resources in support of ground forces. Interdiction strikes, per se, normally did not occur.

when ordnance was delivered from altitudes exceeding 10,000 feet was unacceptable for air support in close proximity to friendly units. Consequently, for all practical purposes, that type of close air support ended following the cease-fire, and there was an accompanying weakening of ties between the ARVN and the VNAF.[116] A related factor was the inability to assess strike results. Since strikes were not in immediate proximity to ground units, ground commanders were reluctant to send out long-range patrols for assessment of bomb damage, and operating altitudes and reconnaissance limitations precluded assessment from the air. Further, little use was made of the concept of "immediate response." Instead, nearly all targets were pre-planned, the only operational flexibility being the take-off time.[117] The MR commander, and his headquarters, selected the targets to be struck, and through tight control of air and ground resources in the MR, established the philosophy governing the role of air strikes in support of the ground battle. All of these factors altered the role of VNAF air support in the eyes of RVNAF commanders.

(S/NFD) Thus, it was unclear whether, in the case of another major enemy offensive, the VNAF and ARVN could reverse the trend and begin to take full advantage of close air support. Under such circumstances, as VNAF pilots pressed their attacks to lower altitudes, and ground crises developed which demanded close air support in near proximity to friendly units, there would surely be a tendency toward increased air strikes in the immediate battlefield area. On the other hand, the targeting process and the lack of close coordination between the VNAF and RVNAF ground units, indeed the lack of effective coordination channels as reflected by weaknesses in the ALO/FAC program,* would be an obstacle to a return to close air support in the immediate battlefield area. Consequently, some military observers stated bluntly that the ARVN would have to plan for a lack of effective close air support during an enemy offensive due to the enemy threat, the low level of available VNAF resources, and the deterioration of ties between the ARVN and the VNAF.[118]

(S/NFD) Other observers, however, felt that more aggressive VNAF delivery tactics, and improvements in organic ARVN capabilities following the enemy's 1972 offensive, would compensate for the reduced close air support capabilities available to support friendly forces.[119] Along these lines it was pointed out that the shift away from close air support in the immediate battlefield area was not without its beneficial results: the shift forced ground units to place increasing emphasis on their own organic artillery and mortars. This was most vividly evident in Military Region I where, subsequent to the cease-fire and throughout 1973, few TACAIR sorties were flown. This was apparently the result of two factors: (1) the desire to avoid provoking high levels of enemy activity in MR I, and (2) the high threat environment, which limited the effectiveness of VNAF TACAIR resources. Regardless of the cause, however, the result of the shortage of air support was evident: while the level of TACAIR sorties flown in MR I was only 20 percent of the average in the other military regions, the rate of friendly

---

*See pp. 59, 60, 99.

artillery expenditure was double the average in the other military regions.[120] An assessment of the situation in MR I was made by a VNAF Commander in an interview with intelligence personnel. The resulting Human Resource Intelligence (HUMINT) report stated:[121]

> (S/NFD) [Interviewee] . . . said that he believed Gen Truong's [MR I Commander] policy of not using air support was having a definite effect on the ARVN, as they were beginning to rely on organic artillery and mortars to provide fire support where requested. [Interviewee] . . . said that previously the ground commanders would call for air support during even a small contact with VC [Viet Cong]/NVA forces and wait until the air support arrived before advancing. Now that the policy on air support is rigidly controlled by the MR-1 commander, ground forces are for the first time learning to use what is immediately available to them, i.e., artillery and mortars.

Not withstanding that optimistic assessment, it was clear that the VNAF was no longer playing an influential role in combat activities in MR I. Whether or not that would change under conditions of a general offensive was open to question.

Fixed-wing Gunships (U)

(S) Between July 1971 and July 1973, VNAF gunship resources grew in both number and sophistication (see Table 2). These aircraft represented a valuable asset for support of Vietnamese ground forces, particularly during nighttime or poor weather conditions. Especially noteworthy was the transfer to the VNAF, during Enhance Plus, of the last AC-119K (Stinger) gunship squadron in the USAF inventory; it represented a significant upgrading of the VNAF fixed-wing gunship fleet, which had been limited to AC-47s and AC-119Gs. The AC-119Ks were equipped with more-sophisticated

TABLE 2: VNAF GUNSHIP SQUADRONS
July 1971 vs July 1973 (U)

Sqdn	1 July 1971 A/C UE	Base	Sqdn	1 July 1973 A/C UE	Base	Qtr of CY for New Activation
817	AC-47/16	Nha Trang	817	AC-47/16	Nha Trang	-
			819	AC-119G/18	Tan Son Nhut	3/71
			821	AC-119K/10	Tan Son Nhut	1/73
				AC-119K/8	Da Nang	
Total Squadrons	Total UE		Total Squadrons	Total UE		
1	16		3	52		

Source for Tables 1-6, (S) CHECO Report, Vietnamization of the Air War, 1970-1971 (U), 8 Oct 71 (S). AFGP, "Military Assistance Progress Report (U)," for the quarterly periods between Jul 71 and Dec 72 (S). U.S. DAO, Saigon, "DAO Quarterly Assessment Report (U)," Jul and Oct 73 (S).

detection devices and armed with 20mm cannons (compared to the 7.62mm miniguns carried by the AC-47s and AC-119Gs).[122] Although even the AC-119Ks would be of limited value for employment in threat areas, they did provide a significant close air support and in-country interdiction potential. The effectiveness of the AC-119Ks in the base defense and TIC-support role was attested to by departing U.S. forces, who insisted that a minimum of ten AC-119Ks remain under U.S. operational control for nightly use in base defense missions over Bien Hoa and Da Nang.[123] A personal 3 November 1972 message from General Vogt, 7AF Commander, to General Clay, CINCPACAF, explained:[124]

> (S) Bien Hoa and Da Nang have been and are expected to continue to be, targets for repeated rocket attacks by enemy. AC-119K has been extremely effective in deterring and/or suppressing these attacks in the past, and believe that continued employment of these assets by 7AF is imperative to survival of these bases until cessation of hostilities. . . . In addition to their demonstrated effectiveness at suppressing rocket attacks, they have frequently been in position to engage the enemy during TICs, and to break the TIC. Those AC-119s operating from Bien Hoa have been additionally valuable in augmenting the defense of the Capitol Military District [i.e., the Saigon area].

(S) By 5 March 1973, USAF crews had flown their last AC-119K training missions with VNAF crews, who by that time were routinely flying combat missions. As of July 1973, a detachment of eight VNAF AC-119Ks were permanently deployed to Da Nang to provide support for RVNAF forces in MR I, which constituted the highest threat environment in South Vietnam. The remaining 10 VNAF AC-119Ks were stationed at Bien Hoa, to centralize maintenance requirements and to enhance protection of the Capitol Military District.[125] The importance of these and other VNAF gunships was heightened by the post-cease-fire shift of fighter resources away from support of troops in the immediate battlefield area. Thus, gunships became the sole provider of close air support for troops in contact with the enemy.

(S) Yet, notwithstanding the potential value of the VNAF gunship fleet, its usefulness to RVNAF forces throughout 1973 was severely curtailed by proliferating AAA and SAM defenses. Again, the VNAF policy was to avoid areas containing high enemy threats, and to fly at high altitudes in all but the lowest threat areas. Accordingly, gunship missions were normally flown at or above 6,500 feet, which represented the upper limit of the 20mm guns on the AC-119Ks and AC-47s. This threat/altitude factor rendered the AC-119Ks only marginally effective by greatly limiting their lethality and accuracy, and negated the usefulness of AC-119Gs and AC-47s in all but low threat areas.[126]

(S) The need for more lethal, accurate, and survivable gunships prompted continuing consideration of the proposal, originally submitted in May 1972, to add AC-130s to the VNAF's gunship inventory. The primary factor arguing against this course of action, and the factor which ultimately resulted in the decision not to replace AC-47s and AC-119s with AC-130s, was the difficulty and expense of maintaining the highly sophisticated systems on the AC-130. A September 1973 message from PACAF to CINCPAC pointed out that the AC-130 would require contract support for its sophisticated sensor systems. The AC-130 was an expensive weapons system to operate and would require highly skilled maintenance personnel, a resource for

79

which the VNAF was already suffering severe shortages.[127] In an 11 December 1973 message, the 7AF/USSAG Commander remarked, "In my judgment, the system is beyond the VNAF capability to manage and operate."[128]

(S) The argument against increasing the sophistication of the gunship fleet was strongly supported by the difficulties the VNAF was already encountering in maintaining and operating the equipment on their existing gunships. First, supply and maintenance problems resulted in a gunship O/R rate which varied between 30 and 60 percent. Second, problems were encountered with the maintenance of on-board batteries, which were needed to handle electrical surge requirements during firing of gunship weapons. As a result, many missions were unable to expend ordnance. Third, on most AC-119Ks missions the manual firing mode, which was inherently less accurate than a properly calibrated automatic mode, was being used because the automatic firing mode was either inoperative or inaccurate. Finally, some of the sensors and other equipment on the AC-119Ks either were not being used or were inoperative. In some cases, contractors indicated that the equipment was functioning properly, but that the crews did not understand how to use it. Regardless of the exact nature of and solution for each of these specific difficulties, the general conclusion to be drawn was that the maintenance and operation of the relatively sophisticated equipment in the VNAF gunships was the underlying cause of problems. Viewed from that perspective, the decision not to transfer AC-130 gunships to the VNAF, but rather to solve the problems being encountered in the VNAF's gunship inventory, was compelling and sound. Nevertheless, the need for a more modern gunship fleet was, in the eyes of USDAO, strong enough to override these

considerations, and as late as November 1973, the proposed addition of
AC-130s to the VNAF continued to elicit strong DAO support.[129]

(S) Despite their problems and employment limitations, it was generally believed that the gunships would descend, when events dictated, to more effective operating altitudes, thus increasing their accuracy and lethality. As was the case for fighter attack resources, however, it was clear that such tactics would result in increased attrition which could be sustained for only a limited period of time.[130]

Airlift (U)

(S) The evolution of the VNAF transport force between 1971 and 1973 provides a classic example of the planning turbulence and dramatic expansion inherent in the improvement and modernization of the VNAF. In June 1971, the VNAF transport fleet consisted of a C-119 squadron, a C-47 squadron, and a newly activated C-123 squadron. By mid-1973, none of these aircraft remained in the VNAF transport inventory, which instead consisted of three squadrons of C-7s and two squadrons of C-130s (see Table 3) -- this despite the fact that as late as October 1972, C-130s had not been a part of the I&M program. This dramatic evolution of the transport fleet occurred in a period of only two years, and in a VNAF already struggling to recover from previous force changes and growth.

(S) The issue of C-130s for the VNAF surfaced as early as October 1971, during the planning that preceded the FSR-73 force structure proposal. At that time, it was recognized by the Air Force Advisory Group that the "VNAF will need a heavy transport capability. C-130 aircraft would be suitable for

TABLE 3: VNAF TRANSPORT SQUADRONS
July 1971 vs July 1973 (U)

Sqdn	1 July 1971 A/C UE	Base	Sqdn	A/C UE	Base	Qtr of CY for New Activation
413	C-119/16	Tan Son Nhut	413	(Deactivated 4/72)		-
415	C-47D/16	Tan Son Nhut	415	(Deactivated 4/72)		-
421	C-123K/16	Tan Son Nhut	421	(Deactivated 1/73)		-
Total Squadrons	Total UE		423	C-123K/16 (Deactivated 4/72)	Tan Son Nhut	3/71
3	48		425	C-123K/16 (Deactivated 4/72)	Tan Son Nhut	3/71
			427	C-7/16	Da Nang	3/71
			429	C-7/16	Tan Son Nhut	2/72
				C-7/3	Phu Cat	
			431	C-7/16	Tan Son Nhut	3/72
			435	C-130/16	Tan Son Nhut	4/72
			437	C-130/16	Tan Son Nhut	4/72
			Total Squadrons	Total UE		
			5	83		

Source for Tables 1-6, (S) <u>CHECO Report, Vietnamization of the Air War, 1970-1971</u> (U), 8 Oct 71 (S). AFGP, "Military Assistance Progress Report (U)," for the quarterly periods between Jul 71 and Dec 72 (S). U.S. DAO, Saigon, "DAO Quarterly Assessment Report (U)," Jul and Oct 73 (S).

this mission."[131] In response to a Deputy SECDEF request to review new VNAF requirements in light of the NVN invasion,[132] COMUSMACV formally submitted another similar, but more detailed, proposal in May 1972. After noting that the VNAF C-123/119/47 force "is adequate to meet normal RVNAF needs, but is insufficient in high surge conditions," the Advisory Group stated that "to satisfy crisis conditions without U.S. support, consideration should be given to providing a larger and faster transport. . . ."[133] Therefore, the Advisory Group proposed replacing the older, difficult-to-support C-123s, C-119s, and C-47s with four squadrons of the more capable C-130 aircraft. Benefits of the action would thus include increased maintenance support commonality as well as operational potential. The JCS submitted the proposal to OSD on 2 June 1972, but recommended against providing C-130s on the grounds they would require a higher maintenance skill level to support, necessitate a long lead time to train aircrews and maintenance personnel, and would have a negative impact on USAF C-130 resources. OSD submitted the study to the National Security Council (NSC), also recommending against providing the C-130s.[134]

(C) Meanwhile, AFGP planners had proposed a far-ranging CROC to modernize the VNAF transport fleet, as well as to provide a solution to modernization of aircraft used in a number of other missions. The original version of the CROC, dated 24 June 1972, listed the various requirements for the airlift, fixed-wing gunship, Electronic Countermeasures/Electronic Intelligence (ECM/ELINT), photo reconnaissance, and maritime air patrol missions. In addition, it analyzed the potential of the C-130 aircraft in each mission, concluding:[135]

> (C) It appears that the best solution to several of the requirements is utilization of one common airframe,

> the C-130, . . . [with] class V modifications to provide
> the required capabilities. Modification would be re-
> quired to perform the ECM/ELINT and maritime [air]
> patrol missions. It is assumed that the existing
> AC-130 assets could be utilized to answer the fixed
> wing gunship requirement. [The] RC-130 aircraft, as
> used in photo mapping, appears to satisfy the requirement
> for a photo reconnaissance aircraft.

The proposal went on to estimate the number of aircraft required for each mission and the number of aircraft replaced, yielding a total of 90 C-130s apportioned in the following manner: airlift, 32 C-130s (replacing 80 other aircraft); fixed-wing gunships, 36 (replacing 52); photo reconnaissance, 4 (replacing 12); ECM/ELINT, 6 (replacing 18); maritime patrol, 12 (replacing 12).

(S) When formally presented to MACV on 12 July 1972 the AFGP CROC had been modified to cover only the modernization of the airlift fleet, per se. The CROC specified:[136] (C)

> (S) The Presidentially directed Improvement and Moderniza-
> tion (I&M) program requires that the Vietnamese Air Force
> (VNAF) attain and maintain self-sufficiency in airlift.
> The Vietnamese Joint General Staff (JGS) has estimated that
> the VNAF must be capable of airlifting approximately 296
> tons of cargo and passengers daily to satisfy the normal
> Republic of Vietnam Armed Forces (RVNAF) requirement. This
> capability has been achieved utilizing the small and
> relatively slow C-119, C-47, C-7, and C-123 aircraft which
> are currently in the inventory. However, during surge
> periods such as the North Vietnamese offensive which
> began in early April 1972, the present force demonstrated
> that it was outmoded and inadequate when tasked to air-
> lift up to 900 additional tons daily.

*   *   *   *   *   *   *

> (S) The present CRIMP does not provide for replacement
> of the current obsolescent VNAF airlift fleet. Unavaila-
> bility of U.S. airlift assets in surge situations will

> overtax the VNAF lift capability and impair battlefield performance. Two 16 U.E. squadrons of C-130s (32 aircraft plus NOA and attrition) should be programmed to replace three 16 U.E. squadrons of C-123 and one 16 U.E. squadron of C-119 aircraft at the rate of one squadron each four months commencing at the earliest possible date.

Action on the CROC was deferred by the Air Staff, since the proposal was considered to be more appropriately dealt with as a force structure change, rather than as a new operational capability.[137]

(TS) The conversion to C-130s was again proposed by the field commander, this time in the Mid-Range Force Structure Plan, informally submitted by MACV in September 1972. Rationale for the proposal was summarized in an October 1972 memorandum:[138]

> (TS) The present VNAF airlift fleet has the capability of hauling 9,000 tons per month and no outsize* cargo capability. During the April-June period, the surge requirements raised that monthly total to 17,825 tons. In order to give the VNAF the capability to meet surge requirements without USAF help and an outsize cargo capability, we are proposing trading 4 squadrons (one C-119, three C-123 squadrons) for two C-130 squadrons. This conversion would give the VNAF an airlift capability of 19,000 tons per month and equally important, release 54 critically needed pilots for duty in other aircraft.

(S) The plan was submitted to the Air Staff, but was never formally introduced into Joint or Service channels for action. AFGP and MACV continued to support the proposal in discussions with visiting high-level government personnel, including members of the National Security Council staff who informally received a copy of the plan during a trip to Saigon. The NSC staff then questioned OSD and the Air Staff concerning the

---

* "Outsize" cargo included large items such as 2 1/2 ton trucks and armored personnel carriers.

feasibility of providing C-130s to the VNAF. At that time the general consensus among OSD and Air Staff personnel was that providing C-130s would be inappropriate. The NSC staff, however, was apparently convinced of the need for C-130s -- the 20 October 1972 SECDEF memorandum which initiated Enhance Plus specified that C-130s be among the aircraft provided to the VNAF.[139]

(S) As noted previously, Enhance Plus planners envisioned storage of a large percentage of Enhance Plus assets until they could be gradually integrated into the VNAF force structure. C-130s were specifically included in that category, and a 26 October 1972 message from CSAF/Logistics recommended storage of 26 C-130s and use of the remaining six for training. Early in November, however, the VNAF, strongly supported by AFGP, 7AF, and MACV, expressed their intent to activate the C-130 squadrons as soon as possible, and to use them to replace the C-47, C-119, and C-123 squadrons. This drew an immediate response from CSAF and SECDEF that Enhance Plus equipment was additive to the CRIMP, not in lieu of other aircraft, and that no authority had been granted to unilaterally adjust the VNAF force structure. The response from the field stated that the Vietnamese intention was to substitute the C-130s for the older aircraft, that in-country storage was impractical, and that U.S. field commanders supported the VNAF/JGS position. The message conceded, however, that the press of time had caused in-country planning and actions to out-distance program authorizations, and noted that a formal, revised force structure plan would be submitted as soon as possible. Shortly thereafter, a formal AFGP force structure proposal was approved by MACV, and submitted to higher authorities.

The proposal was approved in deference to JGS/VNAF intentions and AFGP/ 7AF/MACV support. The objective of the VNAF/7AF/MACV was to attain a 50 percent C-130 OR rate by cease-fire plus 60 days (28 March 1973).[140]

(C) The effects of the decision to activate the C-130 squadrons and deactivate the C-47s, C-119s, and C-123s continued to be felt many months after the cease-fire. As predicted, the trade-off had one immediate and sizeable benefit: it released a large number of aircrews critically needed for activating VNAF fighter squadrons. It also had the obvious long-term benefit of increasing aircraft maintenance commonality by reducing airlift aircraft from five types to two. Nevertheless, there were also some significant and lasting penalties resulting from the conversion. The greatest of these was maintenance.

(S) By the end of May 1973, all C-47s, the last C-119s, and half of the C-123s had been transferred from the VNAF to the USAF. The remaining C-123s were scheduled to be transferred by the end of July. Aircrew transition training to the C-130s had proceeded well, but the C-130 fleet was suffering severe maintenance problems. A DAO report summarized:[141]

> (S) . . . the C-130A fleet has had an excessive out-of
> commission rate. The OR rate averaged around 35% in
> April and May. Primary causes have been wing cracks,
> fuel leaks, engine problems, parts shortages, ground
> equipment deficiencies, limited repair capability,
> and lack of sufficient maintenance skills. There has
> been a concentrated effort by AF Division, VNAF, AFLC,
> plus TDY [Temporary Duty] personnel to improve the
> in-commission rate. In addition, direct Lear Siegler
> augmentation of the VNAF maintenance capability was
> directed by AF Division, DAO. Positive results are being
> achieved . . . [but] data indicates that the OR rate will
> not continue its recent . . . improvement in the
> ensuing months. The reasons for this are:

a. Depot Maintenance: Excessive number of airframes undergoing wing crack repair/PDM [Periodic Depot Maintenance] . . .

b. NORM/NORS [Not Operationally Ready, Maintenance/Supply] Aircraft: . . . VNAF is not expected to reduce the average number of NORM/NORS airframes below 9 in the near future due to the excessive cracked wings and fuel cell problems. Self-sufficiency of the VNAF C-130A fleet is not expected to be attained until late CY [calendar year] 1974.

(C) In addition to the maintenance problems, some C-130 aircrew training problems surfaced in July and August 1973. For example, the C-123s, about to be transferred out of the VNAF, had been resupplying the encircled Tong Le Chan camp since March 1973 by means of the Seek Point ground-based radar system. When resupply of Tong Le Chan switched to C-130s, there was a dramatic drop in the recovery rate of airdropped bundles. This was considered to be primarily the result of C-130 pilot inexperience with the Seek Point radar system, and secondarily the result of a high incidence of parachute malfunctions.

(C) Despite agreement to implement a priority training program, and to implement back-up parachute techniques, recovery rates remained low. Inadequate training sorties appeared to be the major problem. Consequently, the VNAF switched back to resupply with C-123s, and bundle recovery went up dramatically. Remaining C-123s were released when the C-130 crews were considered qualified for Seek Point aerial delivery, and the last C-123s departed Vietnam on 23 August 1973. The effectiveness of C-130 crews in Seek Point deliveries was expected to continue to improve as they gained experience. The maintenance factor, however, was a continuing concern.[142]

(U) As noted previously, many of the maintenance difficulties associated with the C-130As resulted from the condition of the aircraft at the time of their transfer to the VNAF. A September 1973 DAO fact sheet summarized:[143]

> (U) The status of the C-130A aircraft at the time they were transferred to the VNAF was as follows: 11 were overdue Periodic Depot Maintenance; 12 had less than 12 hours to the next phase inspection; 2 were known to have cracked wing fittings, and it was subsequently found that 7 additional aircraft had cracked wing fittings (total 9). Serious fuel leak problems were encountered during May and June 73 which have now been overcome.
>
> (U) Eleven additional cracked wing fittings on ten aircraft were found in June and July. This seriously affected the fleet. . . . All aircraft were repaired by 24 Aug 73. . . .
>
> (U) In spite of the above obstacles, the VNAF C-130A Program is looking up. They are beginning to attain a degree of proficiency in the maintenance of the engines and propellers. They are also becoming more effective in Airframe Maintenance . . . [and] the VNAF C-130 airlift objective of 16 OR aircraft should be achieved in the Nov/Dec 73 time frame. The final factors are the ability of the VNAF to input O3 level trainees for OJT and gradual phaseout of the contractor augmentation and training personnel and improved supply support.

(S) The original decision to deliver C-130As to the VNAF, rather than C-130Es, had been prompted primarily by the desire to minimize the impact of the USAF worldwide airlift capability (i.e., USAF active forces included only AC-130Es, while Reserve forces were composed of C-130As and Bs).[144] However, as a result of the difficulty in maintaining the C-130As at an OR level of 50 percent and with the intent of increasing the potential of the VNAF airlift fleet, an October 1973 RVNAF proposal called for the replacement of C-130As with newer, more maintainable, and more capable C-130Es.[145] The proposal noted:

> (S) VNAF is assuming airborne operations for the entire RVNAF. Therefore, the old C-130As need to be

89

replaced by C-130Es which are modern and have enough
supplies and equipment to increase the operational
readiness to a standard of 71% in order to meet airborne requirements of the RVNAF.[146]

The terse DAO response was as follows:

> (S) There is no possibility of obtaining C-130Es at
> this time. The C-130As are being upgraded through
> IRAN [Inspect and Repair as Necessary] and if properly
> maintained and supported by VNAF, they would meet all
> your needs. But it is re-emphasized that much depends
> on your own flying skill and handling of the aircraft
> and expert maintenance and supply support.

(S) Even assuming maintenance problems could be overcome, or assuming the C-130As were replaced with C-130Es, there was still considerable concern regarding the sufficiency of VNAF airlift capabilities in a crisis.[147] Responding to a question regarding the adequacy of the VNAF to meet RVNAF requirements, the Deputy Chief of the Air Force Division, DAO, Saigon, commented:[148]

> (S) Airlift capability is a funny thing because you
> really don't know what the requirement is. . . . We
> did not build the VNAF to go into a major head-on con-
> frontation with an enemy air force or in a major
> battleground. . . . If you're going to support fire
> bases, infiltration bases, then I think they have more
> than the capability they need. However, if you're
> going to have mass movements of ARVN troops, or mas-
> sive airlift requirements, if you're going to have to
> sustain many, many places that are surrounded and cannot
> get food and supplies other than by airlift, then they
> don't have the capability to fight that kind of war.
> We did not build that for them. . . . If the ARVN can
> take their fair share of the work and keep a lot of
> the roads open, then they might have the capability to
> airlift those things that are required. So, it depends,
> really, on the tactical situation, what kind of war
> you're going to fight, and how much airlift you're
> going to need. . . . If they enter a major offensive
> of the magnitude experienced during the 1972 North
> Vietnamese invasion, I doubt they will have enough
> airlift.

(S) Those comments are perhaps best placed in perspective by acknowledging the general belief that the VNAF, as well as the RVNAF, while having made great strides, would be unable to withstand an all-out communist offensive without external assistance.[149] A 31 May 1973 message specified: "It is recognized by DAO that VNAF is not equipped to cope with an offensive of the scope of the 1972 action without help, not only in airlift but in other areas as well."[150]

Helicopters (U)

(S) Helicopters represented by far the largest single element of the VNAF force structure, and it was the helicopter fleet which experienced the greatest numerical increase in assets between July 1971 and July 1973. Despite the problems attending the expansion from slightly over 400 airframes to nearly 900 (see Table 4), the helicopter fleet was considered effective and responsive to RVNAF needs, and was well on its way to self-sufficiency.[151]

(C) VNAF helicopters provided an essential ingredient to RVNAF combat assault forces -- mobility. As such, they were basic to the RVNAF philosophy and doctrine of military operations. VNAF helicopter resources consisted primarily of UH-1s, but they also had a substantial number of CH-47s. The UH-1s were employed primarily for troop airlift, while CH-47s were used for airlift of supplies and personnel, relocation of artillery, and recovery of downed UH-1s. Helicopters were fragged on a weekly and a daily basis; in addition, helicopters were available on a standby basis to meet emergency requirements, and each Corps had a number of UH-1s on Medical Evacuation (Medevac) alert.[152]

TABLE 4: VNAF HELICOPTER SQUADRONS
July 1971 vs July 1973 (U)

	1 July 1971			1 July 1973		Qtr of CY for
Sqdn	A/C UE	Base	Sqdn	A/C UE	Base	New Activation
219	H-34/25	Da Nang	219	UH-1/38	Nha Trang	-
211	UH-1/31	Binh Thuy	NC	NC/38	NC	-
213	UH-1/31	Da Nang	NC	NC/38	NC	-
215	UH-1/31	Nha Trang	NC	NC/38	NC	-
217	UH-1/31	Binh Thuy	NC	NC/38	NC	-
221	UH-1/31	Bien Hoa	NC	NC/38	NC	-
223	UH-1/31	Bien Hoa	NC	NC/38	NC	-
225	UH-1/31	Soc Trang	NC	NC/38	Binh Thuy	-
227	UH-1/31	Soc Trang	NC	NC/38	Binh Thuy	-
229	UH-1/31	Pleiku	NC	NC/38	NC	-
231	UH-1/31	Bien Hoa	NC	NC/38	NC	-
233	UH-1/31	Da Nang	NC	NC/38	NC	-
235	UH-1/31	Pleiku	NC	NC/38	NC	-
237	CH-47/16	Bien Hoa	NC	NC/NC	NC	-
Total Squadrons	Total UE		239	UH-1/38	Da Nang	1/72
14	413		241	CH-47/16	Phu Cat	2/72
			243	UH-1/38	Phu Cat	4/71
			245	UH-1/38	Bien Hoa	4/71
			247	CH-47/16	Da Nang	1/73
			249	CH-47/16	Binh Thuy	2/73
			251	UH-1/38	Bien Hoa	1/73
			253	UH-1/38	Da Nang	2/73
			255	UH-1/38	Binh Thuy	1/73
			257	UH-1/24	Da Nang	1/73
			259	UH-1/8	Nha Trang	1/73
				UH-1/8	Phan Rang	
				UH-1/10	Phu Cat	
				UH-1/10	Pleiku	
				UH-1/12	Tan Son Nhut	
				UH-1/12	Bien Hoa	
				UH-1/24	Binh Thuy	
				Total Squadrons		Total UE
				25		894

Source for Tables 1-6, (S) CHECO Report, Vietnamization of the Air War, 1970-1971 (U), 8 Oct 71 (S). AFGP, "Military Assistance Progress Report (U)," for the quarterly periods between Jul 71 and Dec 72 (S). U.S. DAO, Saigon, "DAO Quarterly Assessment Report (U)," Jul and Oct 73 (S).

(S) In view of the vast shortfall which would exist when comparing final Vietnamese helicopter resources with those available when U.S. involvement was at a peak, the decision had been made to place management of all RVNAF helicopter resources under the VNAF. Central management of helicopter resources was considered essential -- dedicated helicopter units were a luxury that the RVNAF could not afford--but would such a system be responsive to the RVNAF's needs? The controversy concerning exclusive VNAF management of RVNAF helicopter resources continued to surface in late 1971, and the fear that such a system would not be responsive to the needs of the ground forces was the factor most frequently cited in proposals for dedicated helicopter support of ground units. Despite the fears, central management and control by the VNAF increased the flexibility and responsiveness of much reduced helicopter resources in support of a broad array of RVNAF needs, while decreasing maintenance and support requirements.[153]

(C) The system was flexible, but there was valid, continuing concern that withdrawal of U.S. Army helicopters would leave the RVNAF with a serious shortage of essential helicopter support. A 9 October 1972 AFGP memorandum stated there would be a shortfall in Riverine Patrol and Search and Rescue (SAR)/Medevac missions, and that VNAF resources could provide approximately 63 percent of the then-current level of USAF/VNAF efforts. the AFGP memo then offered the following proposal:[154]

> (C) Addition of 3 UH-1 squadrons and 4 CH-47 squadrons to increase VNAF capability to support ARVN in combat after U.S. withdrawal will provide approximately 75% of current USAF/VNAF efforts.

> (C) Increase of 22 UH-1 gunships in MR IV for riverine patrol missions. Provide one squadron of UH-1Ns (48 UE) for . . . search and rescue/medevac missions.

(S) The initiation of Enhance Plus later that month and the subsequent Vietnamese decision to immediately integrate Enhance Plus assets into their active force resulted, essentially, in the adoption of the AFGP proposal. The nearly 300 UH-1s received by the South Vietnamese during Enhance Plus were used to activate three full helicopter squadrons (each with 12 gunships, 3 command and control aircraft, and 23 troop transports) as well as a squadron and eight flights for Medevac/SAR (109 UH-1Hs), to increase the UE of existing units, and to serve as maintenance backup aircraft. Additionally, activation of two CH-47 squadrons was accelerated.[155]

(S) In late 1973, Colonel James T. Nelson, Chief of the Air Force Division, DAO, Saigon, commented concerning the effectiveness of placing all helicopters under the VNAF, and described the attitude of VNAF commanders toward their responsibility for providing the RVNAF with helicopter support:[156]

> (S) [The] philosophy that anything that flies belongs to the Air Force is their [South Vietnamese] doctrine, and believe me, it's working quite well. The ARVN wanted dedicated helicopters, just like the U.S. Army had when they were in here, and we've had . . . a time convincing them and proving to the ARVN commanders that the Air Force can be responsive to their demands. That is one area in which all the VNAF Generals break their backs to prove to the ARVN that they can respond, in tactical requirements, airlift requirements, and so forth. The desire to prove this capability, I think, is about equal to that of the U.S. Air Force's to prove to the U.S. Army that we can be responsive. I'm proud of them in this respect, and they're doing fine with their helicopters.

Reconnaissance (U)

(S) The VNAF reconnaissance (recce) program consisted of visual recce (VR) by FAC aircraft, photo recce by RF-5s and RC-47s, electronic surveillance by EC-47s, and coastal surveillance by ground-based radars supplemented by FAC VR. Although considerable improvements were made in most reconnaissance areas, remaining shortfalls were a matter of serious concern. Limitations in photo reconnaissance capabilities, and a general inadequacy and task of direction in the VR program remained as obstacles to VNAF self-sufficiency. (See Tables 5 and 6 for VNAF recce resources.)

(C) Visual Reconnaissance/FACs (U). Nowhere was the difference between U.S. and RVNAF command and control more apparent than in the Visual Reconnaissance/Forward Air Controller program. VNAF Liaison Squadrons consisted primarily of O-1 aircraft which were used to satisfy VR and FAC mission requirements, with by far the greatest number of sorties being flown in the VR category. A July 1972 AFGP analysis noted that "the essence of O-1 operations is that the aircraft is primarily dedicated to the ARVN. The ARVN Corps Commander directs the utilization of the aircraft to support ground operations as it deems necessary."[157] Reconnaissance or observation missions were normally flown with an ARVN rather than VNAF observer. The implications of this approach were explained in an AFGP memorandum:[158]

> (C) The VNAF pilot flies the plane with an ARVN Ranger or even Naval observer, depending on the mission. The philosophy of utilizing an observer intimately familiar with the local environment and mission has merit. The drawbacks to the policy are twofold: Present ground rules permit only a qualified VNAF observer to direct air strikes. Targets of opportunity cannot be attacked immediately by a 'mixed' VNAF/ARVN crew. The non-VNAF observer reports intel information directly to his command channels. Very little inter-service cross-talk is presently apparent.

TABLE 5: VNAF RECONNAISSANCE SQUADRONS
July 1971 vs July 1973 (U)

	1 July 1971			1 July 1973		Qtr of CY for
Sqdn	A/C UE	Base	Sqdn	A/C UE	Base	New Activation
716	RC-47D/3	Tan Son Nhut	716	NC/12	NC	–
	EC-47D/1			NC/2		
	U-6A/8			NC/NC	Tan Son Nhut	–
				C-47/2		
			718	EC-47D/20	Tan Son Nhut	3/72
				EC-47D/10	Da Nang	
Total Squadrons	Total UE		Total Squadrons	Total UE		
1	12		2	54		

Source for Tables 1-6, (S) CHECO Report, Vietnamization of the Air War, 1970-1971 (U), 8 Oct 71 (S). AFGP, "Military Assistance Progress Report (U)," for the quarterly periods between Jul 71 and Dec 72 (S). U.S. DAO, Saigon, "DAO Quarterly Assessment Report (U)," Jul and Oct 73 (S).

TABLE 6: VNAF LIAISON SQUADRONS
July 1971 vs July 1973 (U)

Sqdn	1 July 1971 A/C UE*	Base	Sqdn	1 July 1973 A/C UE	Base	Qtr of CY for New Activation
110	O-1A/E/G	Da Nang	110	O-2/20	NC	-
	U-17A/B			O-1/5		
112	O-1A/E/G	Bien Hoa		U-17/7		
	U-17A/B		112	O-1/25	NC	-
114	O-1A/E/G	Nha Trang		U-17/7		
	U-17A/B		114	O-1/25	NC	-
116	O-1A/E/G	Binh Thuy		U-17/7		
	U-17A		116	O-1/25	NC	-
118	O-1A/E/G	Pleiku		U-17/7		
	U-17A/B		118	O-2/15	NC	-
120	O-1E/G	Da Nang		O-1/10		
	U-17A/B			U-17/7		
122	O-1E/G	Binh Thuy	120	O-1/25	NC	-
	U-17A			U-17/7		
Total Squadrons	Total UE		122	O-1/25	NC	-
7	195			U-17/7		
			124	O-1/25	Bien Hoa	3/72
				U-17/7		
			Total Squadrons	Total UE		
			8	256		

* Numbers of squadron unavailable.

Source for Tables 1-6, (S) CHECO Report, Vietnamization of the Air War, 1970-1971 (U), 8 Oct 71 (S). AFGP, "Military Assistance Progress Report (U)," for the quarterly periods between Jul 71 and Dec 72 (S). U.S. DAO, Saigon, "DAO Quarterly Assessment Report (U)," Jul and Oct 73 (S).

(C) The observation missions and resulting intelligence flow described above may have been responsive to the immediate battlefield needs of the ARVN ground commander, but were detrimental to long-term needs and did not constitute an effective VR program. The same July 1972 memo explained:[159]

> (C) There is no country wide program conducted by the VNAF in the U.S. conceptional mode. The ARVN does require VNAF VR support. This type of Visual Reconnaissance consists of a security cover with the FAC orbiting directly over the ARVN unit. . . . In general, the ARVN does not recognize the value in a VR program. The ground commander would rather have a FAC overhead than trying to discover enemy activity in the area of his responsibility. The FACs themselves either fail to give good VR reports or any reports at all. Although one can go out and be shown briefing and debriefing teams and report forms the point of the matter remains that little enemy activity is noted and the form contains only the flight date. Any significant information remains locked up at the local level. Progress has been made in III Corps with the VNAF ALO awareness of possible benefits of a VR program, however, he feels he can not initiate a program unless there are more O-1s and crews available.

(C) The failure to initiate an effective VR program, although necessarily influenced by aircraft limitations and pilot shortages, was most directly attributable to a lack of command emphasis within the RVNAF command and control structure. An August 1972 memorandum explained:[160]

> (C) From past experience, it has been demonstrated that a VR program can be extremely effective. However, it must be energetically and aggressively planned, monitored and coordinated in order to properly function. VNAF basically considers itself a service organization for the ARVN. ARVN should take the initiative to establish a VR program and coordinate with VNAF. VNAF could take more initiative to establish a VR program for its own use, but command guidance must come from VNAF Headquarters Intelligence to get this program moving. VNAF Division and Wing Intelligence sections are set up and well staffed to effectively operate a liaison VR program. However, with no guidance from higher headquarters, very little effort in this area will be realized.

During the remainder of 1972, some progress was made in improving the VNAF briefing/debriefing procedures, thus maximizing the flow of intelligence from strictly VNAF missions, but the inter-service intelligence flow problems remained.[161]

(S) Throughout 1972, the same personnel problems which plagued the ALO* program continued to hamper the progress of the FAC program. As with ALOs, a critical shortage of experienced personnel, and an emphasis on manning the fighter squadrons activated subsequent to Enhance Plus with the most highly qualified VNAF pilots, drained away competent personnel and generally detracted from the effectiveness of the FAC program throughout 1973. VNAF FACs were inexperienced and inadequately trained in fighter tactics. Further, despite earlier, repeated attempts by advisors to emphasize the importance of FAC-collected information, FACs were inexperienced in the intelligence gathering role, and there was no intelligence training program for FACs.[162]

(C) A positive factor in the FAC program, however, was the introduction during Enhance Plus of O-2s into the VNAF aircraft inventory. Thirty-five O-2s were transferred to the VNAF in exchange for a like number of O-1s. The O-2's performance characteristics significantly increased the operational capabilities of the VNAF FAC fleet, particularly in regard to missions over the highlands or in enemy threat areas. The O-2's greater range, load-carrying capacity, airspeed, and loiter time enabled the VNAF to cover larger areas with fewer aircraft. Further, the aircraft's greater survivability substantially reduced the need for A-37s to act as FACs in threat areas which continued to be off-limits to O-1s.[163]

---

*See pp. 59-60.

(S) Photo Reconnaissance (U). The VNAF photo reconnaissance program was labelled as "a problem area of continuing concern"[164] by the Chief of AFGP in August 1971. By late 1973, although there had been an increase in capabilities, Photo Recce potential continued to be limited by inadequate RF-5 cameras and outdated RC-47 aircraft. As of September 1973, VNAF Photo Recce resources consisted of only eight RF-5A aircraft and 12 RC-47s.[165]

(S) As of late 1973, of the eight RF-5s in the VNAF inventory, two were totally unserviceable, leaving only six in service. Although the small number of operational RF-5s represented a gross limitation, the most serious shortcoming of the RF-5 reconnaissance force continued to result from the deficiencies of its KS-92A camera. Although the CROC for an improved RF-5 camera had been initiated in early 1972, by the end of 1973 no tangible progress had been made in equipping VNAF RF-5s with improved cameras. The problem encountered in satisfying the CROC was that the proposed solution -- installation of the KA-95 camera -- required extensive, relatively expensive modification to the RF-5A nose. Other cameras were available which could be installed with less difficulty and expense, notably the KA-77, but these alternative solutions were viewed by PACAF and USDAO as inadequate to meet VNAF mission requirements. Funding was not forthcoming for the more expensive, but the preferred, KA-95 cameras. In late 1973, it became obvious from CSAF messages that there was little or no hope for funding the program, and an alternative solution, such as the KA-77, would have to be pursued. USDAO still considered the KA-77 an unacceptable substitute. In February 1974, in anticipation of the projected arrival of F-5E aircraft, DAO suggested that 18 F-5Es be modified to RF-5Es, and equipped with the desired KA-95 camera. Shortly thereafter, a PACAF ROC proposal was submitted by DAO in pursuance of their earlier suggestion. Unless that PACAF ROC were accepted and satisfied, little could be done to improve the VNAF's limited RF-5 reconnaissance capability.[166]

(S) The RC-47s in the VNAF inventory were C-47s which had been modified for reconnaissance purposes. As of September 1973, primarily as a result of camera shortages, only five of the VNAF's 12 RC-47s were operational. The operational RC-47s were equipped with three types of cameras, providing flexibility to meet the specific needs of the mission being planned, whether it dealt with an area target, point target, or a mapping requirement.[167] The primary limitation of the RC-47 was its vulnerability, which resulted from its low-altitude, low-speed operating characteristics. Thus, the RC-47 provided excellent coverage of MRs III and IV, but was limited in MR II and totally unusable in MR I. Between the RF-5's camera limitations, and the RC-47's threat area restrictions, "detection by photography of infiltration and most other enemy activity in MR I and II is . . . beyond the capability of the VNAF."[168] Unless renewed actions were taken to equip VNAF F-5s with better cameras, this would be a continuing VNAF limitation.

(S) <u>Electronic Surveillance (U)</u>. In the fall of 1971, interest began to mount in a VNAF sensor program. In January 1972, VNAF C-47s, equipped with a Palletized Airborne Relay (PAR), began flying sensor relay orbits. The PAR was capable of being carried on 20 specially modified C-47s; it received and relayed signals from IGLOO WHITE sensors back to a PAR Terminal (PART), where the information was monitored and analyzed by ARVN personnel. The VNAF responsibility was to maintain the C-47 on station, and insure that a good signal output was being generated by the PAR.[169]

(S) Assigning the VNAF a broader role in the sensor activities of the RVNAF, including sensor field planning, sensor implant, and sensor information exploitation in a Credible Chase-type interdiction role, was a subject of discussion and debate throughout 1972. Specifically, VNAF involvement in and support of the PAR/PART program continued to be debated as late as the fall of 1972, and a related 7AF CROC was in being to provide the VNAF with a high-speed sensor implant capability.[170] In December 1972, however, following Enhance Plus, VNAF participation in the PAR/PART program was reevaluated and cancelled:[171]

> (S) VNAF provision of C-47 platform for the PAR portion of the ARVN sensor program was deleted for following reasons:
>
> A. Vulnerability.
>
> B. No VNAF high-speed implant capability.
>
> C. Quality of intelligence from PAR of minimal value . . .
>
> In summary, the PAR/PART system is no longer a VNAF mission and due to the need to modernize the VNAF AOB as rapidly as possible will not be a VNAF mission for the foreseeable future.

(S) Although the PAR/PART program was cancelled, the VNAF retained an active electronic intelligence program which provided a constant input to the intelligence data base. During Enhance Plus the fleet of VNAF EC-47s was increased from 22 to 33 aircraft. Basically, the EC-47 was a C-47 configured with electronic devices, commonly referred to as Bravo equipment. Aboard each aircraft, seven VNAF personnel manned the Bravo equipment to intercept voice communications and to perform the Airborne Radio Direction Finding function.[172] As of late 1973, 23 EC-47s were stationed near Saigon, and 10 at Da Nang. The EC-47s were flying 14 four-hour intelligence gathering missions daily, and the goal was 16 seven-hour missions. Low maintenance manning levels, compounded by the incidence of maintenance required by the aging C-47s, were the primary factors limiting the sortie rate.[173]

(S) <u>Coastal Surveillance (U)</u>. The subject of VNAF Market Time (ocean surveillance patrol) operations had been under discussion since 1971. In November 1971 an AFGP force structure proposal recommended that the VNAF be provided with cargo type aircraft modified for the ocean surveillance role. The VNAF surveillance effort would supplement the Vietnamese Navy coastal interdiction of enemy supply vessels so that U.S. Navy (USN) P-3 patrol aircraft could cease operations off Vietnam and be withdrawn from SEA.[174] At that time, the VNAF was already providing a small number of light observation aircraft sorties, termed Visual Aerial Reconnaissance and Surveillance (VARS) sorties, to patrol the Vietnamese coastline. The missions, however, extended only a few miles from the SVN coastline and were few in number.[175] The concept of the proposed VNAF Market Time squadrons was to provide systematic surveillance [out] as far as 200 miles from the coast.

(S) VNAF Market Time operations were envisioned as a supplement to VNN surface patrols and coastal ground radars. The coastal ground radar system consisted of sixteen radar sites which provided the VNN with the capability of monitoring the entire SVN coastline seaward for a distance of

40 Nautical Miles (NM). The ground radar system was considered highly effective, as far as it went, against steel-hulled trawlers. Market Time was to extend that coverage seaward, provide on-the-spot identification of the ship in question, and help solve the problem of large wooden-hulled infiltrators which were more difficult to detect with coastal radar.[176]

(S) Enhance Plus provided RVN with C-119s, which were to be modified with radar and other equipment necessary for the ocean surveillance role. Originally, a squadron of the modified aircraft, RC-119Ls, was to be activated in March 1974. However, a delay in aircraft modification and a reevaluation of the threat prompted the Advisory Group to recommend deletion of the RC-119L squadron in an 11 January 1973 message. That recommendation was supported by COMUSMACV and CINCPACAF. The proposed deletion was based on the following factors: modification problems would delay squadron activation and operational readiness until at least May 1975; the contract for proposed modifications was about to be finalized and would cost nearly four million dollars; the performance of the RC-119L in the Market Time mission was unproven; the RC-119Ls were potentially vulnerable during the identification phase of a mission (projected to be flown at 2500 feet above the ocean); land ingress routes, over which the enemy could move personnel and supplies with relative ease, would become increasingly available as U.S. interdiction forces departed; and a system capable of meeting the threat out to at least 40 NM from the SVN shoreline was already in existence (VNN patrols and coastal radar, and VNAF VARS flights).[177]

(S/NFD) The Commander, U.S. Naval Forces, Vietnam, did not concur in the deletion of the squadron, parimarily on the basis of the following: the "wooden-hulled threat"; the fact that existing U.S. Navy air patrol missions had demonstrated their effectiveness in supplementing coastal radars, VNN patrols, and VNAF VARS flights; the probability that the terms of a cease-fire would make it difficult to reinstate the VNAF maritime air patrol mission if deleted from the force structure prior to the cease-fire; and the belief that a cease-fire would turn VNAF attention from support of ground units to land and sea interdiction.[178] CINCPAC recommended retention of the squadron, but suggested modification of the squadron be held in abeyance pending further definition of the threat. In April 1973, the JCS approved the VNAF 66-squadron force (including the RC-119L squadron), but recommended additional review of the requirement for the squadron.[179]

(S) The need for the RC-119L squadron was again evaluated, and in May 1973 Hq USSAG recommended, and CINCPACAF concurred, that the squadron be deleted. The Commander-in-Chief, Pacific Fleet, did not concur on the basis of the significance of the threat and the desirability of relieving the USN Market Time commitment. CINCPAC supported the deletion recommending the following: termination of the modification contract, with the option of reimplementing it at a later time; retention of the C-119s in-country as attrition aircraft for gunships and transports, or for later modification; reevaluation of the modification option on a continuing basis; and reduction of the USN patrols as VNAF visual reconnaissance increased. The JCS approved the CINCPAC course of action, specifying that USN P-3 patrols continue and that the operational capabilities of the RC-119L squadron, and the potential requirement for the squadron, be reviewed after the prototype test and evaluation in September 1973.[180]

(S) Late in 1973, the Director of the Air Force Division, DAO, Saigon, addressing RC-119L squadron, commented:[181] (U)

> (S) We, in the U.S. Air Force and the VNAF, in assessing the validity of the requirement for this unit, questioned the validity of the threat. There has been but one attempted incursion of an infiltration by a heavy ship that far off-shore [out to the 200 mile limit to be covered by the RC-119L squadron] in the past three years. We have Navy coastal radars that go out 75 miles and feel that this is adequate, and with tactical air responsiveness we can cover any potential infiltration. In addition, the modification of the C-119 has never been testflown, that is. . . . no airplane's ever been modified with the 133 radar, and we do not know if it is really flyable. There is a seven million dollar program to accomplish this. Due to the lack of threat and the high cost we have been able to convince everybody through DOD not to activate the 66th squadron, the RC-119L. However, this requires a formal amendment to NSDM [National Security Council Decision Memorandum] 168. The Secretary of Defense has yet to . . . [obtain the NSC's approval].

VNAF Intelligence (U)

(S/NFD) The VNAF intelligence organization and its capabilities remained essentially unchanged from the beginning of FY 72. In a sense, the question of VNAF intelligence capabilities became moot in that targeting of air resources was more rigidly in the hands of the MR commander than ever before. Although VNAF intelligence nominated a number of targets, the MR commander and his staff selected the targets to be struck.[182] On some occasions targets nominated by ARVN intelligence and selected by the MR commander were considered by the VNAF to be unproductive.[183]

(S) The VNAF faced another problem in that the intelligence sources available as a basis for targeting were severely restricted. It has already been shown that, for all practical purposes, the VNAF did not have a VR program. Further, the small amount of information which was available from VR missions in support of the ARVN was largely restricted to terrain close to friendly positions. Remaining VNAF intelligence sources consisted of Photo Intelligence (PHOTINT), Signal Intelligence (SIGINT), and Human Resource Intelligence (HUMINT). It was estimated that 90 percent of VNAF intelligence was based on PHOTINT, and 10 percent was derived from SIGINT; the amount based on HUMINT was negligible. Thus, VNAF intelligence was essentially reliant on the photographic reconnaissance program, the shortcomings of which have already been enumerated.[184]

(S) A final significant problem was the lack of VNAF expertise in munitions selection. Once the Advisory Group left, the VNAF had no significant operational advice on munitions, and no munitions technical data or source, such as the Joint Munitions Effectiveness Manual, upon which to base computations of number and types of munitions for a particular target.[185]

Proposed Improvements to VNAF Combat Capabilities (U)

(C) As a tool for updating and improving the combat capabilities of the VNAF, CROCs played an important role in the I&M program. Considering, however, the length of time it could take to complete CROC actions, and the turbulence in the existing and planned VNAF aircraft inventory, there was a tendency for CROCs to be overtaken by events before their completion.

(S) Enhance Plus and the subsequent cease-fire had a severe impact on the CROC program. The influx of aircraft and equipment resulted in drastic scheduling and cost changes to previously validated programs. As typified by the SEEK POINT radar-directed delivery system, new equipment was rushed in-country before provisions were completed for installation, training, and operation. This influx, coupled with the withdrawal of U.S. forces and advisors, created management problems* in overseeing the orderly, efficient accomplishment of CROC actions involving large sums of money and extensive manpower.

(S) Following Enhance Plus, both 7AF and PACAF carefully reevaluated the many existing VNAF CROCs to determine which of those were still considered essential. These reviews were initiated in light of (1) clearly stated cease-fire provisions regarding the introduction of any new capabilities into RVN, (2) the cost impact of Enhance Plus additions (for example, the F-5 force grew from 40 plus to 150 plus aircraft) and the attendant decrease in the ability to fund and complete modification actions within a reasonable time frame, and (3) the fact that funding for VNAF programs was directly and seriously depleting already scarce USAF modification funds. The list of CROCs resulting from the initial 7AF review are enumerated in Table 7, which also reflects the progress made in CROC completion during 1973. Although funding and technical problems delayed or precluded completion of a sizeable number of the CROCs, a great deal was accomplished

---

*(S) For example, it should be noted that during the months following the cease-fire, actions to complete many VNAF CROCs consisted primarily of locating kit materials lost or misplaced during the massive influx of equipment into RVN. The inability of limited numbers of civilian contract personnel to determine the warehouse location of these kits, or to even determine whether kits had been received, continued to present a major management obstacle to the completion of these requirements.

TABLE 7

VNAF CROC/ROC STATUS

PART A--VNAF CROCs which were, as of 20 Nov 72,
still considered essential by 7AF.

CROC #	TITLE	STATUS
27-70	VNAF C-119G Propeller Reversal System	Partially completed, then dropped in Jan 73. C-119 airlift aircraft returned to U.S. as a result of activation of C-130 squadrons.
42-70	Improved Motor for the USAF/VNAF 2.75" Folding Fin Aircraft Rocket (FFAR)	Problems with rockets discovered during testing. CROC cancelled in favor of TAC ROC 15-68.
56-70	Increased Firepower for VNAF UH-1H Helicopters (VNAF 19 Tube Rocket Launcher)	Delivery of 200 units per month commenced in Nov 73.
61-70	Additional UH-1 Gunship Capability for the VNAF	Completed in late 1973.
64-70	VNAF All-Weather Bombing Capability (SEEK POINT)	First units delivered before the cease-fire. Continuing maintenance and support problems, and contractor efforts, throughout 1973 and into 1974.
65-70	VNAF C/AC-47 Aircraft Fuel Cell Explosion Suppressant (Class V Modification)	Completed in early 1973.
5-71	VNAF UH-1 ASC-10 Command and Control Radio Modification	Completed in Feb 73.
7-71	20mm Guns for VNAF A-37 Aircraft	Converted to PACAF ROC [Required Operational Capability] 4-73.* Still active and unfunded as of Jan 74.

*An 11 Sep 73 Air Staff directive specified that all CROCs would either be converted to ROCs, or deleted.

CROC #	TITLE	STATUS
14-71	Modernization of Communications for VNAF Aircraft	Shipment of equipment completed by mid-1973.
18-71	VNAF RF/F-5A/B Capability to Accommodate AIM-9E (Class V Modification)	Funded. As of Aug 73, all 40 mod kits received in country. Aircraft undergoing modification at Bien Hoa at the rate of two per week. Estimated completion date, 15 Oct 73.
2-72	VNAF High Speed Sensor Implant Capability	Dropped as a result of the cancellation of the PAR mission in Dec 72.
5-72	Improved Camera System for VNAF RF-5 Aircraft	Converted to PACAF ROC 5-73.* Still active and unfunded as of Jan 74.
7-72	RHAW [Radar Homing and Warning] Equipment for VNAF F/RF-5 Aircraft	Converted to PACAF ROC 2-73.* Still active and unfunded as of Jan 74.
8-72	Vietnamization of Interdiction	A major portion of this CROC was to provide the VNAF with an LGB delivery system. CROC was cancelled.
15-72	ECM for F/RF-5 Aircraft	Converted to PACAF ROC 3-73.* Still active and unfunded as of Jan 74.
24-72	AN/AAD-5 Infrared Recce Set (Increased Reconnaissance Capability for the VNAF)	Cancelled. No longer considered essential.
27-72	IRCM (Infrared Countermeasure) Capability for VNAF Aircraft	As of Oct 73, 668 of 883 flare dispensers had been delivered. IR [Infrared] suppressant paint was also being provided. Continuing actions were planned under PACAF ROC 1-73.*

*An 11 Sep 73 Air Staff directive specified that all CROCs would either be converted to ROCs, or deleted.

PART B--New ROCs approved by early 1974

CROC #	TITLE	STATUS
8-73	Paradrop Computer Program for VNAF AN/TPB-1A Radar	ROC was developed to improve the accuracy of SEEK POINT airdrops.
1-74	F-5E MER (Multiple Ejection Rack)	The MER would greatly increase the F-5Es' air-to-ground capabilities.
2-74	Mod of 44 VNAF A-1 Aircraft with SST-181	SEEK POINT-related. Previously, 26 A-1s had been modified under CROC 64-70. This ROC covered the VNAF's remaining 44 A-1s, and would result in an all-weather bombing capability for all VNAF A-1s.

SOURCES: Letter: Reevaluation of Combat ROCs (U), AFGP/DO/LG, 20 Nov 72. (C)

Pertinent PACAF/XOOQ CROC AND ROC files.

in the year following Enhance Plus. Clearly, VNAF capabilities were significantly enhanced through the CROC program.[186]

(U) The various operational forces and mission capabilities covered in this chapter reflect the ability of the VNAF to meet its operational requirements. The potential of the VNAF to support and sustain its operational capabilities is the subject of the next chapter.

CHAPTER IV

SUPPORT FUNCTIONS (U)

(U) A number of major activities are included under the "support functions" heading: the training function, which was at the heart of the Vietnamization process; the logistics system, which provided supply and maintenance support for operational units; the transfer and maintenance of U.S. facilities, which became increasingly important as the VNAF continued its expansion and U.S. forces withdrew; and communications-electronic capabilities, which were essential for effective air operations. In all of these functional areas, the VNAF faced monumental challenges, registered noteworthy accomplishments, but experienced continuing serious problems throughout FY 73 and beyond.

Training (U)

(S) Pre-Enhance Plus (U). By July 1971, the VNAF training program was well-established, and was headed for self-sufficiency for those weapon systems possessed by the VNAF and for the personnel levels projected in the CRIMP. A previous CHECO report noted that "except for pilot training and a few highly technical skills, VNAF self-sufficiency in training appeared assured by mid-1971. . . . By June 1971 it was apparent that the most critical facet of establishing VNAF self-sufficiency--a sound and viable training program--was achieved."[187] The VNAF training program, however, had yet to face those challenges, then unforeseen, which would result from VNAF force structure expansion, revision and modernization of VNAF weapons systems, Projects Enhance and Enhance Plus, and the cease-fire agreement with the concomitant total withdrawal of U.S. military forces from Vietnam.

(S) The training of personnel to support and operate an increasingly sophisticated and complex Air Force required long lead times. Meeting requirements in a timely manner demanded efficient utilization of training facilities, which was in turn dependent upon availability of sufficient numbers of trainees. As noted earlier in this report, the JGS failed to allow early VNAF recruitment to fill VNAF trainee needs relating to the FSR-73 force structure expansion. That delay added months to the training lead-time requirements, which were already estimated to be two years for the 14,000 personnel added by FSR-73.[188] A 29 December 1971 letter to COMUSMACV from Maj Gen James H. Watkins, the Chief, AFGP, stated:[189]

> (S) At this time, the VNAF training schools are operating at approximately 20% of capacity. . . . Due to the lack of student inputs, Hqs VNAF has solicited approval of the JGS to start recruitment to fill these training vacancies but, to date, have [sic] been unsuccessful.
>
> * * * * * * *
>
> (S) The magnitude of the increase of the force structure, along with the multitude of tasks which must be performed during the next year are sufficient challenge to the ingenuity and resourcefulness of the VNAF. Imposition of an unnecessary delay in obtaining qualified support personnel by failure to permit recruitment to fill training pipelines endangers our entire mission. . . .

Unfortunately, swift JGS approval of early recruitment was not forthcoming; VNAF training facilities continued to operate well below capacity until May 1972, when the JGS finally allowed "early"* recruitment of 2,000 personnel.[190]

---

*(S) This amounted to recruitment of personnel only two months earlier than would have otherwise been the case.

(C) At the same time that VNAF training facilities were experiencing a lack of trainees, the scope of the USAF integrated training program was drastically declining. The phase-out of integrated training reflected the increasing withdrawals of USAF personnel from Vietnam. From a monthly participation of more than 1,000 VNAF personnel in January 1972, the integrated training program steadily declined, yielding only 65 trained VNAF personnel in the last quarter of 1972. Since the establishment of the integrated training program in 1970, a total of nearly 6,200 VNAF personnel had completed training.[191]

(C) In the meantime, VNAF formal in-country training courses were meeting a wide range of training requirements including pilot, navigator, air/ground operations school, maintenance, comm-electronics, weather, and military training. In-country contractors provided training courses in some functional areas, including civil-engineering and vehicle maintenance. The formal training courses were enhanced by VNAF OJT upgrading which was pursued at a vigorous rate throughout 1972. The VNAF efforts were supplemented in highly technical or new areas by USAF Mobile Training Teams deployed to Vietnam from the CONUS. These teams trained VNAF instructors in their particular specialties before returning to the CONUS. Finally, a small number of VNAF personnel were trained in the CONUS.

(C) Despite these efforts, however, the intensified expansion and development of the VNAF under FSR-73 and Project Enhance, and the accompanying influx of new recruits into the VNAF manning structure, had accelerated the dilution of VNAF managerial capabilities, skill levels, and the pilot force. In the course of four years (1968-1972), VNAF manning had tripled and aircraft levels had multiplied by a factor of five. Further, the VNAF force contained more sophisticated weapon systems, and was charged with greatly increased operational and logistical support responsibilities. Twenty percent of the VNAF force was in initial training, and the remaining force was heavily concentrated at the lower skill levels. Among enlisted personnel and noncommissioned officers (NCOs), manning at the various skill levels reflected the high ratio of unskilled personnel. Thus, manning at the "9" skill level (the VNAF's highest) was only 1.6 percent of the authorized; and at the "5" skill level it was 51 percent of authorized; but at the "3" (or basically unskilled) level, it was 165 percent of authorized.[192] While primarily the result of the VNAF's rapid growth, the overmanning at the three level was exacerbated by VNAF personnel policies. Trainees who upgraded to the five skill level incurred an additional service commitment without any increased compensation. This "penalty" for skill upgrading was finally removed by the JGS in September 1972, thus opening the door for increased upgrading of skill levels during subsequent months.[193]

(S) By late 1972, VNAF personnel manning had passed 50,000, and an additional 12,000 recruits were scheduled for induction by July 1973. Two-thirds of the force had less than three years in the VNAF. Training these inexperienced and new personnel would be a monumental task, made all the more urgent by the acute shortage of trained maintenance personnel and pilots--this shortage was considered to be the "driving constraint" on the VNAF's progress.[194] It was a demanding task, but I&M planners expressed confidence in the ability of the training program to meet the challenge.[195] Then, in anticipation of a possible cease-fire agreement, Enhance Plus was initiated--the training program faced yet another traumatic expansion.

(S) <u>Post-Enhance Plus (U)</u>. Enhance Plus had only a modest impact on VNAF personnel strength, which rose by some 3,500 men; the introduction of new, more-sophisticated weapons systems, however, together with the decision to activate all projected squadrons as soon as possible, greatly magnified personnel limitations and problems. To help expedite the mammoth initial transition necessitated by Enhance Plus, and to help provide the VNAF with the capability to absorb the training capabilities demanded by the new weapons system, a concentrated transition training program was initiated while USAF resources were still in-country. USAF training augmenters were provided by in-country units and were supplemented by teams from the CONUS. The goal of the program was to leave a well-trained nucleus of VNAF instructors for each weapons system received under Project Enhance Plus, thereby enabling the VNAF to continue the 18-month training out process, with some civilian contractor assistance.[196] The VNAF manpower pool needed as a basis for the training program was formed in the following manner: C-123, C-119, and C-47 transport squadrons were deactivated, releasing aircrews and maintenance personnel for C-130, F-5, and A-37 squadrons; crew ratios for all VNAF aircraft were reviewed and adjusted, and, where possible, crew members were drawn out of existing units; AC-119G crews and maintenance personnel were cross-trained for AC-119Ks; A-37 aircrews and maintenance personnel were cross-trained to F-5s; experienced O-1 pilots were cross-trained to help fill the reduced A-37 manning and to fly O-2s; some O-1 observers were trained as O-1 pilots; and the CONUS pipeline was used to provide additional trainee inputs.[197]

(S) By the end of November 1972, just four weeks after Project Enhance Plus was directed, selected USAF training personnel and equipment were in place in Vietnam, initial VNAF trainees had been identified and provided, and training had begun. The first trainees, eight C-130A crews, completed transition training on 24 December 1972. Thereafter, a steady stream of aircrews and maintenance personnel continued to complete training for O-2s, C-130As, AC-119Ks, F-5As, and A-37s. The F-5A training involved the longest lead-time, with the last personnel not scheduled to complete training until December 1973. However, the bulk of the Enhance Plus training would be completed by March, at which time only the F-5A and A-37 training programs would be incomplete. The total number of trainees involved included 38 O-2 pilots and 60 maintenance personnel, 32 C-130A crews and 451 maintenance personnel, 15 AC-119K crews and 62 maintenance personnel, 157 F-5 pilots, and 274 A-37 pilots*.[198]

(S) The number of VNAF aircrews and maintenance personnel provided by these Enhance Plus training programs was well below the number of personnel required to fully man the various squadrons. Nevertheless, the program provided crucial mission assistance in overcoming the initial hump of training requirements and in providing the VNAF with a relatively experienced, well-trained cadre for activation of Enhance Plus squadrons. Of at least equal importance, it helped provide experienced VNAF instructors capable of teaching subsequent trainees when they became available. Indeed, a fundamental limitation of Enhance Plus training was the continuing unavailability

---

*Immediate maintenance requirements were to be met by contractor augmentation and available VNAF maintenance personnel. VNAF maintenance training was to be accomplished through OJT on VNAF training capabilities. Numbers of personnel were not specified.

of suitable trainees--the required number of qualified, experienced trainees simply could not be extracted from existing VNAF resources without severely degrading the operational capabilities of the units affected. Time and stability were required to overcome the critical shrotage of trained, experienced VNAF personnel. It was hoped that the anticipated cease-fire would provide an environment conducive to continued VNAF progress in these areas.

(S) <u>Post-Cease-Fire (U)</u>. By the time that the Agreement on Ending the War and Restoring Peace in Vietnam went into effect on 27 January 1973, steady progress had been made in filling initial transition training needs. The VNAF training program was still reeling, however, from the effects of Enhance Plus and earlier expansions. Added to that, in anticipation of the cease-fire, a massive transfer of remaining U.S. facilities had occurred on paper; implementation of the cease-fire and the subsequent withdrawal of U.S. forces made those transfers a reality.[199] The need for trained VNAF personnel to support these facilities, to supply and maintain equipment and aircraft, and to effectively operate VNAF squadrons only became more acute with the cease-fire. Although there was a decrease in the intensity of combat after the cease-fire, the desired degree of stability and peace was never realized. The VNAF found themselves facing not only their massive training task, but also confronted by the need for continuing support of combat operations. The VNAF would have to proceed with heavy recruitment and basic/upgrade training, which would encompass as much as 50 percent of its active force, while at the same time meeting continuing operational requirements. To assist them in that task, and to handle other aspects of U.S. involvement, in-country U.S. resources would consist of only 50 military, 1,200 DOD civilian, and approximately 5,000 contractor personnel.[200]

(S) The bulk of the post-cease-fire training was handled by the VNAF, but valuable assistance was received in two ways: By CONUS training for pilots, instructors, and technicians in highly complex areas; and by in-country contractor OJT training with emphasis on providing the VNAF with the capability to support its new weapon systems. The total FY 74 CONUS training program involved only about 1,250 students, but the personnel trained were considered essential to help the VNAF overcome pilot shortfalls, and to provide them with highly qualified instructors and a core of personnel well-trained in high skill-level specialties. To help overcome the pilot shortage, and to provide future pilot training needs, the VNAF established Undergraduate Helicopter Training at Binh Thuy, Da Nang, and Bien Hoa, and Undergraduate Pilot Training at Nha Trang and Phan Rang.[201]

(S) The contractor OJT training was more difficult to define in terms of training goals and numbers of trainees. The basic difficulty was that contractor efforts had a two-fold objective: (1) to provide the VNAF with an immediate operational capability, and (2) to conduct the necessary training to transition to totally self-sufficient VNAF operations, thus allowing contractor phase-out. Initially, it was envisioned that self-sufficiency would have to be attained within one year from the cease-fire. Events proved this a clearly unrealistic goal, as basic VNAF training requirements alone dictated greater than a two-year lead-time, and contractor numbers were insufficient to pursue both training and operational capabilities. During the months following the cease-fire, considerable turmoil occurred as a result of the conflicting requirements for support of operations and training. At the Air Logistics Command, for example, the emphasis was first placed on production from the VNAF as augmented by the contractors. It then shifted to training, with a subsequent negative impact on production and support to VNAF units. Consequently, training adjustments were required to increase production. Essentially, the small number of U.S. personnel available and the extent of training and experience required by the VNAF were the limiting factors. These factors precluded the possibility of concurrently training, producing, and filling the void in VNAF middle management, and thereby attaining self-sufficiency within the desired time constraints. Nevertheless, considerable phase-out of contractor support was accomplished in some areas by late 1973. On the day of the cease-fire there were 5,237 U.S. contractors in Vietnam; by September 1973 there was 2,823.[202]

(S) By mid-1973 it was clear that steady progress had been made in the expansion of VNAF training capabilities, and that the VNAF was nearing self-sufficiency in all but the most complex, high-skill-level training. In June 1973, in his end-of-tour report, Maj Gen Jumper, Chief, AFGP, summarized VNAF training programs as follows:[203]

> (S) . . . Except for a few specialized areas, the VNAF is quite self-sufficient in training capability. The capability exists to conduct over 170 in-country formal courses annually, with a production capacity of over 19,000 people. . . . There is training available to cover most recurring needs. Very little three- or five-level training is not done in-country and what little has been done in CONUS is rapidly phasing out. . . .

*   *   *   *   *   *   *

(S) . . . The VNAF has adopted many US training techniques to its own purposes. For example, it has formed and dispersed a few Mobile Training Teams which enable specialists to travel to the units where instruction is needed and train in the operational atmosphere. It has adopted USAF standards for monitoring and measuring the effectiveness of its OJT programs. And it is establishing in-country instructor training and professional service schools. In general, except for pilot training, the VNAF can be said to be self-sufficient in all but staff level instruction and training in the use and maintenance of new equipment and systems. . . .

(S) It was equally clear, however, that despite intense and continuing in-country VNAF and contractor training efforts, the skill and experience level of the VNAF work force would remain considerably below the desired level for some time to come. By September 1973, although VNAF manning had reached nearly 62,000 on the way to the projected 65,000 man force, the manning picture remained serious. While enlisted strength was 99 percent of authorized, officer manning was only 74 percent of authorized. Furthermore, nearly 17,000 VNAF personnel were in the training pipeline--one out of four assigned personnel. Concentration of personnel at the lower skill levels continued to be one of the VNAF's most pressing problems. Even the best training could not convert a raw recruit into a skilled, experienced airman overnight. Experienced technicians and managers would come only with a combination of training and time. The inevitable paucity of middle managers would continue to be one of the greatest impediments to VNAF self-sufficiency. Once again, time, a measure of stability, and continued emphasis on training would be required before the VNAF could rise to the level of competence required for self-sufficiency.[204] Yet, with the attainment of VNAF end-strength nearly in sight, intense training efforts during the next year promised significant dividends. Whereas previous personnel accomplishments were diluted by the continuous flood of inexperienced recruits, by late 1973 the VNAF had finally reached the point at which real progress was possible in upgrading the skill level of the VNAF force.

(C) <u>Vietnamese Capacity for Training (U)</u>. A section on the progress and limitations of VNAF training programs would be incomplete without addressing the basic foundation of these programs--the capacity of the Vietnamese trainee to absorb training. There were many factors mitigating against Vietnamese training programs: the massive number of recruits, the lack of continuity in the flow of trainees, expansion of tasks in numbers and complexity, reduced U.S. in-country assistance, and others. The Vietnamese capacity for training, contrary to popular opinion, was not one of these factors. If anything, Vietnamese personnel, especially considering their agricultural background, exhibited a surprising propensity for technical training. In July 1972 end-of-tour report, a former Advisory Group Plans and Program director offered the following comments:[205]

> (C) In dealing with the Vietnamese Air Force (VNAF) on a daily basis it readily became apparent that U.S. opinion concerning the technical capacity of the VNAF airman was based on a false assumption. That assumption was that an agricultural people would require a great deal of time and training to be able to handle relatively rudimentary technical assignments. Our experience over the past year, which was a period of accelerated growth for the VNAF, revealed that the VNAF airman is capable of almost any technical assignment we are willing to train him for despite his primarily agricultural background.

(C) It was equally true, however, that it was a challenge to motivate the Vietnamese to train to their full capacity. Essentially, to be effective, trainees had to understand that when they finished their training they would be responsible for operating or supporting the particular system in question.[206] As long as they knew they would be on their own on a specific date, and that no further assistance would be available, training was a success. On the other hand, if the trainees felt that U.S. personnel would continue to be available to assist, they would project the appearance of not understanding. This point was brought out in an interview of the Director of the Air Force Division, DAO, in which the Vietnamese were compared with the Nationalist Chinese and South Koreans during their respective transitions to modern Air Forces:[207]

> (C) I saw the transition of the Chinese, after World War II, in becoming a nation and growing, and setting up a logistical base and becoming a self-sufficient organization. I am also familiar with the efforts after the Korean War in getting South Korea to do the same thing. It has taken between 15 and 20 years for each of these nations to achieve a capability of standing on their own two feet to a high degree. If anything, I would have said the Vietnamese' back should have been broken long ago, but they have been able to absorb it, and . . . at a 300% faster rate than either the Chinese or the Koreans. It is amazing what these people can do. They learn well when they learn something. I think we take too much for granted in assuming that they know things that we learned as children . . . but we have to go back and teach them. We forget our differences in culture. However, I have also learned, through my years of association in this country, that they have a tremendous capacity and capability of accomplishing a task. Once they're forced to do it, they can do it, but as long as somebody else will do it for them, they are going to let the other people do it . . . ., and I think any of us would do that. But, when you tell them to stand on their own two feet, sink or swim, they are always there and can stand up and be counted. . . . They have the talent and, I think, they have the intelligence. I think we have really underestimated their intelligence potential. So, with patience, and time and stability, I think they'll hack it.

Logistics (Supply and Maintenance) (U)

(C) The VNAF logistics system was the foundation upon which VNAF operational capabilities were based. Its responsibilities included maintenance and repair of VNAF aircraft and equipment, and procurement, storage, and distribution of materiel (including equipment, spare parts, and consumables such as POL, munitions, and normal supplies.) To meet these responsibilities, the VNAF logistics organization consisted of an Air Logistics Command, located at Bien Hoa AB, and maintainenance and supply wings at each of the six VNAF Air Division. The Air Logistics Command was the hub of the VNAF logistics system. It was organized in three major subdivisions to provide depot-level maintenance of equipment, central logistics management, and procurement, storage, and distribution of supplies. To meet supply needs, the ALC served as the supply depot for the Air Division supply wings, and centrally managed requisitioning, inventory control, and distribution of spares and supplies to units at the nine VNAF bases. To meet maintenance needs, the ALC provided depot-level repair, overhaul, and rebuild of VNAF aircraft and equipment,* while organization and intermediate maintenance (field level maintenance) was performed at the base level. Continued development and improvement of the VNAF's supply and maintenance capabilities were imperative, since the degree to which the VNAF logistics

---

*(C) As of late 1972, the ALC's maintenance program was still in its infancy, but with the help of USAF and contractor augmentees, it was developing rapidly. A program to develop VNAF depot level maintenance capabilities had not begun until 1970. Up to that time depot level maintenance had been routinely accomplished by the USAF. Depsite its short history, however, the ALC's maintenance program had made remarkable progress toward self-sufficiency in helicopters, fighters, and light aircraft.

system met its responsibilities directly influenced the degree to which operational squadrons could perform their mission.[208]

(C) Many problems occurred during the development of the VNAF logistics system. One factor central to efforts to solve those problems was computerization of the ALC, a continuing effort which was beset with seemingly chronic problems. Resolution of computer problems was mandatory for the development of depot capabilities which in turn was essential to the efficient operation of the logistics system as a whole. Yet, the very emphasis required for depot capabilities detracted from the development of base capabilities. Despite the difficulties, the VNAF was able to achieve solid progress in the growth of their logistics system. Nevertheless, self-sufficiency--while much closer than before--was still a distant goal.

(S) <u>Mid-1971 Through Late 1972 (U)</u>. Despite continuing improvements in and expansion of VNAF supply and maintenance capabilities, VNAF Operationally Ready*, Not Operationally Ready Spares, and Not Operationally Ready Maintenance rates for late 1971 and throughout 1972 reflected a decline in the ability of the VNAF logistics system to support operational needs.[209] The primary factors causing the decline in logistics performance were the

---

*(S) Operational Readiness was defined as the percentage of possessed aircraft which were capable of accomplishing their primary mission. It should be emphasized that the VNAF O/R system was based on possessed aircraft, rather than UE; when an aircraft was in field or depot maintenance, it was not considered possessed. Further, the decision as to which aircraft were considered possessed was made by the local commander, not by VNAF headquarters. In some cases, aircraft which had not yet been sent to the depot or which were NORS were designated by the unit commander as not being possessed. Not only was the number of non-operational aircraft obfuscated by the "not-possessed" designation, but the number of aircraft considered O/R was also inflated; that is, the number of aircraft reported as O/R during a specific period was greater than the actual number O/R at a given time. The result of this situation was deceptively high O/R rates. VNAF headquarters recognized this inflation and informally used a conversion factor to adjust O/R rates submitted by the units.

expansion of the VNAF aircraft and equipment in number and complexity, undermanning in the supply and maintenance areas, the withdrawal of U.S. military support personnel, and the NVA invasion. Actually, the VNAF supply and maintenance disciplines had undergone steady improvements, but the rate of expansion and improvement could not keep pace with the rapid growth of VNAF needs.

(C) USAF Auditor General reports identified numerous shortcomings in the VNAF supply and maintenance areas in 1971 and 1972, but indicated that significant progress was being made in overcoming many of these obstacles and in developing an effective logistics system.[210] A continuing problem, which would have to be overcome if self-sufficiency in logistics were to be realized, lay in the Vietnamese attitude toward maintenance. An Auditor's report written in October 1971 pointed out a commonly observed Vietnamese attitude: ". . . many personnel in the RVNAF do not fully realize that continued operation of available equipment can only be assured with the concomitant feature of proper maintenance."[211] The report also stated:[212]

> (C) Since 1969, we have issued six reports on various RVNAF Logistics programs. In each of these reports, we pointed out wasteful management practices. Also, the files of U.S. Advisors are replete with memorandums and letters . . . pointing our instances of poor supply discipline, inadequate maintenance of equipment and slovenly storage practice.

This attitude toward preventative maintenance and supply discipline was considered a serious obstacle to Vietnamization of logistics during 1971 and 1972, and it represented one of the fundamental challenges to the I&M program during 1973.

(S) *Enhance Plus and Its Aftermath (U)*. Under Enhance Plus, the South Vietnamese were provided with enough aircraft, equipment, and supplies to survive one year of total isolation. That approach had been taken to cover the possibility that the cease-fire might prohibit resupply of Vietnamese forces for one year following the cease-fire, but that constraint did not materialize in the cease-fire agreement. The massive influx of materiel, however, left the VNAF logistics system completely overwhelmed with a year's supply of equipment, spares, and consumables. The volumes of equipment and supplies exceeded the capacity both of VNAF warehouses and of accounting controls. Large quantities of supplies were hastily stacked out-of-doors, and accountability for the material was lost. At the same time, the withdrawal of U.S. forces from Vietnam necessitated the assumption, by the VNAF, of many logistical functions previously performed by U.S. personnel. This, together with the expansion of the VNAF squadron strength and the types and sophistication of equipment, exceeded the VNAF's capability to absorb, control, and properly maintain the assets provided by the United States.[213]

(S) Adding to the logistical problems created by the volume of materiel delivered during Enhance Plus, were difficulties relating to the condition of aircraft delivered and the shortage of AGE and spares for some assets. The poor condition of C-130 aircraft has already been discussed.* Although the condition of F-5As was generally better, severe corrosion was found on about one out of five aircraft. Even more serious than the F-5A corrosion problem was a critical shortage of AGE and spares. Virtually no F-5 spares were available for delivery during Enhance Plus, and a quantity of AGE sufficient to support only one squadron was all that could be provided. Available AGE was also limited for the C-130 and A-37 aircraft.[214]

---
*See p. 89.

(S) To complicate matters for an already overburdened supply system, the VNAF airlift capability was severely curtailed as C-123s and C-119s were phased out to allow activation of C-130 units. Inadequate airlift of VNAF supply items resulted in increased supply shortages at the unit level. The loss of accountability for materiel, problems with the supply system computer (located at the Air Logistics Command at Bien Hoa), and the reduced availability of airlift all combined to seriously impair the responsiveness of the VNAF supply system. Cannibalization increased, which only served to complicate matters. Adding to these difficulties was the critical shortage of skilled VNAF personnel in the supply and maintenance areas. The end result was a large maintenance backlog, together with increased NORS/NORM rates and low OR rates.[215]

(C) Thus, at the time of the cease-fire, a bleak VNAF logistics outlook faced the newly formed DAO. For years the emphasis had been on helping the VNAF pursue self-sufficiency in operating its aircraft. The greatest task now facing the DAO was to help the VNAF develop its capability to support and maintain their aircraft with a minimum level of U.S. assistance, at minimum expense, and in minimum time. In late January 1973, the Chief of the Air Force Advisory Team at the ALC summed up the task facing the U.S. and VNAF personnel and called for a detailed plan of action:[216]

> (U) During past eighteen months, major changes in improvement and modernization (I&M) program have greatly affected force structure of VNAF with major impact on logistics mission and ALC workload. There is no single document which reflects all these changes or incorporates . . . information needed for development and operation of this single VNAF logistics support center. . . . Continual acceleration and expansion

of this program has left Vietnamese and U.S. logisticians in a state of confusion. This confusion can only be corrected through formulation of a master planning document which addresses all significant aspects of logistics. . . .

(U) [The] primary goal of Air Logistics Command is to develop maximum logistical capability to effectively and efficiently support VNAF. . . . To achieve [this] goal, VNAF must reduce dependency on outside sources to a minimum. . . . [The] long range success of VNAF Vietnamization...is largely dependent upon achievement of this goal. . . . Support of VNAF by ALC, now, and in post-withdrawal period, relates directly to their national survival and future industrial development. It is imperative [that] a comprehensive review be made of current status of ALC, that all aspects are evaluated, and a master charter be developed. . . .

(U) In early March 1973, a master plan for the expansion and improvement of VNAF logistics was published. Known as the V-Log, the plan provided a background summary, current assessment, and a "road map" to be used by the DAO with the objective of developing a self-sufficient VNAF logistics system. The background summary stated:

(U) Previous planning envisioned VNAF logistic development through the 1975 time frame using required advisors (military, civilian, and/or contractor) in achieving a high degree of self-sufficiency. Increased hostilities, opening of new VNAF bases and the recent peace agreement required a new direction in many areas of logistics planning to compensate for dilution of VNAF skills, VNAF manning deficiencies, one year tenure of DOD civilians and expedited completion of facility modifications. Logistics planning during the initial phases of Enhance Plus did not provide for the increased force structure of the VNAF to their objective 66 squadrons. Planning was for storage of the majority of these aircraft and when decision was reversed to activate the new squadrons, the VNAF were not equipped logistically to do so. Previous planning placed considerable emphasis on production of reparables...rather than expedited and/or concurrent VNAF training. . . .

The V-Log then presented an assessment of each element of the VNAF logistical system:[218]

(U) Facilities: VNAF base facilities are adequate except for the ALC at Bien Hoa. However, base level facilities may not be adequate to support the 66 squadron structure. ALC warehouse space is extremely short. . . .

(U) Materiel Management: The VNAF have a trained cadre of personnel assigned, but it is limited. They need more people and an extensive training program, both OJT and formal. The 1050-II computer, though not the desired or optimum instrument for depot management, is adequate for the current and near-term projected workload. . . . The VNAF have day-to-day problems. . . . Aggressive action is required by all responsible agencies and the VNAF.

*　　*　　*　　*　　*　　*　　*

(U) In the past two years, the total number of line items stocked in the depot has increased from 114,000 to 170,000 and the number of repair cycle items with a projected repair requirement has grown from 300 to 1900 line items. This expansion is attributable both to the increase in the VNAF's force structure . . . and to the significant increase in the ALC's planned repair capabilities.

*　　*　　*　　*　　*　　*　　*

(U) Depot Maintenance: The Depot Maintenance at the ALC is in a transition stage from an Organizational and Intermediate capability to a depot repair capability. . . . They are not getting people or required training (49% assigned). . . . Planning has been previously oriented toward some production capability and augmentation of the VNAF manpower force while training was receiving a secondary priority. . . . Recommendations: a. Get more VNAF people. b. Emphasize training. . . .

(U) Supply: . . . The effects of Projects Enhance and Enhance Plus have literally bogged down the supply functions at the ALC and 90,000 requisitions are still outstanding with approximately 80,000 due outs.* Warehouses are filled to capacity at Bien Hoa. This

---

*Due out--Requisition has been submitted through supply channels and processed, and the ordering agency has been notified that the item is officially on order.

aturation has almost eliminated inventory accuracy
and numerous items and boxes are stacked outside. . . .
In summary, the supply system has ground to a stop
impacting both the ALC and base logistic systems.

(U) <u>Transportation</u>: ...Original project Enhance
Plus planning was for the C-130 aircraft to be additive
to the C-123s and C-119s airlift force while the C-130s
would be maintained in flyable storage until transition
training could be accomplished for the VNAF. . . .
Logistics support for immediate flying of the C-130s
was not planned nor provided as is now apparent in the. . .
high NORS rate. The resultant impact is that the VNAF
cannot effect the distribution of required material
assets to the bases which is resulting in a high NORS
rate for all VNAF aircraft and support equipment. . . .

(U) The approach to be taken in the months ahead to improve VNAF capabilities was summarized as follows:[219]

(U) <u>Concept</u>: The VNAF's combat capability must
be maintained and supported concurrently with expansion
of the logistics base. Priority of effort will be devoted to establishing effective maintenance and supply
systems to serve assigned weapons systems and associated
equipment. The ultimate objective is to achieve a viable
logistics management system which provides the VNAF the
maximum in-country self-sufficiency consistent with cost
constraints.

(S) The phrase "maximum in-country self-sufficiency" reflects a principle which requires clarification. Total self-sufficiency, in the strictest sense of the term, was never an objective of the Vietnamization program, for "full self-sufficiency is a concept that cannot be realized by a small, basically agrarian economy in the throes of a modern conventional war."[220] Accordingly, it was envisioned that there would always be areas in which continued logistical support by the United States would be required. South Vietnam would be dependent for the foreseeable future on outside financing, materiel resupply, and repair and overhaul of a number of types of critical military equipment.[221] Nevertheless, a "maximum" degree of self-sufficiency was the objective. For example, the expressed goal was to make the

Vietnamese logistics system approximately 80 percent self-sufficient in responding to its maintenance requirements, the remaining 20 percent to be satisfied by offshore contractors or CONUS support. Specifically, the plan was for the VNAF to become totally self-sufficient in maintaining [its] UH-1 helicopters, the VNAF's most numerous airframe. Essentially, the objective was to also attain total self-sufficiency in tactical fighters, including A-1s, A-37s, and F-5s. This goal was to include complete overhaul of engines, and a jet engine overhaul facility (designed to overhaul or repair jet engines used on the F-5, A-37, C-123, UH-1, and CH-47 aircraft) was constructed at Bien Hoa and began operation in December 1972. Further, total maintenance self-sufficiency was being sought for light utility aircraft such as O-1s, O-2s, and U-17s, which employed small reciprocating engines. However, in regard to larger, multi-engine aircraft such as the C-7s, C-130s, C-119s, and C-47s, the VNAF was to be responsible only for field-level and intermediate maintenance. For these aircraft, offshore contractor facilities were to be utilized for higher level maintenance such as IRAN and extensive repair work.[222]

(C) <u>Air Logistics Command Computerization Problems (U)</u>. The VNAF logistics system was structured around the capabilities of UNIVAC 1050-II computers. The 1050-IIs were to provide centralized inventory control and requisitioning, and to satellite each base account to the ALC. A 1050-II was originally installed at Bien Hoa in July 1970 to automate the VNAF supply system. By December 1971, the VNAF had three separate computer systems: one for processing supply transactions, another for preparation of supply reports, and the third for forecasting and preparing depot repair schedules. In May 1972, the computer systems were reorganized and realigned to establish two computer systems: one to support satellization of the VNAF bases and one to serve as a dedicated depot computer (this second system contained two 1050-IIs). The last of nine bases, Phan Rang AB, was satellited in August 1972, and the computer system configuration remained essentially the same through the cease-fire.[223]

(S) The computer configuration at the ALC was, however, far from optimum. This inherent difficulty, combined with the need to account for the flood of materiel provided prior to the cease-fire, led to the suspension, as of 15 March 1973, of all requisitioning actions in Vietnam (except NORS grounding requisitions) until the South Vietnamese logisticians could recover from and properly account for, the supplies and materiel inundating their logistics system. By July, considerable progress had been made in accounting for supplies, moving them into warehouses, and drawing down supply levels toward a goal of a 180-day stock level. Unfortunately, when the decision was made to start requisitioning actions again, the 1050-II computer systems at Bien Hoa began experiencing severe problems resulting in extended periods of downtime and attendant havoc in the VNAF's logistics system.[224]

(S) The computer problems stemmed from a number of factors, including electrical power surges, electrical cable decomposition, and hardware malfunctions, all compounded by a change in contractors for support of the computer equipment. The VNAF was totally dependent on U.S. commercial contractors for maintenance of its computer equipment. In March 1973, the then current contractor lost the contract for support of the VNAF computers to a lower bid by another company. Departing contractor personnel were very bitter; they performed minimum maintenance, and when they left they destroyed all the test decks, technical data, and switching gear for the computer, claiming contractor proprietary rights.[225] When the new contractor took over in July, the computer immediately went down and a complete overhaul was required. Other unforeseen difficulties added to the hardware problems. For example, a 400-foot section of a primary communication cable feeding the computer was being eaten up by fuel seepage from a Petroleum, Oil, and Lubricants (POL) bladder subsequently installed near the underground cable. The cable was a special type which the VNAF had not been trained to repair. Through contractor assistance, the VNAF were trained and the cable was repaired. At about the same time, the air conditioning equipment for the computer facility overheated and was extensively damaged. (Air conditioning was essential due to the sensitivity of computer equipment to the large amount of heat generated during computer operations.) Then, late in July, when it appeared that many of the problems were being overcome, two unexplained power surges heavily damaged the primary and back-up memory drums, totally paralyzing the computer system. During the periods of extended computer shutdowns, the VNAF supply system was crippled. Accumulated backlogs were partially eased, however, by flying VNAF tapes and card decks to Clark AB for processing on their 1050 computer and by manual processing during computer outages.[226]

(S) By the end of September, the ALC computer situation was rapidly improving. Additional contractor personnel were in-country attacking remaining hardware problems, computer maintenance has improved, and the backlogs were being reduced. It was equally evident, however, that some inherent computer deficiencies would remain.[227] The basic problem was that the VNAF 1050-II computer equipment was designed for a base supply system, and fell short of the requirements demanded of a depot-level system. The Deputy Director of the DAO Air Force Division branch at the ALC commented:[228]

> (S) [The ALC needs] . . . depot-type hardware; a 360, 370, 380, an 1107, 1401 whatever. . . . The 1050 system was configured...as kind of a bandaid-patched, cut-and-paste operation. . . . It still has the basic USAF base and organization maintenance programs and logistics program, and I believe that when we made the decision to computerize we should have computerized based upon system requirements which would have dictated the hardware, rather than say 'Hey, we've got an excess 1050, let's put it up there and capture the depot account.' It was originally put in . . . just to mechanize the depot account. Now it's running the whole VNAF logistics system--and it's cumbersome.

(S) The Chief of the DAO Air Force Division branch at the ALC was equally candid in his appraisal of the 1050-II configuration and its role in the VNAF logistics system:[229] (U)

> (S) ...The computer itself set back the supply system here at least one-half year in its development. . . . We're trying to train the Vietnamese how to run the computer. In my year here, at any one time this influence [American] is lacking to the least bit, the Vietnamese become very reluctant to pursue the use of the computer, they have not realized . . . that the information which goes into a computer is exactly that which comes out of the computer; put bad data in, bad data comes out. . . . It's an interesting subject as to whether or not the computer really is an advantage for the Vietnamese. We're teaching them to do something by computer mechanisms that has been done manually for many years, and in some instances . . . very efficiently and effectively . . . although it takes manpower. . . . I would say that the pasting together, the bandaid'ing of...the 1050-II computer, trying to

> increase its capability to handle a depot operation
> here is foolhardy. . . . If we are going to resign
> ourselves to the fact that a computer is needed here
> I think that we need to put in a computer that is going
> to give long-lasting benefits rather than pasting to-
> gether something that, in my opinion, has too many
> limitations and is nothing but a big base computer to
> begin with.

(S) <u>Base Capabilities Versus Depot Capabilities (U)</u>. To help overcome the VNAF's shortage of managers and skilled technicians, USAF personnel and contractors augmented VNAF units throughout 1972. In an effort to insure that this managerial and technical augmentation was most efficient and would assist the growth of the VNAF's logistical capabilities, priorities were established for various aspects of the program. First priority was placed on development of Air Division logistical functions such as base supply and field and organizational maintenance. The development of a centralized logistic management command to support and manage depot-level logistics functions was assigned second priority. Thus, while facilities and equipment were provided to both the bases and the ALC, the VNAF manning priority was given to the expanding Air Division to support their operational flying missions and base logistic development. Since the major constraint on the VNAF was the shortage of middle managers and trained, skilled technicians, the result of these priorities was that by the end of 1972 ALC manning stood at only 50 percent of authorized personnel.[230]

(S) In light of the ALC's severe manning problem, Enhance Plus and the subsequent 66-squadron force structure proposal were a cause of concern to I&M planners. This concern was reflected in a 17 January 1973 message from AFLC to CSAF:[231] (C)

(S) The logistics impacts that would result from approval of the proposed 66-squadron VNAF force structure on . . . [the] Improvement and Modernization (I&M) program have been a subject of concern here since originally proposed by the AFGP.

*   *   *   *   *   *   *

(S) [Of greatest] . . . concern is the impact on our development program for the Air Logistics Command (ALC) at Bien Hoa. This impact relates to the VNAF manning of the ALC and availability of VNAF personnel for training. At our last I&M conference in February 1972, General Minh personally assured me that 800 additional personnel would be assigned to the ALC in 1972 with the possibility of 1,000 additional in 1973. The turmoil created by Project Enhance made this commitment impossible to fill. Not considering Enhance Plus, the ALC is now approximately 54 pct manned which is little or no improvement over the status one year ago. In the event the new structure is approved, manning priority will go to the Air Divisions as in the past. This will not only obviate any input to the ALC but will further drain off experienced personnel at the ALC to fill critical operational unit requirements. We have indications the latter is already occurring. Considering a post-cease-fire twelve month time limitation for contractors to complete training, the immediate availability of trainable personnel and a reliable personnel assignment program are critical. The activation program if approved, in our evaluation, will preclude significant further progress toward self-sufficiency at the ALC due to the lack of adequate VNAF personnel.

(S) Considering the dire ALC manning situation, manning priority shifted to the ALC. In January 1973, the JGS authorized the recruitment of 1,000 personnel for the ALC. In addition, authorization was granted to recruit 544 16-year-olds for the ALC. By July 1973, ALC manning had increased to 88 percent. As previously mentioned, however, this increase was achieved almost exclusively by the assignment of untrained recruits, while officer and NCO manning remained at their earlier, critically low levels. Thus, although training tasks at the ALC had increased drastically, and the middle management shortages had become more acute, a positive step had been taken in that recruits had been provided and progress toward development of programmed ALC capabilities could be renewed.[232]

(C) The shift in manning priority to the ALC, however, had its inevitable effect on maintenance and supply capabilities at the bases.[233] Personnel shortages were made all the more severe by on-going squadron activations. A 31 May 1973 message from the DAO to CINCPACAF summarized the impact of continuing squadron activations on VNAF logistical support:[234]

> (C) .... The VNAF activated three A-37 squadrons effective 1 May 73, and have two F-5A squadrons scheduled for activation 1 Jun. We negotiated with the VNAF in an effort to delay these activations due to personnel, AGE and other logistical constraints. However, they have made the decision to adhere to [their activation schedule].... These activations will be with reduced UE ... within the entire fighter squadron force rather than bringing aircraft out of flyable storage. In other words, their total active aircraft force will not change.... Manning will be particularly critical. A recent survey revealed that manning in the maintenance and supply wings at the bases ranges from a high of 67 percent of authorized to a low of 42 percent authorized. Manning priority is being afforded to the ALC so these activations will further dilute their base level maintenance capability.... No contract augmentation is planned in support of these five squadrons and the VNAF have been so advised. We will support these activations within our capability but due to the constraints mentioned above, it is highly probable that OR rates will suffer.

(S) The relative priority of base-level and depot-level development was thus of continuing concern throughout 1973. An even more fundamental question was raised by the Deputy Director of the DAO Air Forces Division branch at the ALC when he examined the approach that the U.S. had taken in building the ALC to provide depot-level capabilities:[235]

(S) I think the major problem [in Vietnamization] has been the rapid expansion thrown at a people who don't have the technological schooling, the technical background, [or] the industrial base to support an Air Force. Because of that, I think that in the development of the VNAF the next problem we faced was concentrating on building a logistic system before we had the basic rudiments and skills of a tactical organization. We jumped in and built a logistic system for them and built a depot--I was involved in that. Hindsight being 20-20, I would think that the first step in building an Air Force of this magnitude as rapidly as we did should be to concentrate on the operational air divisions first, train a logistic capability for those air divisions, maintenance skills, supply skills, transportation skills, and all the support skills that go along with that, because that really is a lower level of skill than what one will find at a depot. I think had we established that base, and then . . . supported them on the direct support concept, supplied them right into the bases, there would have been some problems, but I don't think to the magnitude we encountered. Then I believe I would have started a depot and established materiel management aspects, and then taken from the good skilled base that we had and upgraded them into that [depot] capability on a normal-step, slow process, I believe I would have turned Bien Hoa into a large base maintenance/base supply activity for two things: to effect logistics distribution and repair, but also to train the people and then put them out in the air divisions. That, I believe, would be more logical progression. . . . Trying to build the logistic depot and concentrating on it with greater emphasis than we did the air divisions was one mistake. The second mistake was the mechanization process that we put the logistic system through.*

(U) The comparative emphasis placed on the ALC, versus the bases, was also addressed by other DAO personnel. A DAO fact sheet, dated 30 September 1973, outlined the capabilities of VNAF base/depot maintenance personnel, and underscored the need for renewed emphasis on base maintenance per-
236
sonnel:

(U) All nine bases have limited capability to accomplish organizational and intermediate . . . aircraft and support

---
*See the discussion of the 1050-II computer systems, above.

equipment maintenance. All are playing catch-up maintenance. Personnel manning and skill levels are the limiting factors.

*   *   *   *   *   *   *

(U) The depot at Bien Hoa is well on the way to achieving the planned objectives. However, when the USAF Advisory effort departed during the January through March 73 time frame, it created a temporary void. We have discovered that, in applying the priority for ALC manning, the maintenance of aircraft at the bases did not progress. Conversion of the contractors' efforts from augmentation to training efforts has left the VNAF with the problems of extensive crash/battle damaged aircraft repair and a massive training program. . . . The primary effort is to achieve a cadre of trained VNAF Logistics personnel through the contract training program to provide a solid base for future growth. The contract training will be conducted in concert with production training relying heavily on hands-on OJT. Time and VNAF personnel manning are the biggest constraints.

(S) <u>Progress Toward Logistics Self-Sufficiency (U)</u>. The DAO Quarterly Assessment, 24 July 1973, summed up the progress of the VNAF logistics system to that date:[237] (U)

(S) Maintenance capability is limited due to lack of skill while the supply capability is constrained by poor supply discipline. Given the proper emphasis and time along with stability this situation should improve.

(S) Supply is a continuing problem compounded by lack of an adequate number of middle managers along with a wide variety of complicated equipment, slow repair capability of complex end items, and inadequate identification and distribution of available resources. This problem is also amenable to solution; however, it will require time and training until the personnel become experienced. The matter of supply discipline . . . is . . . of utmost priority. It is a problem that can only be solved by the RVNAF leaders.

(S) By late 1973, the limitations outlined above were still the basic problems facing the Vietnamization of logistics. In October 1973, the DAO noted in its Quarterly Assessment that many actions had yet to be accomplished before the VNAF could attain the desired degree of logistics/self-sufficiency. In describing the state of development of the various elements of the VNAF logistics system, they began using terms such as "months and years" of development, which formally recognized the basic contention of many Vietnamization planners; namely, that true logistics self-sufficiency could not reach fruition without the time required to raise VNAF experience and to mold middle managers. The assessment summarized the progress of Vietnamization of logistics at both the base and ALC levels:[238]

> (S) . . . [At the base level,] material support manning and skill levels are still the primary limiting factors hampering maintenance operations. Limited technical knowledge, management ability and availability of middle managers inhibits the effective utilization of maintenance personnel.
>
> (S) [At the depot level,] construction slippages of pertinent ALC facilities, from 2 to 6 months, will impact on both programmed training and production. Although the ALC has some of the finest facilities in SEA, maximum utilization by the VNAF is many months in the future. This deficit can only be filled by VNAF, at the conclusion of extensive training, and after several months/years of practical experience.
>
> (S) Manning at ALC has increased significantly since February 1973 (from 49% to 91%). . . . The increases have predominantly been with unskilled personnel, which imposes an intensive training requirement. . . . Although the current manning figure is impressive, the officer manning remains constant at 50%, and the NCO [Non-Commissioned Officer] manning is equally bad. There are significant voids in both top and middle management, which can only be rectified by months and years of development, or by drastic reductions of operational units. The DAO and contractor personnel are presently helping to fill the management voids, but many areas are lacking due to U.S. personnel complement constraints.

*   *   *   *   *   *   *

(S) Through[out] the VNAF, two basic problem areas can be observed:

    (1) The lack of adequately trained middle management personnel.

    (2) The logistic support effectiveness to operate/maintain and sustain the 66 squadron force.

In both areas, numerous actions are underway to try to overcome these limitations.

(C) A November 1973 Government Accounting Office audit noted that the VNAF logistical system was "not responsive." The system's unresponsiveness--and the requirement that U.S. contractors use the Vietnamese logistical system--was cited as one of the reasons for extending several of the U.S. contractor training courses for VNAF personnel. The DAO was reluctant to authorize alternate methods of supply for U.S. contractors; and was intent on making the VNAF system responsive. The DAO contention was that a delay of a few months in a few contracts would be worthwhile if VNAF logistical responsiveness was improved as a result.[239]

(S) As of late 1973, there were numerous cases of supply shortages in VNAF operational units. This, too, was attributed to the "unresponsiveness" of the supply system. Investigations of such allegations, however, showed that it was not always the system itself which was unresponsive, but that VNAF personnel at the unit level were sometimes the cause of the shortages. The Deputy Director, Air Force Division, explained:[240]

> (S) . . . It gets back to system discipline, middle management and knowledge of the system. At Da Nang they have somewhere between 40 and 45% fill on the benchstock items, and in talking to the VNAF there I'm sure that they don't really understand how to get [supplies]. . . . Now, as a parallel to that . . ., [at Nha Trang] they have the same system, weapons

> systems, and I see an 80-85-90% fill in their bench-
> stock. . . . They know the system . . . [and] they're
> going to get response. Many times the Air Divisions will
> say (and I'm not defending the ALC because we have our
> problems here too) . . . "We've had that requisitioned
> and we didn't get it." Well, upon investigation I find
> out they thought it was on requisition, or the requisi-
> tion had been cancelled, or they had been supplied and
> they hadn't cancelled their requisition. So this is
> supply discipline. . . . [It takes] time.

(S) A fair assessment of the VNAF logistics system as of the end of 1973 was that VNAF supply and maintenance capabilities were continuing to progress steadily, but that self-sufficiency was still a distant goal. The VNAF's capacity to accelerate their progress was severely limited by an acute shortage of experienced, skilled technicians and managers in their recently developed force structure.[241] The Deputy Director, Air Force Division, DAO, underscored the importance of these factors: "Some of our AFLC aircraft repair people have been in the business 20-25 years. . . . By comparison, many VNAF logisticians [are] right out of high school . . . [and] have been in the business maybe 18 months at most."[242]

(S) To place VNAF progress in perspective, it is enlightening to compare the problems which the VNAF confronted with those being encountered by USAF units in SEA--the similarities were striking. Even more striking, however, was the immensity of the VNAF's problems in comparison to those of USAF units. A 29 December 1972 message from 13AF addressed some of the logistical difficulties which were facing USAF units in SEA and causing concern among USAF managers:[243] (S)

> (U) . . . We are drawing inexperienced people into the
> most demanding tasks that now exist in the USAF. This
> lack of experience is evident across the spectrum from
> top management to the specialist on the line. Senior

and middle managers are being assigned to control weapons systems they are not experienced on or even familiar with. Three level technicians are being assigned to support a mission that requires a 100 pcnt effort from an experienced specialist.

(U) Our SEA units are tasked to respond to ever changing real time requirements. To expect a manager whose experience has been mainly airlift, for example, to flawlessly effect the mission change of an F-4 unit from air to ground to air to air is not realistic. Nor is it realistic to expect the cadre of experienced technicians we do possess to support a maximum effort while training people on an unfamiliar weapons system. . . . [We have] an arbitrary standard of 94 pcnt of UDL [Unit Detail Listing] strength as our manning goal and in this 94 pcnt liberally sprinkle three levels. As has been clearly demonstrated numerous times in CY72, our assigned manning cannot support our mission requirements and maintain the standards of quality we expect. Nor can we provide the training and supervision three level technicians require.

(U) It is the 13AF/LGM position that manning at anything less than 100 pcnt of UDL strength is unsatisfactory. Further, the percentage of inexperienced/unqualified personnel assigned must be kept at less than 5 pcnt. . . . Only when we are manned with sufficient, experienced people can we expect to support the ever changing type and quantity of combat missions and still produce safe, quality airplanes. Additionally, freeing our people from the time consuming task of training will allow us to assign the qualified technician to the job and get it done quickly and properly the first time. Also recommend that the policy of assigning entry level maintenance officers to SEA or officers without experience on the respective weapons systems to top management positions in SEA be discontinued. SEA is not the environment to train a maintenance officer any more than it is the environment to train a three level airman.

If the cited factors of inexperience, undermanning, and training were thus causing maintenance difficulties even for the seasoned logisticians in USAF units, they plagued the VNAF to an immensely greater degree. Clearly, those tasks would continue to demand intensive VNAF and DAO efforts in the months and years ahead.

Facilities (U)

(C) The years 1972 and 1973 were years of contrast for facility transfer and support. During 1972, the moderate transfer of facilities to the VNAF was barely able to keep pace with rapidly expanding VNAF needs. Then, at the end of 1972, in advance of the cease-fire agreement, all remaining facilities were suddenly transferred to the VNAF on a mass basis. The resulting impact on the VNAF's capability to support its facilities was far-reaching and would continue in evidence many months after the cease-fire.

(U) <u>Facilities Transfer</u>. As U.S. withdrawals from South Vietnam proceeded during late 1971 and early 1972, and expansion of the VNAF continued, transfer of U.S.-occupied facilities became an item of ever greater importance and concern. A letter written early in 1972 reflected the increasing emphasis being placed on facility transfers by the Commander, 7AF:[244]

> (U) The most obvious way we can assist the VNAF is by insuring that they and their supporting agencies are given the equipment and facilities essential to further timely development. . . . Facilities . . . are a matter within our control, and are an area in which we can do much to improve the efficiency of the VNAF. It is incumbent on every 7AF commander to release as rapidly as possible those facilities earmarked for VNAF use. In some instances, temporary crowding of USAF personnel or shops will make available to VNAF badly needed quarters or work facilities. I will expect 7AF units to make such sacrifices as a matter of routine. . . .
>
> (U) Vietnamization is one of the highest priority goals of national policy. Our role in support of national policy can be significant through the simple means of doing all we can to provide the VNAF the tools they need to do their job. As in so many military matters, the attitude of your people towards this important program will be a reflection of your own attitude. I feel certain I will have your complete support.

(S) A major I&M objective was to transfer facilities to the VNAF on an orderly basis, as they became surplus to the requirements of dwindling U.S. forces. The NVN invasion, Project Enhance, and further acceleration and expansion of VNAF growth all added elements of complication and conflict with respect to that basic objective. The invasion resulted in a delay of the withdrawal of some air units from South Vietnam, with a concomitant delay in the transfer of facilities. At the same time, acceleration of scheduled unit activations and expansion of the VNAF force structure increased the urgency of transferring facilities to the VNAF.[245]

(S) Lack of VNAF facilities was most acute at the three major VNAF air bases, Tan Son Nhut, Bien Hoa, and Da Nang, which were still under U.S. control. These bases were scheduled to retain their status as major U.S. installations until the withdrawal of remaining U.S. forces at the time of a cease-fire. In the meantime, as incremental reduction of U.S. forces proceeded, points of consolidation were essential to maximize security for remaining U.S. personnel. The decision was made by MACV to use the three major air bases as final consolidation points for U.S. forces in Vietnam. The U.S. Army consolidation at these USAF bases occurred from mid-1972 through late 1972. This created the requirement for more space for U.S. forces just at the time the VNAF's needs were greatest. For example, the situation at Tan Son Nhut was described by the DCS/Plans (XP), 7AF:[246] (S)

> (C) An increased emphasis on Project Enhance and VNAF Improvement and Modernization (VNAF I&M) created VNAF demands for more . . . facilities at Tan Son Nhut. A time-phased consolidation of Air Force activities/functions to and around the 7AF Hq compound was instituted

to provide the required facilities. Midway through
the consolidation program, MACV directed suspension of
facility turnover to the VNAF. This action was necessary because of the impending move of USARV [U.S. Army,
Vietnam] to the Saigon/TSN area. 7AF/XP obtained MACV
recognition of the requirement to continue making
facilities available to the VNAF in support of the I&M
program. 7AF was tasked, however, to meet USARV relocation requirements while providing facilities for the
VNAF. Increased emphasis on consolidation efforts and
concurrent drawdown of AF personnel at TSN allowed 7AF to
accommodate both VNAF and USARV requirements.

(C) . . . Two basic problem areas were encountered.
First, USARV did not present a complete requirements
package; requirements were identified on a piece-meal
basis making it difficult to distribute facilities to
both USARV and the VNAF on a planned basis. The second
problem stemmed in part from the first. On several
occasions, the VNAF received informal indications that
several facilities would be made available to them. Subsequent USARV requirements prevented the planned turnover to the VNAF causing a decrease in Air Force
credibility.

(S) In an end-of-tour report, Major General James J. Jumper, Chief, AFGP, summarized the facility transfer situation which prevailed at the three bases throughout the second half of 1972: [247] (U)

(S) . . . The space needed to accommodate the VNAF increases at the major installations was not available.
MACV necessarily gave top priority to U.S. forces for
facility allocation. As USAF units phased out, the
facilities were immediately allocated to U.S. Army units,
who were standing in line to consolidate their field
units under the protective umbrella of the well secured
air bases.

(S) Because of this situation, the major facility
planning efforts up to cease-fire were mainly geared
to continuing negotiation with the staffs of 7th Air
Force, MACV, and USARV. It required constant prodding of all U.S. units to continually consolidate their
organizations and personnel as they reduced in size by
the recurring incremental reductions, thus allowing
transfer of the vacated facilities to the VNAF.

(S) AFGP did enjoy total support from 7th Air Force--
the Command Section on down. Their efforts were
highly beneficial to the VNAF in obtaining the maximum possible facilities.

(S) The space situation at the bases became an acute problem as Enhance Plus deliveries started in early November 1972. At about the same time, in anticipation of an impending cease-fire, the JCS directed title transfer of nearly all U.S.-owned facilities to the Government of Vietnam. Title transfer was to be completed by 10 November, the anticipated date of the cease-fire. In accordance with this decision, U.S. installations were transferred on a mass basis on 6 November 1972; on paper, nearly all installations had been transferred to the VNAF. In actuality, however, a memorandum of understanding between MACV and the JGS provided for continued occupancy of transferred facilities by U.S. military and contractor personnel until the facilities were no longer needed. Further, consummation of the transfers required an inventory of individual facilities on an installation subsequent to the title transfer. This provided a means for retaining U.S. ownership of selected facilities, if required.[248]

(S) Final inventory and transfer of USAF facilities began on 14 November 1972. Even those facilities which were still occupied by USAF forces were transferred, but the inventoried property was carried on a hand receipt pending departure of USAF personnel. Most U.S. Army and Navy facilities on USAF installations were also transferred to the VNAF. Some facilities, however, were retained by the American embassy and the U.S. Agency for International Development, while others were transferred to the ARVN. Of highest transfer priority were utilities, ramps, and aircraft revetments, together with all other hardened facilities; next were facilities vacated and declared surplus to U.S. requirements; and last were those still occupied by U.S. forces.²⁴⁹

(C) By the cease-fire date, 28 January 1973, the inventoried transfer to the VNAF of all but a handful of U.S. facilities had been completed. During the months of November 1972 through January 1973, more than 3,000 U.S. facilities,* valued at 175 million dollars, were transferred to the VNAF. The magnitude of that activity is put into stark relief when viewed in light of the value of facilities transferred from 1 July through 30 October 1972, which, by comparison, totaled 13 million dollars.²⁵⁰ Table 8 lists, by base, the facility transfers under CRIMP, and those during the final months before the cease-fire. Table 9 enumerates, by case, the transfers by each U.S. service.

(S) <u>Civil Engineering (U)</u>. The VNAF Civil Engineering (CE) function, already undermanned and receiving inadequate support from VNAF supply and transportation channels, was strained by the VNAF's expansion to nine bases during 1972, and overwhelmed by the subsequent massive transfer of U.S. facilities during the three months preceding the cease-fire. Extensive contractor support was required after the cease-fire to compensate for serious shortages of skilled VNAF CE personnel. Furthermore, the CE force was handicapped by a "startling"²⁵¹ lack of VNAF supply support. The VNAF civil engineers were forced to place almost total reliance on ARVN supply channels to obtain the equipment and supplies necessary to maintain

---

*The term "facilities" is all-encompassing and includes all Civil Engineer-constructed items.

TABLE 8

TRANSFER OF U.S. FACILITIES TO THE VNAF (U)

Base	Cumulative Number of Facilities Transferred by 1 Nov 72	Transfers Between 1 Nov 72-28 Jan 73	Total
Da Nang	358	1,460	1,818
Tan Son Nhut	545	1,120	1,665
Bien Hoa	1,050	278	1,328
Nha Trang	518	109	627
Binh Thuy	341	39	380
Pleiku	382	24	406
Phu Cat	475	22	497
Phan Rang	518	17	535
Soc Trang	279	0	279
Total	4,466	3,069	7,535

Source: Based upon COMUSMACV OPLAN J215, COUNTDOWN, After Action Report (U), AFGP, 22 Mar 73, Tab 8. (S)

TABLE 9

BY-SERVICE TRANSFER OF U.S. FACILITIES TO THE VNAF--
1 NOVEMBER 1972 THROUGH 28 JANUARY 1973 (U)

Base	USAF	USA	USN	Total
Da Nang AB/Monkey Mountain	914	494	52	1,460
Bien Hoa AB	278	-	-	278
Tan Son Nhut AB	685	423	12	1,120
Nha Trang AB	109	-	-	109
Binh Thuy	31	8	-	39
Pleiku	1	23	-	24
Soc Trang	-	-	-	0
Phu Cat	-	22	-	22
Phan Rang	-	17	-	17
Total	2,018	987	64	3,069

Source: Based upon COMUSMACV OPLAN J215, COUNTDOWN, After Action Report (U), AFGP, 22 Mar 73, Tab 8. (S)

facilities. In recognition of this problem, a November 1972 PACAF message pointed out that the quantity of material actually being issued through the VNAF for Civil Engineering was "inadequate to maintain even mission essential facilities, utility plants, and systems."[252] General Jumper summarized the VNAF CE problems as follows:[253]

> (S) The old adage, "It is necessary to crawl before you can walk," did not apply to the VNAF Civil Engineering self-sufficiency in 1972. Giant steps were forced on the embryo civil engineering organizations by the total base transfers and assumption of complete responsibility for Base Civil Engineering at five air bases. An aggressive self-sufficiency training program to produce 900 qualified technicians by the end of FY 74 [is being pursued to meet] . . . the requirements at the four other bases. . . .
>
> * * * * * * *
>
> (S) Significant problems are the lack of supply and transportation and VNAF funding limitations on needed contracts to accomplish required facilities maintenance and minor construction requirements. . . . There is also a problem of civilian/military mix whereby the VNAF do not have BCE [Base CE] civilian technicians due to pay scale inequities.

(U) By the end of 1973, there had apparently been little improvement in the CE supply support situation. In a 28 September 1973 message to DAO, PACAF stated: "Deterioration of VNAF bases . . . is of deepest concern to PACAF. A key item contributing to inability of the VNAF to properly maintain its airfields is an almost total lack of supply support to the Civil Engineering function."[254] The 9 October 1973 response from the DAO shared the concern for supply support, but expressed optimism that the JGS was making real progress toward solving the problem:[255]

> (U) . . . Considerable progress currently being made in the area of common item support. This area covers material

> provided by the ARVN and includes most of the supplies used by the VNAF base civil engineers. Investigation/analysis proved all parties concerned to be at fault. Believe you will soon see considerable progress in this area of lateral support.

(U) The DAO 9 October message took exception, however, to the PACAF allegation that VNAF facilities were deteriorating, pointing out that the "main problem is there are larger facilities/real estate and more buildings than the VNAF need or can possibly maintain without extensive contractor augmentation."[256] The DAO, the VNAF, and the JGS recognized that fact and its significance in light of the weather effects in SEA, the limited Vietnamese budget, and the constraints on both U.S. contractor and VNAF manpower ceilings. Therefore, the DAO, VNAF, and representatives from the PACAF staff planned to conduct a facility utilization survey at each base. The goal of the survey would be to identify the minimum level of essential facilities required for mission accomplishment, with the objective of either eliminating or preserving the excess facilities.[257] The facility utilization survey was scheduled for completion in December 1973, and a 1 September 1974 goal was listed for disposing of, or preparing for permanent storage, those facilities identified as excess.

(C) In the October 1973 Quarterly Assessment, DAO summed up the status of various aspects of the VNAF CE program. Among continuing needs, that of training ranked first: "Training of VNAF-BCE personnel is of utmost importance. Presently, the skill level of assigned personnel is very low. Further training of BCE skills is required to attain a position of self-sufficiency."[258] The DAO noted that contractor training and assistance

154

had been extended in the areas of power production and facility maintenance, and U.S. contractors continued to assist the VNAF in upgrading fire and rescue equipment. The establishment of a preventive maintenance program at each base was also being stressed, and contract extensions were being prepared to facilitate success of these programs. With regard to manning, recruitment of local engineers and administrative support personnel was continuing, although somewhat hampered by the low pay scale for Vietnamese civil servants. VNAF manning at the bases was being augmented and brought up to strength. Necessary construction programs were continuing, although some slippages were occurring.[259]

(U) Summing up the progress of VNAF CE toward self-sufficiency, the 9 October 1973 DAO message quoted earlier stated:[260]

> (U) . . . The VNAF have made considerable progress in the past six months. However, they still have a long way to go before they can achieve any semblance of self-sufficiency. . . . We . . . will continue to press for the maximum degree of VNAF self-sufficiency. . . .

Communications-Electronics (C-E) (U)

(C) Responsibilities of the VNAF C-E function encompassed (1) the entire Tactical Air Control system, including the Tactical Air Control Center, Direct Air Control Centers, Tactical Air Control Parties, and the Airlift Control Center with its Airlift Control Elements, (2) the Aircraft Control and Warning (AC&W) radars and associated equipment, and (3) the SEEK POINT equipment discussed earlier. In addition, each Air Division also had C-E personnel who were responsible for command and control equipment, base and weather communications, and navigational aids (NAVAIDs). There was also a

C-E training center responsible for the equipment and facilities necessary to operate the in-country C-E school at Nha Trang, and, in 1972, a C-E organization was formed at the ALC to perform depot functions, including IRAN.[261]

(C) During late 1971 and early 1972, the VNAF C-E force underwent great turmoil: "Equipment and facilities programmed to be transferred to the VNAF over a three year period were thrust upon it in the short period of 10 months."[262] The acceptance of facilities formerly used by U.S. personnel and the unprogrammed activation of two VNAF bases, Phu Cat and Phan Rang, extended the VNAF C-E force to the limit. At the same time that U.S. withdrawals and facility transfers were accelerating, and new VNAF bases were being activated, the VNAF C-E force was transitioning from a training status to an operational mode. U.S. contractors were employed to help overcome the C-E shortfalls in personnel numbers and skill levels. By June 1972, approximately 85 percent of assigned personnel had completed training and were considered qualified in their particular AFSCs. It was estimated, however, that the full authorized strength would not be reached until late 1973 or early 1974.[263]

(C) During 1972, the C-E force made truly great strides in its transition from a training status to an operational organization responsible for expanded numbers and types of equipment and facilities. This progress was made during a period of accelerated growth, and was partially eclipsed by the massive transfer of facilities and equipment to the VNAF in the post-Enhance Plus, pre-cease-fire time frame. It was not surprising that such an evolving organization would be confronted with serious problems. Following

the cease-fire, the Chief of the AFGP summarized the status of the VNAF
C-E program as follows:[264]

> (C) . . . The VNAF C-E force has accomplished a great deal in the past nine months, more than in any comparable period in its history. It has major problems in its top and middle management and in the support areas, i.e., supply, civil engineering, test equipment, and publications. These major problems are interdependent as the lack of leadership and executive ability at the top results in the lack of motivation and initiative to correct discrepancies outside the prime area of responsibility even though the facilities and equipment are totally dependent upon these elements.
>
> (C) The VNAF has developed the fundamentals of a viable C-E force; however, I have reservations on its ability to continue to build unless personnel changes are made, especially at the top management levels within the C-E community.

(C) In a large measure, many of the other, non-personnel-oriented problems confronting C-E were traceable to a lack of logistics support. A 15 August 1973 DAO talking paper summarized the impact of logistics problems in (1) equipment calibration at the depot, (2) supply support, and (3) civil engineering support:[265]

> (C) . . . Problem areas common to all sites have been identified. Of major concern are PMEL [Precision Measuring Equipment Laboratory], supply, and back-up generator support.
>
> (C) PMEL equipment transportation support leaves much to be desired. Accurate and reliable test equipment is extremely vital to maintenance of all NAVAIDs and other Communications-Electronics facilities, and must be available on site at all times. . . . Delays of up to six (6) months are being encountered in getting the equipment to the PMEL and returned. In many instances, by the time the equipment is returned to the site, it is due for calibration again. . . . The equipment should always be couriered, and the long delays create a hardship on the VNAF courier who must defray his TDY expenses out of his own pocket.

> Consequently, site personnel are not sending equipment to
> the PMEL. Their rationale being that test equipment of
> questionable accuracy is better than none at all.
>
> (C) Supply support is very unsatisfactory. Receipt of a
> requisitioned item involves from 4-6 months. Due to this
> delay, site personnel obtain parts from whatever source is
> available--scrounging parts from battle-damaged equipment,
> cannabaliz[ing]. . . .
>
> (C) Diesel fuel is rationed at all bases. This rationing
> is superimposed on the approved established allocation
> by various levels of command. . . . [resulting in an in-
> adequate supply for generators].
>
> (C) Frequent instability of base and generator power is
> causing damage to C-E equipment. This is further com-
> pounded by no-notice losses of base power. Applied voltage
> is either excessive or too low. This causes damage to and
> gradual deterioration of C-E equipment. This particularly
> true of the NAVAIDs facilities back-up generators. Many
> of the generators are past due for overhaul. Some are
> inoperative.

(C) Nowhere were the VNAF C-E problems graver and more visible than in the NAVAIDs and AC&W areas. An 11 August 1973 DAO memorandum warned that the condition of VNAF Tactical Air Navigation (TACAN) sites was "deteriorating," and to a greater degree than indicated by daily TACAN readiness statistics.[266] Inadequate supply support was cited as the major factor hindering maintenance at the TACAN sites. Each site had two TACAN units using a common antenna. When one unit went down, the other unit could be switched on, thereby maintaining TACAN operations. Increasingly, however, the shortage of spare parts caused cannibalization of the alternate unit. Any subsequent failure of the operational unit caused unavoidable down-time, and timely repair became more and more difficult. One critical item, the TACAN antenna, was in extremely short supply--there were no usable* spares

---
*There were two in-country spares, but neither was operable.

in-country. Thus, when an antenna failed, the site was totally disabled until a suitable spare could be obtained. For example, as of August 1973, the TACAN at Binh Thuy had been non-operational continuously since 22 June, and the TACAN at Tan Son Nhut since 7 June, both due to antenna problems.[267]

(C) The antenna problem was a case in which lack of supply support was decisive. The TACAN antennae rotated at a constant speed, dictating that their bearings be balanced or replaced at specified intervals. Some of the antennae had been in continuous use for as long as six years. Unfortunately, ALC personnel had not been trained or equipped to service the antennae, and procedures for off-shore repair had not been established. Thus, when USAF units departed, the VNAF had no way of replacing or repairing defective antennae. Furthermore, no usable spare antennae were available in-country. Apparently, little thought had been given to providing the VNAF with these critical spares. Following the cease-fire, the DAO assisted the VNAF in developing a limited maintenance capability for the antennae, and any major repair was to be performed in the CONUS at the USAF's Sacramento ALC. Even then, however, maintenance efforts were frustrated by the lack of spare antennae--although numerous operational antennae were in need of maintenance, there was no possibility of repair until spares were received from the CONUS. Removal of an operational antenna for depot servicing or shipment to the CONUS for repair would have rendered the site non-operational.[268]

(C) TACAN sites also suffered from physical deterioration. Progressive corrosion, already in progress long before the VNAF took over the sites, threatened to impair operations unless corrected. Frequent failure of air conditioners was also a problem at the sites. Within a few hours of air conditioner failure, excessive heat and humidity would cause serious TACAN and radar maintenance problems. Therefore, the sites had to shut down if the air conditioning remained out. Damage sometimes occurred because the equipment had become too hot before it was shut down.[269]

(C) Test equipment, essential to the accuracy of the TACANs, continued to be subject to excessive delays when shipped to the PMEL for calibration. As before, the primary factor causing the delay was transportation.[270] Finally, the sites suffered from a lack of the support equipment used for lifting, moving, and installing heavy components high above the ground.

(C) In late 1973, the NAVAID/AC&W problems became of increasing concern to both the DAO and PACAF. Site inspections by PACAF and DAO personnel revealed that a growing percentage of C-E equipment was inoperable or only marginally operational. (See Table 10) The October 1973 DAO Quarterly Assessment summarized the problem and proposed a three-phase program to provide both short- and long-term solutions.[271] (U)

> (C) Excessive outages being experienced with the NAVAIDs and AC&W facilities are a major concern. Air Defense and Safety of Flight dictate the need for reliable Flight Facilities throughout the RVN. The condition of NAVAIDs and AC&W systems has gradually deteriorated over the years. Several factors have contributed to the present conditions. The equipment is old (1950 State of the Art) and has been in a harsh environment for some five to seven years, generally without depot type overhaul or upgrade. Preventative maintenance has not been effective in stopping deterioration. A shortage of experienced VNAF technicians has compounded the problem. A systematic approach that provides for both short and long-range benefits is required. A DAO recommended program has been forwarded for CINCPACAF and Air Staff consideration. The program has been developed for three phase action.

TABLE 10

NAVAIDS/AC&W SITE STATUS
AS OF NOVEMBER 1973   (U)

	Inoperative	Marginally Operational	Operational
TACANs	5	2	4
GCA*	3	1	3
GCI**: Height Finders	3	-	2
GCI: Search Radars	2	2	1

* GCA--Ground Controlled Approach

**GCI--Ground Controlled Intercept

Source: <u>DAO Saigon Trip Report (19-24 Nov 73) (U)</u>, USSAG/DOT, 3 Dec 73. (S)

(a) Phase One: Immediate action to return . . . facilities to fully operational status. . . .

(b) Phase Two: Consists of a program to . . . [replace the VNAF's unserviceable or old mobile systems] and major assemblies of AC&W radars with serviceable items. . . . Selected, highly critical assets would be changed out by 1 January 1974.

(c) Phase Three: [Existing] . . . TACAN systems should be converted to . . . [a] configuration [which is] housed in a permanent structure. This would enhance maintainability and improve reliability of equipment. The feasibility of replacing obsolete equipment with more modern sets would be evaluated during the Phase Two analysis. Personnel augmentation will be required in specific specialties to inspect equipment and develop an exchange program. . . .

(C) VNAF site technicians, in general, are able to accomplish normal day-to-day maintenance. However, assistance is still required for complex problems, and to maintain certain system components. . . . Both site and Depot personnel require solid-state training. . . . VNAF motivation and initiative have improved considerably. Overall, training efforts and programs are well-received. . . . Supply and test equipment calibration/repair problems, however, continue to plague all sites in varying degrees. The VNAF is still experiencing a shortage of qualified NCOs in the management areas, and seven level supervision. As a result of the various training programs, this situation is gradually improving.

During October, this three-phase program was adopted and became known as Commando Gopher.

(C) At the close of 1973, the future of the VNAF C-E force, on the basis of planned Commando Gopher actions, was hopeful. If initiated and pursued to its conclusion, the program would remove many of the basic obstacles to progress in the NAVAIDs and AC&W area, one of the most critical VNAF C-E functions. The future of the C-E force as a whole was also hopeful. It was envisioned that as training continued, and skill and experience accrued, a larger measure of self-sufficiency should become attainable.

(U) The various VNAF operational capabilities, and the ability to support and maintain those capabilities, were the tangible objectives of the VNAF I&M program. The nurturing and growth of VNAF self-sufficiency, however, was strongly influenced by a number of less tangible factors which are addressed in the next chapter.

CHAPTER V

FACTORS AFFECTING VIETNAMIZATION (U)

U.S. Advisors (U)

(S) The Air Force Advisory Group was at the heart of the Vietnamization process--it was largely through advisors that VNAF progress towards self-sufficiency was promoted and monitored. Late in 1971, as U.S. withdrawals accelerated, the question arose as to whether Advisory Group strength should be keyed to reductions in U.S. troop strength. In answer, the AFGP emphasized that the responsibilities, roles, and size of the advisory force should be directly related to VNAF capabilities and progress toward self-sufficiency, rather than tied to a ratio of in-country U.S. forces. In fact, in many ways the tasks facing the advisors multiplied as U.S. forces withdrew and the VNAF assumed facilities, equipment, and missions previously handled by U.S. personnel. AFGP also pointed out that, ideally, advisory units should phase out only as individual VNAF units attained self-sufficiency. In a very real way then, the desirable size of the advisory force mirrored the state of VNAF development--the more numerous the obstacles impeding VNAF self-sufficiency--the greater the number of advisors required.[272]

(C) Yet despite their crucial role in the Vietnamization process, there were recurring indications throughout the Vietnamese conflict that the U.S. advisors were often ill-prepared for the tasks facing them. A May 1972 7AF Auditor General report emphasized the importance of advisors, praised the dedication of most advisors, but criticized the continuing lack of preparation of advisors for their demanding role in Vietnam:[273]

(U) The responsibility of advising Vietnamese Air Force officials--who are simultaneously fighting a war and building an air force--is a complex and demanding challenge. Admittedly, no magic formulas or rules define what an individual must do to be a good advisor. Nonetheless, the overall success in developing broadly based Vietnamese management capabilities depends on the day-to-day actions of each individual advisor. Detrimental actions--no matter how well intentioned--compromise the successes achieved. Each advisor is an informal ambassador for the United States and should fully understand the goals and objectives established for his effort.

*   *   *   *   *   *   *

(U) Without question, [the] vast majority of USAF advisors/contractors were dedicated men, sincerely concerned about making meaningful contributions to the VNAF I&M program. [The] same individuals usually indicated, however, that they could be even more effective.

(U) . . . Most advisors indicated that weaknesses in their orientation and preparation for the advisory responsibilities was the factor which most significantly reduced effectiveness. Approximately 29% . . . indicated that they received no orientation or guidance before starting work, and [an additional] 60% indicated general dissatisfaction with short cultural orientation lectures received . . .:

    a. Pressure of other events tended to draw management attention away from the orientation of new personnel. There was no overall coordination, supervision, or monitoring of efforts to ensure that newly assigned personnel were being adequately informed of their responsibilities. . . .

    b. USAF advisors were generally most outspoken about the lack of effective guidance on effective dealings with the Vietnamese and on the lack of any orientation to the language. They believe this seriously hampers effective dealing with their counterpart[s]. These same problems were also confirmed by a number of Vietnamese officials who hoped for better relations with American advisors. . . .

c. Work oriented preparations have also been under-emphasized. Many advisors . . . received no instructions on what was expected of them--they just picked up their responsibilities as they went along. Probably the most important aspect of any orientation program is the effective communication of the AFGP mission, current objectives, the unique aspects of advising VNAF officials, and past efforts to improve specific facets of an individual functional area. . . . We have noted advisors who were working innocently at cross-purposes with broader goals and objectives established at high level--primarily because they were unfamiliar with what was expected. There was also a tendency to re-invent the wheel because of the lack of clear communication about past problems and past attempts to solve them. . . .

d. The most difficult problem is that the continual turnover of personnel and the rapidly changing nature of the VNAF I&M program makes information outdated fairly frequently. . . .

(U) There has been increased attention on screening and assigning the best advisors available . . . [however,] a significant number (28% of replies) of people were being improperly utilized in their positions. The job did not match their experience . . . [and] personnel records do not contain all of the information needed to select good advisors from records along. At present there is no requirement for a personal interview with [a] potential advisor though we believe this would be of significant value.

(U) One of the continual subjects of objection has been the short tour and the lack of accompanied status for advisors. This has the serious effect of permitting an advisor to leave the country after he has developed enough experience to be effective. . . . In just [the] short time we have been here, problems once developed and corrected occurred again because of inexperienced personnel.

(U) In addition to the formal findings listed above, the individual comments of some of the advisors and their Vietnamese counterparts interviewed during this and previous audit surveys were also instructive. For example, one senior NCO stated, "I've seen many advisors including Team Chiefs who have almost a hatred of the Vietnamese people and no respect for them."[274]

Others interviewed commented they were working far out of their specialty. Remarks such as these prompted a December 1971 USAF Auditor General report to conclude:[275]

> (U) There appears to be a disturbing number of advisors who feel they are mal-assigned as advisors or who feel that other advisors are not suited for their responsibilities. Many of these problems appear to be caused because the specific attributes of the advisor--professional experience, tolerance for the Vietnamese, or desire to advise--do not always appear on official personnel records.
>
> (U) We readily recognize . . . [that] the vast majority of the advisors . . . are exceptionally qualified. The difficulty is that one mal-assigned advisor can easily undo the many contributions of effective advisors.

(U) Comments made by the advisors' VNAF counterparts were even more enlightening. Nearly all of those interviewed stressed the tendency of the U.S. advisor to do the job himself, rather than teaching his counterpart to do it. While American advisors were rated excellent "technically," their counterparts emphasized that "advisors have to understand the Vietnamese and appreciate the need for step-by-step training so that we can do the job." Some of those interviewed also expressed the belief that advisors generally had a "low opinion" of the VNAF. While the comments expressed above were based on only a small number of interviews, they nevertheless served as a constant reminder to the Advisory Group that vigilance was required in insuring that the advisory image remained high in the eyes of the VNAF.[276]

(U) Perhaps the most striking aspect of the advisory effort, however, was the cyclical, recurring nature of the problems confronting the advisor. A Rand study published in 1965 had underscored many of the problems and needs of advisors in their relations with their Vietnamese counterparts.

Incredibly, many of the findings of the report were still valid more than seven years later, at a time when the U.S. advisory effort was phasing out of Vietnam. The study offered the following recommendations, which serve as a fitting conclusion to this report's coverage of the advisory effort in Vietnam:[277]

SELECTION CRITERIA

(U) To ensure strong motivation for the task, it would be well to place advisory service on a voluntary basis if at all possible.

(U) Whether service is compulsory or voluntary, a careful screening process should be devised to test a candidate's suitability from the point of view of (a) professional equipment; (b) adaptability to foreign cultures; (c) . . . disposition, especially in the case of prospective field advisors, to share dangers, hardships, exotic food, and primitive shelter with members of an oriental civilization; (d) existing linguistic skills or the ability to acquire languages easily; (e) the possibility of "culture fatigue" in a man who, though otherwise qualified, has had too many overseas assignments and is not keen on another.

DESIRABLE EMPHASIS IN THE TRAINING OF ADVISORS

(U) Language being the single most important factor in breaking down cultural barriers, language training far more intensive than at present should be given to all field advisors. . . .

(U) In preparing personnel for cultural hurdles they will have either to remove or bypass, training programs must insist on the importance of respecting the Vietnamese cultural identity wherever it does not go against the interest of the counterinsurgent [sic] effort, and must stress the patterns that are most strikingly different from ours: the preference for indirectness that is evident in the language itself and in the general style of discourse; the more relaxed and fatalistic attitude toward time; the importance of tradition and ritual, including the cult of the ancestors; a relative indifference to human beings not part of one's kinfolk and intimate environment; the importance of taboos; native attitudes toward health and hygiene, with special attention to folk-medical beliefs; and the most common criteria of the good life.

(U) To accomplish this kind of indoctrination, students in predeployment courses ought to have some instruction in the history, economics, government, sociology, ethnic composition, major religious sects, and general customs of the country as well as on the special characteristics of the region to which they are being assigned.

*   *   *   *   *   *   *

(U) In addition to acquainting students with the official structure of the Vietnamese military, predeployment instruction should contain important information in the informal, unwritten aspects of the system . . . [to] include, for example, the strong heritage of French military thinking among officers and their preference for French tactics and techniques; the decision-making mechanisms within the army; the status and prerogatives of the different military ranks; the principle of reward and punishment that governs promotions and hence conduct in the military; and a definition of a given counterpart's precise role within the hierarchy, with emphasis on the limits it imposes on his autonomy.

(U) Far greater attention than heretofore needs to be given to all facets of civic action. Prospective advisors must be impressed with the importance of civic action in the counterinsurgent [sic] effort. . . .

<u>ADMINISTRATIVE CONSIDERATIONS</u>

(U) . . . every effort should be made to reduce bureaucratic demands on the advisor, especially paper work, to the minimum necessary.

(U) Because it takes several months for an advisor to work effectively with his counterpart, the possibility of extending the length of tours should be studied. . . .

(U) Professional equality and other bases for mutual respect being of great importance in advisor/counterpart relations, both rank and military occupational specialty ought to be matched wherever possible. . . .

(U) Vertical communication within the American echelons should be encouraged with the aid of better opportunities

through which advisors can maintain rapport with their
superiors by reporting to them and airing their problems
as needed.

(U) Lateral communication would be greatly enhanced
by the organization of periodic group sessions of
advisors at the same level, preferably attended also
by several representatives from higher echelons, in
which experiences could be exchanged and common difficulties discussed and solved. . . .

Transition to DAO (U)

(S) Total withdrawal of U.S. forces, assimilation of Enhance Plus equipment, expanded activation of unprogrammed squadrons without the skilled manpower force required for such expansion, and continuing combat commitments represented an unprecedented challenge to the VNAF. Perhaps the greatest paradox of the advisory effort in Vietnam was that at the time when the VNAF was facing its ultimate challenge, and therefore when advisory assistance was most needed, the Advisory Group was withdrawn. The terms of the agreement to end the war in Vietnam specified that no U.S. advisors would remain in Vietnam. Those remaining after the cease-fire would act as "technical assistants," but not as "advisors" per se. Replacing MACV and the Advisory Group was the DAO, which fell heir to the long-standing goal of promoting VNAF (indeed RVNAF) self-sufficiency, but faced the task without the benefit of advisors.[278]

(S) The use of contractors provided the primary means of augmenting and training the VNAF in the skills they needed to pursue self-sufficiency. The DAO guided and monitored the contract programs, deciding when progress toward self-sufficiency warranted completion of one contract, or required extension or creation of another. The limited number of U.S. personnel allowed in-country, and the self-imposed U.S. intention of permitting DOD civilian and contractor support in-country for only 12 months (at the end of which, it was hoped, RVNAF self-sufficiency would be realized), were the primary limitations on contractor support of the RVNAF. The formidable task of conversion from the MACV/AFGP force to the DAO organization was an initial stumbling block which further complicated matters.[279]

(S) Following the signing of the cease-fire agreement, numerous civilians began to arrive in-country to replace their military counterparts, many of whom had already departed; indeed, overlap with departing personnel was not generally possible. Unfortunately, careful recruitment of personnel apparently had not taken place.[280] The Chief of the Air Force Division, DAO, summed up the personnel situation.[281]

> (S) Unfortunately, as with any organization created overnight, there were very weak people hired in key positions. There were also some outstanding people hired. But the DAO did not have the opportunity of coming in and transitioning with their predecessors; the predecessors would just up and leave and the civilians were on their own. They had the enormous task of getting oriented, . . . and they had no idea what their jobs would be--and the military was of no assistance to them. There were no continuity folders left for the people and there was groping for courses of action.

(S) The Chief of the DAO's ALC Branch also emphasized the impact of the transition process, and had some suggestions for avoiding such difficulties in the future. While some transition problems would be inevitable in such situations, he noted that a more organized approach to recruitment and transition would surely help avoid some of the difficulties:[282]

> (S) The transfer of responsibilities from MACV to DAO, the rapid phase-down of the military within 60 days after the cease-fire, and the influx of DOD civilians and an increased contractor force within country caused a certain

amount of confusion during the first four months of
transition from January 28th of 1973 before we really
got oriented. . . . Because of the lack of interest on
the part of the military due to their phaseout and the
input of the DOD civilians to take the military's place,
the amount of time it took to orient, put people in the
right position, bring them up to speed as to what their
objectives were . . . these things all took time. . . .
In the event that we would ever have a military confrontation again and replace that military force with a DOD
civilian force, an extreme amount of recruitment should
take place well in advance of a transition such as we
experienced here last February and March. I think that
personnel of the military force that are best qualified
at that particular time to have knowledge of the types
of individuals who should replace them should form teams,
go back to the states and recruit at all the installations
where DOD civilians would be interested to come to Vietnam.
I think that the recruitment that was done for the DAO was
done helter-skelter, I think there was no rhyme or reason
in the selection of people. . . . All possible actions
should have been taken to insure that the best qualified people would come here to expedite the performance
of our objectives.

(S) . . . We should continually update our roadmaps, our
milestones of objectives. . . . The roadmaps . . . left
behind by the MACV were totally inadequate. There should
be some assurance that documents like the V-LOG are a
continuing item of interest anytime we start into a program like this in the future, and that emphasis is placed
on the participants to see that that document is continually updated so in the event that we do have a rapid
withdrawal, those remaining people . . . will at least
know what is left to be accomplished.

(S) Once the nearly formed DAO became well-organized and established, and the immensity of the tasks confronting the South Vietnamese were in focus, it became obvious that attainment of self-sufficiency within one year of the cease-fire was not possible. As mentioned previously, VNAF personnel and middle management problems, the recent expansion of the force struc-ture, and the lack of military stability following the cease-fire made continuing assistance to the VNAF mandatory for a number of years to come.

Following a visit to Washington, D.C., in October 1973, the U.S. Ambassador to South Vietnam summarized the factors surrounding U.S. assistance to the VNAF during the previous year, and established the need for intensifying U.S. assistance aimed at the development of VNAF logistics capabilities:[283]

> (S) Enhance . . . and Enhance Plus were deliberately designed to provide a reasonable military inventory before the January 27 effective date of the cease-fire which limited future military hardware items to a one-for-one replacement basis. It was recognized that certain digestive difficulties were inherent in this process, but the decision [was] made at the highest levels that the inventory levels on that date were to be a floor as well as a ceiling and we would take such subsequent actions as might be necessary to help the VNAF to overcome the digestive problem.
>
> (S) It was assumed by some, in the euphoria surrounding the conclusion of the Paris agreement and the return of the POWs [Prisoners of War], that the DRVN [Democratic Republic of Vietnam] would reasonably respect the agreement. Consequently, the approach on our part to the solution of the VNAF operational readiness problem was perhaps more relaxed than prudence might have dictated. Certainly, in view of the massive DRVN violations and dangerous military build-up in the South, accelerated action was clearly called for.
>
> (S) . . . Subsequent increases by the DRVN in the scale of military action . . . [convinced] me that we simply must again accelerate the improvement of the VNAF logistics capabilities. Therefore, during my visit to Washington the previously operative restraints requiring phaseout of contractor personnel were removed.

(S) Consequently, the decision was made to drop the one-year time constraint and to instead key reduction of post-cease-fire U.S. assistance to progress in Vietnamizing remaining functions and tasks. A 27 October message from the JCS stated:[284]

> (S) In view of the state of developments in SEA and the status of implementation of the cease-fire agreement, higher authority has directed that plans be made to

maintain the civilians assigned to the DAO, Saigon, at full strength subject to annual review. While observing the principle of nondegradation of U.S. support and assistance to the RVNAF, higher authority wishes to insure that U.S. . . . manning levels are sound and economical from a management viewpoint. Accordingly, DOD and civilian contractor spaces should only be reduced as functions and tasks are Vietnamized, completed, transferred to other agencies or activities, or eliminated. A residual DAO, Saigon will be retained with sufficient DOD civilian personnel to insure the accomplishment of essential mission objectives and completion of Vietnamization.

VNAF Morale (U)

(C) The need to provide VNAF personnel with a measure of economic security was the greatest single factor affecting VNAF morale. Economic hardship resulting from the low VNAF standard of living was a long-standing problem which continued to grow throughout 1971 and 1972. To place the issue of VNAF income in perspective, it should be viewed in light of the Vietnamese culture. A May 1972 AFGP study outlined the impact of the cost of living, the family unit, traditional family commitments, and "moonlighting" on the VNAF standard of living:[285]

> (C) a. <u>The Family Unit</u>. The typical Vietnamese family household of seven individuals includes parents, brothers, sisters, often grandparents, and of course the individual's own wife and children. The broad composition of this basic family unit adds two unique ingredients to the family economic structure. First, all members who are able normally generate income and contribute to the group survival. Secondly, because of the Asian cultural tradition of close family ties, PCS [Permanent Change of Station] movement of the military member often results in a move for the entire family. The consequence of this uprooting is severe economic hardship through loss of family non-military income until new means of income are established. . . . Although many VNAF families are separated by PCS of the military member, it is an unacceptable penalty to Vietnamese family integrity and a morale factor of great significance.

b. _Traditional Family Commitments_. Status virtually demands that VNAF members above the rank of Sergeant own at least a small motorcycle. . . . While the cost of a small Honda may be inconsequential in many societies, it is indeed a major and unavoidable expense in this society. Family commitments for burial sites and elaborate, symbolic religious markers often result in long term indebtedness.

c. _Moonlighting_. . . . It is impossible to accurately assess the impact of moonlighting on job effectiveness. The wide variations in availability and type of employment, hours worked, salaries and individual differences preclude a meaningful statistical analysis. . . . [Our] opinion is that moonlighting is practiced by more than 25% of the VNAF personnel; however, because of personal pride, the possibility of criticism, or the loss of face, the true extent of moonlighting is not really known.

d. _Cost of Living_. . . . The average airman's salary is $17.28 (U.S.). The monthly cost of feeding one individual on the Vietnamese economy is $15.00 (U.S.). This leaves a balance of $2.28 (U.S.) for housing, clothing, burial commitments, transportation, and to feed the other members of the household! . . . It is not difficult to perceive that the average Vietnamese airman and junior officer must rely on other sources of income merely to meet the cost of the absolute necessities. . . . Financial distress is a common occurrence. One cannot escape the conclusion that improved pay for the VNAF is a must.

*   *   *   *   *   *   *

(U) 4. . . . TDY pay seldom equals the extra expenses of meals alone, and there are no provisions for collecting advance TDY pay. It is common practice for VNAF members to draw advance full regular pay in order to finance their TDY periods.

*   *   *   *   *   *   *

(U) 7. Because of the size of the military force and the large disparity between wage and price indexes . . . a simple answer to the overall VNAF standard of living problem is not possible. Obviously, the magnitude of the pay increase required to bring the military in line with the civilian working class is beyond the capability of

> the GVN [Government of Vietnam]. . . . It is only fair, however, to try to resolve the inequities militating against an individual's welfare while performing unusual and hazardous duties for his Government. . . . [A] practical and meaningful way to indirectly increase salaries for VNAF personnel without becoming embroiled in an RVNAF pay struggle is to provide adequate Base Quarters for all grades in both married and bachelor categories. VNAF personnel do not receive a housing allowance, but Base Quarters are provided when available without cost to the individual. This represents a sizeable increase in effective income. . . . Many benefits are accrued by on-base living such as increased security for the member and his family and an easing of transportation requirements. Morale for all categories would undoubtedly improve.

(S) It is difficult to overemphasize the impact of economic considerations on VNAF morale. In July 1972, the Director of Plans and Programs, AFGP, listed the three factors he considered most important to the achievement of VNAF self-sufficiency after U.S. withdrawal. The second and third factors were modernizing the VNAF and solving the middle management problem, respectively. Listed first was providing "a measure of personal and family security."[286] He believed that providing housing, medical attention, and financial security for the families would result in "a tremendous increase in individual productivity and overall effectiveness of the VNAF."[287]

(C) One activity which was pursued to improve the RVNAF living standard was the dependent shelter program. U.S. participation in the project, which had been initiated by the GVN in 1961, gradually increased over the years. By 1969, a total of 85,000 housing units had been completed, but as of early 1970 only 49,000 had survived the ravages of war and the weather. During CY 1971 through 1975, the U.S. was committed to support the GVN in the construction of another 100,000 units. (In addition, the U.S. Navy and Air Force had initiated separate projects for dependent shelter which totalled approximately 5,500 units.) By late 1973, approximately 30,000 RVNAF housing units had been completed through a combination of military and contractor engineers and occupant self-help, and continuing construction was underway at an accelerated pace. These units were essentially a dirt floor, four walls, and a roof. Although extremely austere, the shelters provided a home for a man and his family. Those lucky enough to obtain one of the shelters thus avoided the major expense of providing off-base quarters.[288]

(C) The dependent shelter program alone could not solve the VNAF standard of living problem. Of all the factors contributing to the low standard of living, inflation was the one with the most severe impact. An August 1973 DAO fact sheet pointed out that since 1964, the real purchasing power of the soldier and civil servant had declined [by] 78 percent! In contract, wages in the private sector had roughly kept pace with inflation. As a result, soldiers and civil servants were forced to maintain family income by the only two means available, moonlighting and corruption. Even these choices were unavailable for many due to their low position and the recession in the GVN economy following the withdrawal of U.S. forces.[289]

(C) In an effort to bolster the GVN economy, DOD had three economic support programs in-country. In-country procurement of goods was the major program; its goal was to provide a guaranteed demand which would facilitate the expansion of existing and establishment of new, industries serving domestic and export markets. Military construction by Vietnamese contractors was a second means of providing economic support. Finally, transfer of in-country U.S. scrap to the GVN provided a foreign exchange resource. In the aggregate, however, these programs represented only about a third of the yearly three to four hundred million dollars that U.S. forces had spent for goods and services in Vietnam prior to their withdrawal.[290]

(C) Despite the severe economic problems faced by RVNAF personnel, morale (at least as reflected by desertion rates) remained stable during 1973. Of the various services, the desertion rate for the VNAF was the lowest. Nevertheless, the October 1973 DAO Quarterly Assessment reemphasized that the negative impact on morale by economic hardships was still a very real and acute problem:[291]

> (C) (1) Continuing inflation causes the inadequate military pay to become a greater source of discontent.
>
> (C) (2) As always, cultural traditions and family obligations cause considerable hardships on military personnel who are forced to relocate. Unit moves are often accompanied by increased desertion and AWOL [Absent Without Leave] rates.
>
> (C) (3) The unstable economy aggravates the tendency toward corruption among personnel at all levels. This situation also results in favored treatment for those who can afford it at the expense of those who cannot.
>
> (C) (4) Inadequate dependent housing continues to be a source of irritation.

(C) The across-the-board raises needed to make military pay comparable to that of civilians was beyond the fiscal means of the Government of South Vietnam (GVN). Nevertheless, a number of small steps had been taken to bolster the morale of servicemen. The most significant began in September 1973, when each serviceman started receiving a monthly allowance which at that time was sufficient to meet a single person's rice requirements. Also during 1973, for the first time in five years, the Armed Forces were allowed annual leave totalling fifteen days per person. In addition, a variety of "morale" programs were sponsored, including newsreels, libraries, musical instruments for units, athletics, and programs for Armed Forces holidays.[292]

(S) As noted above, the VNAF desertion rate was the lowest of all services. The Director of the Air Force Division, DAO, stressed that despite the very serious standard of living problems, the VNAF was a proud and elite corps. Recruitment, when compared to the other services, was extremely selective. In fact, he noted that in some cases VNAF recruits had paid 10,000 Piasters (equivalent at that time to 20 U.S. dollars) for being selected from the numerous volunteers--a voluntary tour in the VNAF was that much more attractive than being drafted into the ARVN. Also cited as an example of VNAF morale was an incident which occurred during February 1973 at Phu Cat AB. Phu Cat, while considered a hardship assignment in VNAF eyes, was one of the best-disciplined bases in the VNAF. At the time of the cease-fire, a Viet Cong force was in the city of Phu Cat. The ARVN had been given the assignment of recapturing the city, but they were unsuccessful. The VNAF base commander gathered his airmen together, equipped them with flak vests and weapons, attacked the city, and drove out the enemy force. This outstanding example of discipline and spirit was a source of pride to the VNAF.[293]

(S) Not all units, however, exhibited such a high level of morale and discipline. In the opinion of some, discipline in the VNAF's recruit-laden force structure could prove to be a serious problem. Paradoxically, the relatively well-educated individuals being recruited into the VNAF, while obviously desirable from a personnel/training standpoint, could have a negative impact on VNAF discipline and morale. The Director of the ALC, DAO, explained:[294]

> (S) I think that we'll see in a very few months or perhaps a year's time span there will be much discontent and unrest within the Vietnamese Air Force by virtue of the fact that the people that they have been recruiting recently are of a caliber that certainly doesn't appreciate the low pay that they receive. . . . Outside . . . their families could better afford things compared to what they are receiving in the military. . . . Certainly the lack of middle management . . . is going to have an impact. When you do not have proper supervision . . . then you lose a lot in discipline. . . . They are going to face this lack of discipline for many months and perhaps years until they become well-trained, and realize a significant increase in their middle and top level management.

Despite these problems, however, the consensus was that the VNAF enjoyed higher morale than any other service. "It's a proud corps, . . . it is the elite corps."[295]

CHAPTER VI

POST-CEASE-FIRE ASSESSMENT (U)

(S) By the end of 1973, a great deal of progress had been realized in achieving the goals of the improvement and modernization program for RVNAF forces. Yet, the question of the ultimate success or failure of the Vietnamization program remained untested and unresolved. It was clear, however, that in the long run the survival of South Vietnam would hinge on a number of military, economic, and political variables over which the RVN and its military forces had little control--not the least of which was the willingness of the United States to provide continuing high levels of economic support and military assistance.

Military Activity and the Enemy Threat (U)

(S/NFD) The cease-fire agreement in South Vietnam did not bring peace; by late 1973 combat activity was still widespread, though occuring at lower levels than before the "cease-fire." Overall, the DAO felt that the enemy had "the tactical edge" in post-cease-fire combat. The RVNAF, however, had also scored some gains and in most cases were stubbornly defending GVN-controlled territory.[296] The Defense Attache, in the October 1973 DAO Quarterly Assessment, summed up the more significant activities:[297]

> (S) At the end of the quarter both sides continue military operations to reduce enemy influence in the areas where they claim control. The RVNAF made some progress in clearing the coastal lowlands of MRs I and II and in reducing the area controlled by the enemy in MR IV. GVN forces were also successful in recapturing Trung Nghia and Polei Krong in Kontum

Province, but were not successful in reopening LTL [Interprovincial Road] 1A to Phuoc Long Province in MR III. Le Minh Ranger Base in Pleiku Province and the RF [Regional Forces] base on Bach Ma Mountain in Thua Thien Province were lost to the enemy.

(S/NFD) Of greater concern than the post-cease-fire combat activity was the development of the NVA's military potential within South Vietnam. It was rated as the enemy's "strongest military position in the history of the war."[298] Following the cease-fire, Hanoi moved large amounts of war materiel through the Demilitarized Zone into MR I, from Laos into the Kontum-Pleiku area, and through Laos and Cambodia to the Parrot's Beak area in MR III near the Saigon corridor.[299] The alarming growth of the enemy threat in South Vietnam was summarized by the same quarterly assessment quoted above:[300]

> (S/NFD) Since the cease-fire, Hanoi has improved its military position in South Vietnam by:
>
> a. Deploying 9 AA [Anti-Aircraft] and 1 SA-2 Regiments to MR-1, 2 AA Regiments to MR-2, and 1 AA Regiment to MR-3.
>
> b. Deploying the equivalent of 3 armored regiments to South Vietnam.
>
> c. Deploying the equivalent of 5 artillery regiments to South Vietnam.
>
> d. Shifting some 20,000 rear service personnel to South Vietnam.
>
> e. Extending and improving in-country Lines of Communication toward primary objective areas.
>
> f. Establishing new and expanding old base areas.
>
> g. Pre-positioning sufficient supplies inside South Vietnam to support and sustain a major country-wide offensive.

(S/NFD) The exact manner in which the North Vietnamese intended to exploit their military potential was another question. It was DAO's assessment that the North Vietnamese had three primary options which they could pursue to achieve their overall objective in South Vietnam. The first option--a political one--was the creation of a recognized government within South Vietnam capable of competing with the GVN in the economic and political spheres. The second was to conduct a phased, but limited, military offensive to gradually create a military, economic, and political situation beyond the capability of the GVN to control. The final option was to conduct a major military offensive designed to cause a catastrophic, immediate collapse of the armed forces and the government. The first option could be used in support of either military course, and the phased offensive could be escalated into a major offensive.[301]

(S/NFD) A major factor affecting Hanoi's choice of options was Soviet and Chinese economic and military aid. Following the cease-fire, it was believed that Moscow and Peking were emphasizing economic and reconstruction assistance rather than massive military aid, although there was a lack of firm intelligence on the extent of post-cease-fire arms shipments to North Vietnam. Admittedly, any assessment of the probable Soviet/Chinese reaction to a North Vietnamese offensive was "fraught with unknowns and uncertainties."[302] Nevertheless, it was generally held that, in the event of a major offensive, increased shipments would not occur because they would imply support of the offensive. On the other side of the coin, however, North Vietnam was believed to already have sufficient stockpiles in South

Vietnam and the border areas to support a major offensive for an extended period. A critical unknown to Hanoi was the U.S. reaction to a Communist offensive. With these and other factors as a background, the DAO reached the following conclusions in their October 1973 Quarterly Assessment:[303]

> (S/NFD) DAO Saigon believes that Hanoi has all the armor, artillery and logistics in South Vietnam necessary to pursue any of the three possible courses of action. Further, we believe that the enemy is preparing to commit the manpower to raise the combat forces to levels that will permit initiation of either military option.
>
> (S/NFD) Although we have seen several reports alleging that the enemy has already decided to resume the military offensive early next year, and although we consider his actions to reinforce his military capability strong indications that these reports may be valid, we have not received enough information to permit us to conclude that such a decision has, in fact, been made. The political and economic offensive continues. The military reinforcements are moving into South Vietnam and Southern Laos. Improvements in the logistical infrastructure are proceeding apace. The enemy's most likely course of action is a phased military offensive, supported by the political and economic offensive, keeping open his option to attack with concentrated force to seize the decisive objective.

RVNAF and VNAF Capabilities (U)

(S/NFD) Following the cease-fire, the RVNAF as a whole was improving, although progress was hampered by the continuation of combat operations. The RVNAF concentrated on improving its logistics and training, and on coping with budget constraints, corruption, and the impact of inflation on morale. As reflected by increased unit readiness and manning strength, some dividends were being realized from the logistics and training efforts. Middle-level management was improving, although corruption was a primary hinderance to progress in this area. Corruption and inflation were also hampering the improvement of RVNAF morale and motivation; yet, considering the circumstances, morale did seem to be holding fairly well.[304]

(S/NFD) On balance, the RVNAF was faced with formidable problems, but was nevertheless considered capable of tenaciously defending GVN territory against limited enemy offensive operations. However, the consensus among both RVNAF and DAO officials was that the RVNAF could not withstand a total Communist offensive without U.S. air support.[305]

(S/NFD) As an element of the RVNAF, the VNAF's capabilities to perform during a Communist offensive were assessed in late 1973. Yet, this assessment was very subjective. Experts in the Vietnamization program expressed both optimism and pessimism concerning the ability of the VNAF to function effectively during a period of intensified conflict. Essentially, however, the consensus was as follows: With respect to their combat potential a few years earlier, the VNAF had made amazing progress toward a formidable, self-sufficient force. A major, country-wide Communist offensive would in all probability elicit a vigorous response from the VNAF in support of ground forces; to make such support effective, however, VNAF pilots would have to press their attacks to lower, more vulnerable altitudes, and the VNAF would have to surge to the limit of its combat potential. The ability to maintain this surge would be a critical limitation; although estimates varied widely, a two-month surge was generally considered the extent of VNAF capabilities. Critical to this assessment was the premise that, at least initially, the performance of the VNAF would be an important factor in determining the RVNAF's capacity to withstand a Communist offensive. At the same time, the problems remaining in the VNAF, and the limitations inherent in its size when compared to that of the U.S. air armada previously available in SEA, would dictate a much lower level of air support than that available for ground forces during the 1972 Spring Offensive. As a consequence of these considerations, it was the consensus of U.S. observers and Vietnamese officials that if the RVNAF were to avoid outright defeat or the loss of major portions of RVN territory, U.S. air support would be required shortly after the initiation of a sustained, country-wide NVA offensive.[306]

Assessment of Progress and Outlook for the Future (U)

(U) With the problems and inherent limitations remaining in the VNAF at the end of 1973, and in view of the formidable tasks still to be accomplished in coming years, had the I&M program been unsuccessful? Following a USAF General Officers' Review of the Vietnamization program, a March 1973 CSAF message was dispatched to DAO, Saigon, detailing the status of the improvement and modernization of the VNAF, as discussed and agreed upon in the Review. The message aptly began by assessing the progress which had already been realized, and made a matter of record the widely shared conviction which had so often gone unstated in correspondence dealing with the Vietnamization program:[307]

> (U) For the record, and lest any newcomer or other noninformed [sic] individual assume from the very significant amount of work outlined in this message for accomplishment over the next several months, that

most of what is discussed is new or that little has
been done over the past several years--nothing could
be further from the truth. All who have been associated with this program over the past 2-4 years . . .
recognize that very significant, in some cases spec-
tacular, progress has been made by the Vietnamese toward their goal of self-sufficiency. Viewed from the
perspective of the task given the Vietnamese and the
DAO, and the conditions and timing for its accomplishment, the progress in the last year has been remarkable.

(C) Notwithstanding the incontestable gains made in the Vietnamization program, some expressed a pessimistic view of the adequacy of VNAF and RVNAF progress toward a strong disciplined, self-sufficient military force. In the words of the Chief of the DAO's ALC Branch:[308]

(C) [The belief that the objectives of the United States
in Vietnam could be achieved by pursuing a post-cease-
fire strategy which featured a marked decrease in American
participation in Vietnam, and a phase-out of residual
forces within one year's time,] . . . was predicated upon
erroneous information that resulted from not-too-factual
reports, surveys, and analyses of distinguished visitors
to the country. . . . [This] caused a condition to exist
at the policy level in our government that . . .
[fostered] erroneous or false beliefs with regard to the
degree of Vietnamization. . . .

(C) . . . [In future situations such as Vietnam] we should
continually update our roadmaps, our milestones of objectives, to insure that we don't get caught in the same box
that we got caught in here in Vietnam, wherein we relied
too heavily on false reports that said Vietnamization was
here and that our influence [was no longer needed.]
. . . Those types of reports should be scrutinized in
more depth; I don't think that they should be taken for
face value as it appears that they were. . . .

(C) . . . On January 28th of this year, when the peace
treaty was signed, if the country had in fact realized a
period of peace and coexistence with the Viet Cong and the
North Vietnamese . . ., then our influence here, or our
stay here, would not have been required. I think that the
overall objective of Communism is still domination of all
of Southeast Asia, . . . and I don't think that just the

signing of a peace treaty . . . by any stretch of the
imagination is going to cause that interest and desire
to fade away. . . . The American influence has to stay
here to supplement . . . [the RVNAF] with expertise
that they do not have. I think any early withdrawal of
American influence here would just open the door to Communism and . . . their forces would gather and quite
easily overtake the South Vietnamese government.

*   *   *   *   *   *   *

(C) . . . The basis for any successful military operation
is . . . discipline, and I don't see this too extensively
in the VNAF. . . . We can provide all the facilities
in the world--the parts, the equipment, tools, all the
things that go to enhancing Vietnamization--but one
thing that we can't give them . . . is discipline. . . .
They are going to face this lack of discipline for many
months and perhaps years until they become well-trained,
and realize a significant increase in their middle- and
top-level management. . . . If put under an extreme
amount of pressure (which I would imagine that this
country will be placed under shortly in the event of a
new offensive, and I would imagine that a new offensive
would be of greater magnitude than in the past), without
the discipline required to hold together a military
force, I think that it would be just a matter of time
before the VNAF would flounder. . . . Perhaps we could . . .
[forestall] this sort of thing if we provide qualified
American DOD people that would continue to . . . insist
upon the development of discipline. . . . Right now
it's a matter of the survival of this country. . . .
It's important that the United States be willing and
ready, and will respond to assist South Vietnam if it is
attacked in the near future; otherwise, I think that the
VC and the North Vietnamese . . . will overthrow the
Government of South Vietnam.

(C) The passing of time held potential advantages and liabilities for both Hanoi and Saigon. South Vietnamese forces continued to gain strength and to progress toward self-sufficiency; but North Vietnamese forces also sought to strengthen their military posture. On the economic and political front as well, time could work to the detriment of either side. Inflation, for example, might either worsen or slacken, depending on RVN economic policies, the strain of continuing conflict on the economy, and the level of U.S. economic support. Whatever the economic or political developments, however, the Communists retained the option of initiating a military confrontation. Meaningful, substantial progress in the improvement and modernization of South Vietnamese ground and air forces was an essential ingredient in deterring the North Vietnamese from that option, or in forcefully responding if that option were pursued. Continued U.S. support of Vietnamization was a prerequisite to RVNAF improvement and modernization, and was the cornerstone of South Vietnamese survival.

APPENDIX: VNAF SQUADRON ACTIVATIONS AND DISPOSITIONS

		Page
Table 1:	VNAF Squadron Activations, July 1971 - July 1973	191
Figures 1-4:	VNAF Force Disposition by Military Region, October 1973	193
Figure 1:	Aircraft Strength-1st Air Division, Da Nang AB, Oct 73	193
Figure 2:	Aircraft Strength-6th Air Division, Pleiku & Phu Cat ABs; Aircraft Strength-2nd Air Division, Nha Trang & Phan Rang ABs, Oct 73	194
Figure 3:	Aircraft Strength-3rd Air Division, Bien Hoa AB: Aircraft Strength-5th Air Division, Tan Son Nhut AB, Oct 73	195
Figure 4:	American Strength-4th Air Division, Binh Thuy & Can Tho ABs, Oct 73	196

Sources: (S) AFGP, "Military Assistance Progress Report (U)," covering the quarterly periods from July 1971 through December 1972.

(S) U.S. DAO, Saigon, "DAO Quarterly Assessment Report (U)," July and October 1973.

TABLE 1: VNAF SQUADRON ACTIVATIONS
July 1971 - July 1973 (U)

Sqdn	Type Aircraft	Base	Quarter/CY of Activation
819	AC-119G	Tan Son Nhut	3/71
423	C-123K	Tan Son Nhut	3/71 (Deactivated 4/72)
425	C-123K	Tan Son Nhut	3/71 (Deactivated 4/72)
427	C-7	Da Nang	3/71
243	UH-1	Phu Cat	4/71
245	UH-1	Bien Hoa	4/71
239	UH-1	Da Nang	1/72
241	CH-47	Phu Cat	2/72
429	C-7	Tan Son Nhut/Phu Cat	2/72
431	C-7	Tan Son Nhut	3/72
124	O-1/U-17	Bien Hoa	3/72
718	EC-47D	Tan Son Nhut/Da Nang	3/72
532	A-37	Phu Cat	4/72
534	A-37	Phan Rang	4/72
536	F-5A	Bien Hoa	4/72
435	C-130	Tan Son Nhut	4/72
437	C-130	Tan Son Nhut	4/72
538	F-5A	Da Nang	1/73
540	F-5A	Bien Hoa	1/73
821	AC-119K	Tan Son Nhut/Da Nang	1/73
247	CH-47	Da Nang	1/73
251	UH-1	Bien Hoa	1/73

(TABLE 1 CONTINUED)

Sqdn	Type Aircraft	Base	Quarter/CY of Activation
255	UH-1	Binh Thuy	1/73
257	UH-1	Da Nang	1/73
259	UH-1	Spread among all bases except Da Nang	1/73
546	A-37	Binh Thuy	2/73
548	A-37	Phan Rang	2/73
550	A-37	Da Nang	2/73
542	F-5A	Bien Hoa	2/73
544	F-5A	Bien Hoa	2/73
249	CH-47	Binh Thuy	2/73
253	UH-1	Da Nang	2/73
920	T-37	Phan Rang	2/73

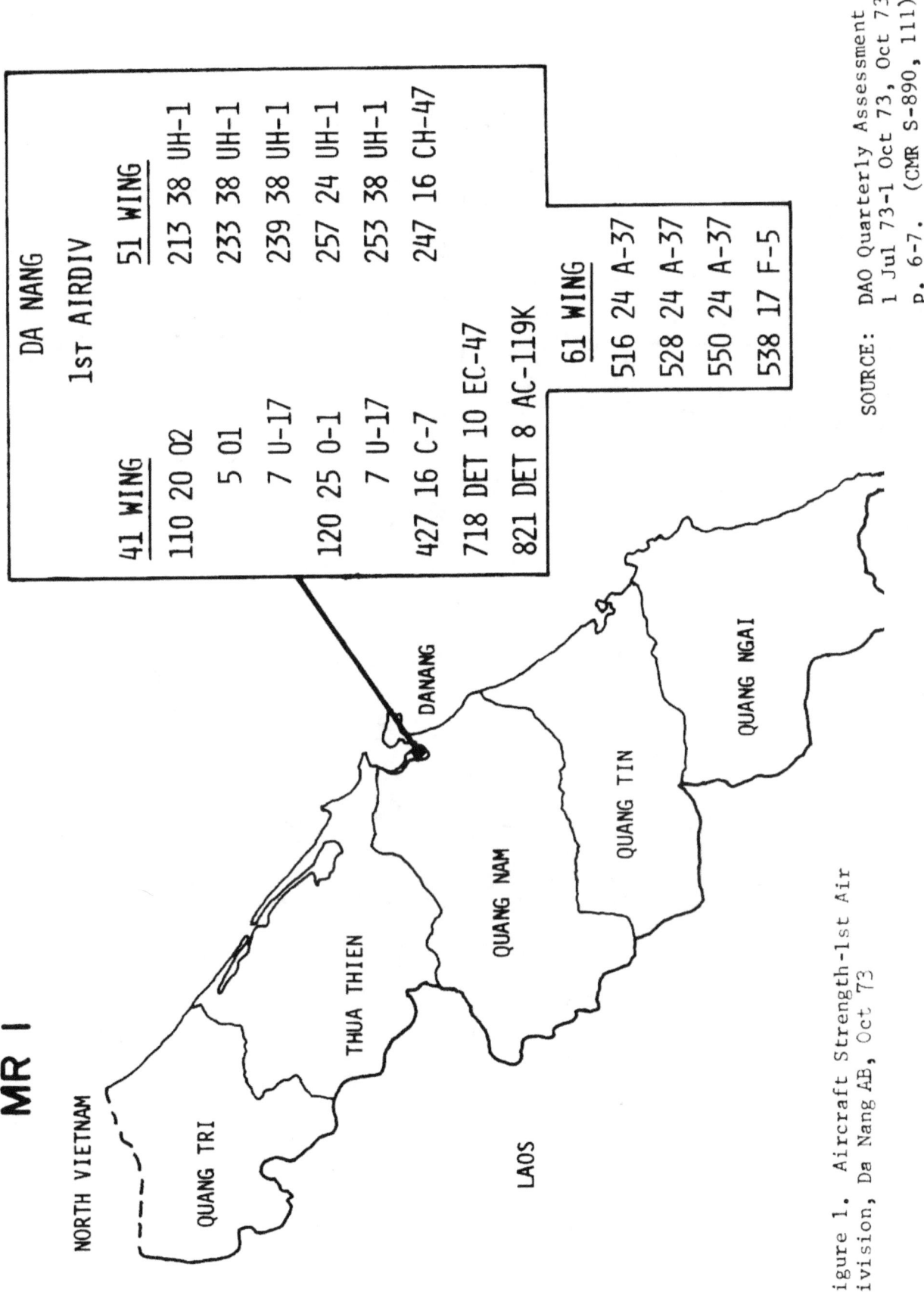

Figure 1. Aircraft Strength—1st Air Division, Da Nang AB, Oct 73

SOURCE: DAO Quarterly Assessment 1 Jul 73–1 Oct 73, Oct 73, p. 6-7. (CMR S-890, 111)

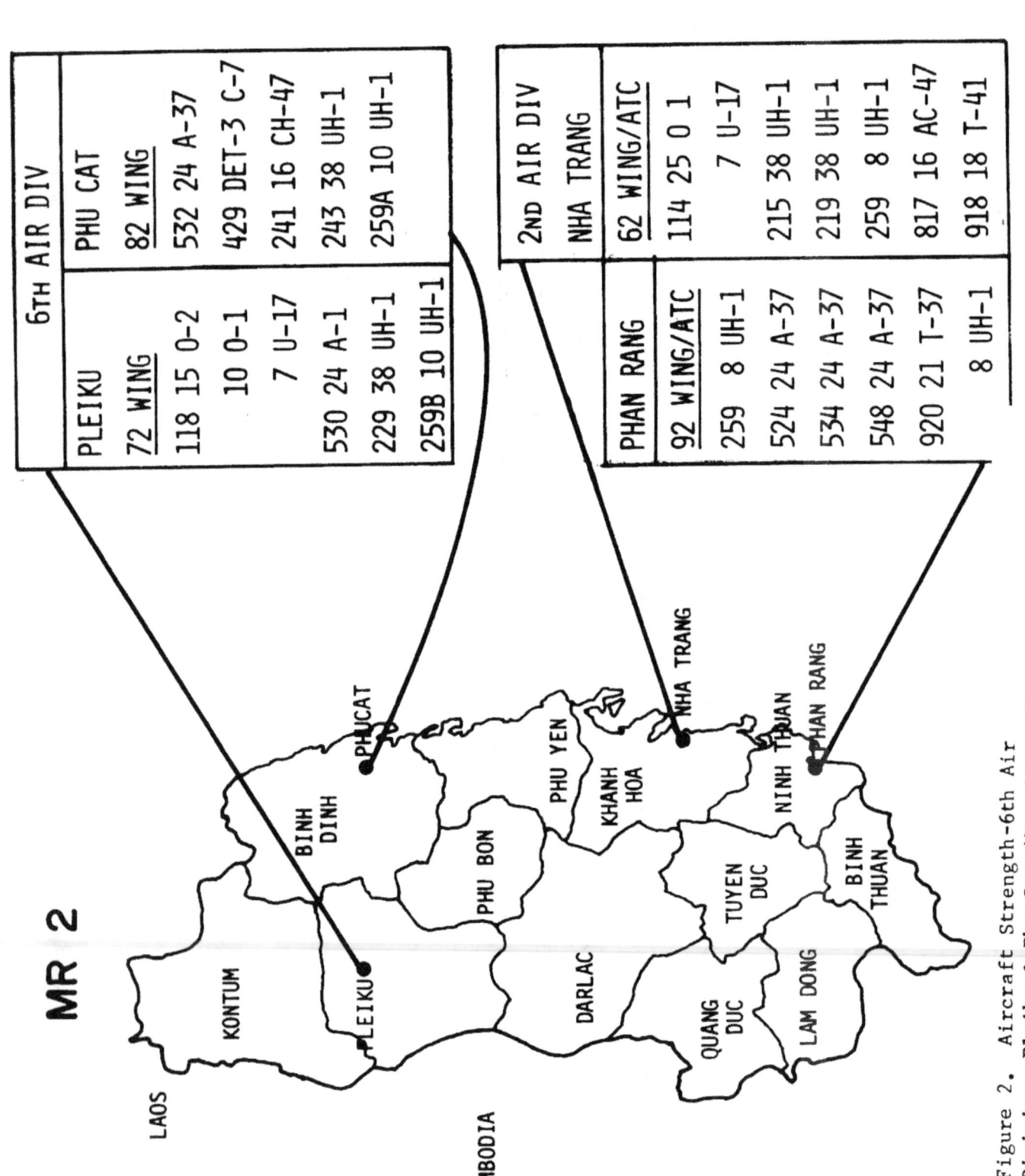

Figure 2. Aircraft Strength-6th Air Division, Pleiku & Phu Cat ABs; Aircraft Strength-2nd Air Division, Nha Trang & Phan Rang ABs, Oct 73

SOURCE: DAO Quarterly Assessment 1 Jul 73-1 Oct 73, Oct 73, p. 6-7. (CMR S-890, 111)

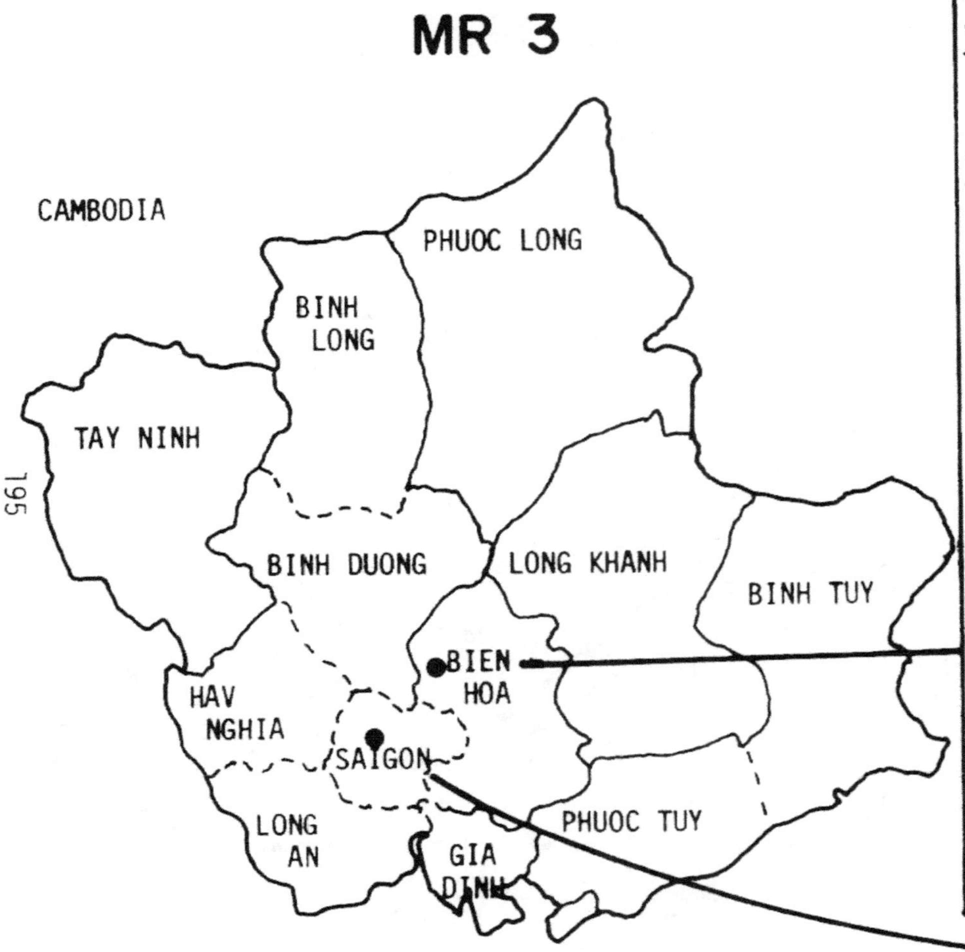

MR 3

BIEN HOA

3RD AIR DIVISION

23 WING
- 112 25 O-1
-        7 U-17
- 124 25 O-1
-        7 U-17
- 514 24 A-1
- 518 24 A-1

63 WING
- 522 23 F-5A/B
-        7 RF-5
- 536 17 F-5
- 540 17 F-5
- 542 17 F-5
- 544 17 F-5

43 WING
- 221 38 UH-1
- 223 38 UH-1
- 231 38 UH-1
- 245 38 UH-1
- 251 38 UH-1
- 237 16 CH-47
- 259E 12 UH-1

TAN SON NHUT

5TH AIR DIV

33 WING
- 314   4 VC-47
-        4 UH-1
-        2 U-17
- 716 12 RC-47
-        2 EC-47
-        2 C-47
-        8 U-6
- 718 20 EC-47
- 431 16 C-7
- 259G 12 UH-1

53 WING
- 819 18 AC 119G
- 821 10 AC 119K
- 435 16 C-130
- 429 16 C-7
- 437 16 C-130

Figure 3. Aircraft Strength-3rd Air Division, Bien Hoa AB; Aircraft Strength-5th Air Division, Tan Son Nhut AB, Oct 73

SOURCE: DAO Quarterly Assessment 1 Jul 73-1 Oct 73, Oct 73, p. 6-7. (CMR S-890, 111)

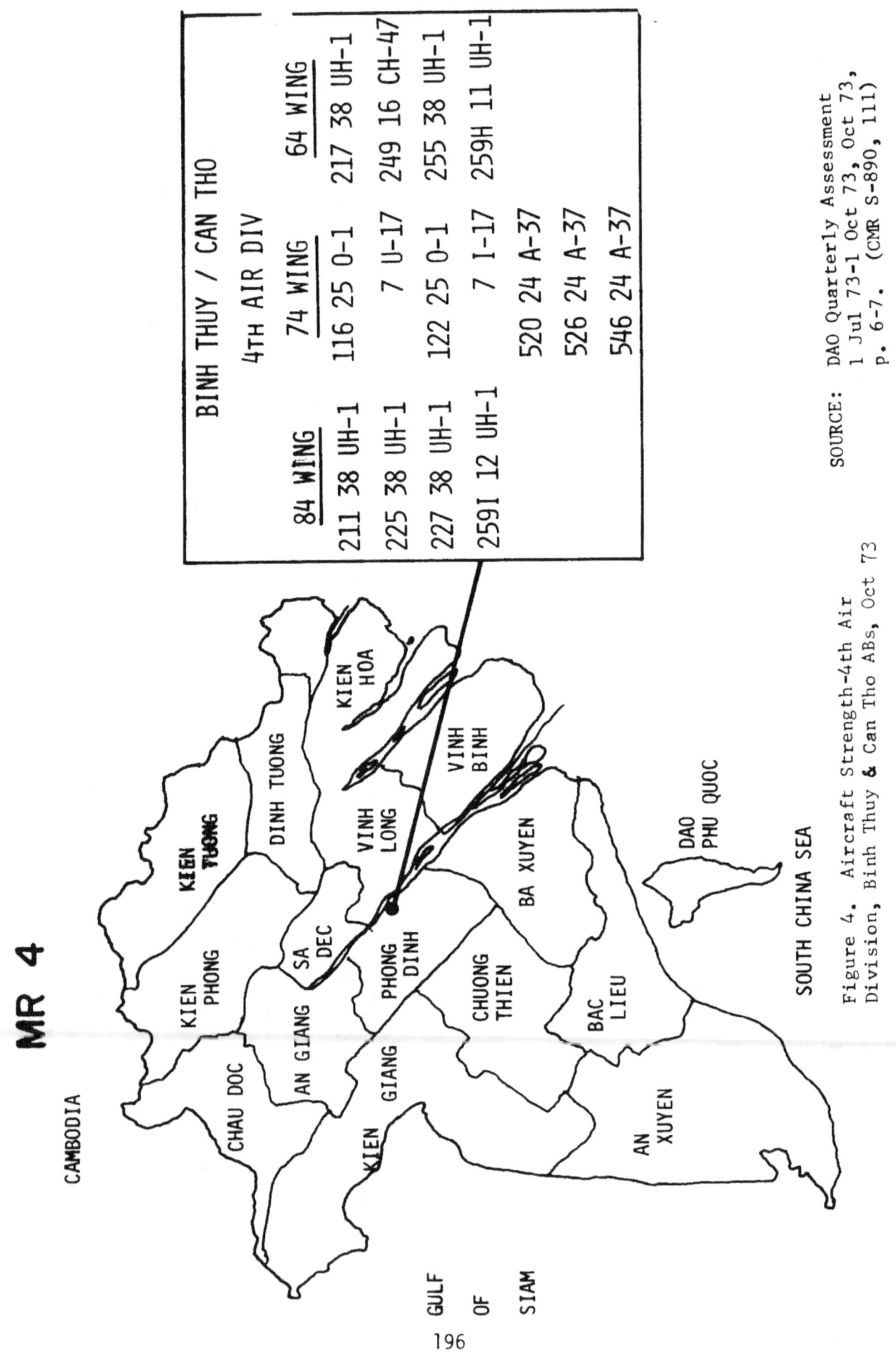

Figure 4. Aircraft Strength-4th Air Division, Binh Thuy & Can Tho ABs, Oct 73

SOURCE: DAO Quarterly Assessment 1 Jul 73-1 Oct 73, Oct 73, p. 6-7. (CMR S-890, 111)

FOOTNOTES*(U)

1. (S) CHECO Report, <u>Vietnamization of the Air War 1970-1971 (U)</u>, 8 Oct 71, pp. 4-5.

2. (TS) Ltr, Maj Gen Leslie W. Bray, Jr., DCS Plans & Ops, USAF to Maj Gen Ernest C. Hardin, Jr., Vice Cmdr, 7AF, 29 May 71, with 4 atchs: (1) Summary of Issues & Actions (U); (2) SEAsia Sortie Rates (U); (3) Credible Chase Briefing (U); (4) Draft Memo for SECDEF (U). (Hereafter cited as "Background to Secretary's Visit (U)." [CMR TS-103, 209]

    (S) <u>Vietnamization of the Air War 1970-1971 (U)</u>, p. 6.

3. (S) Conference Summary: Semi-Annual VNAF I&M/USAF Withdrawal Conference (14-15 July 1971) Summary (U), USAF (SDC), 30 Jul 71. (Hereafter cited as "Withdrawal Conference (U).") [CMR S-510, 37]

4. Ibid.

    (TS) Background to Secretary's Visit (U).

    (S) Msg: CINCPAC to JCS, Subj: "RVNAF I&M Program (U)," 190558Z Apr 71. [CMR TS-101, 26-27]

5. Ibid.

6. (TS) Background to Secretary's Visit (U).

7. Ibid.

8. Ibid.

    (S) Withdrawal Conference (U).

9. (TS) Background to Secretary's Visit (U).

    (TS) "RVNAF I&M Program (U)," 190558Z Apr 71.

10. (S) <u>Vietnamization of the Air War 1970-1971 (U)</u>, pp. 41, 43, 85.

    (S) Msg: AFGP, Subj: "VNAF Capabilities (U)," 270122Z Jul 71. [CMR TS-102, 204]

11. (S) <u>Vietnamization of the Air War 1970-1971 (U)</u>, p. 43.

---

* The security classification of material extracted from sources cited in this report may be lower than the overall classification of the sources indicated below, but it is no higher than the classification assigned to the corresponding paragraph of the text.

12. (S) Withdrawal Conference (U).

13. (S) Msg: "VNAF Capabilities (U)," 270122Z Jul 71.

14. (S) Memo, AFGP/XP, "RVNAF Improvement and Modernization (U)," 21 Jul 71, with 3 atchs: (1) Response to 4c (U); (2) Response to 4d and 4g (U); (3) Response to 4e (U). (Hereafter cited as "RVNAF I&M (U).")
[CMR TS-191, 144]

15. Ibid.

16. (S) Vietnamization of the Air War 1970-1971 (U), pp. 45, 85.

17. Ibid.

18. Ibid.

19. Ibid., pp. 50-51, 87.

20. Ibid.

    (S) Memo: "RVNAF I&M (U)."

21. Ibid.

22. (S) Background to Secretary's Visit (U).

23. (S) Vietnamization of the Air War 1970-1971 (U), p. 39.

24. Ibid., pp. 36-40, 83.

25. Ibid.

    (S) Memo: "RVNAF I&M (U)."

26. (S) Vietnamization of the Air War 1970-1971 (U), pp. 55-56.

27. (S) Withdrawal Conference (U).

28. Ibid.

    (S) Vietnamization of the Air War 1970-1971 (U), pp. 59-65.

29. (S) Vietnamization of the Air War 1970-1971 (U), p. 11.

30. (S) Backaground to Secretary's Visit (U).

31. (S) <u>Vietnamization of the Air War 1970-1971 (U)</u>, pp. 11-20.

32. Ibid., p. 20.

33. Ibid., pp. 66-69.

    (S) Withdrawal Conference (U).

34. (C) Ltr, 7AF/CS, Brig Gen Otis C. Moore to 7AF/DO, Subj: "Special Survey (U)," 19 Jul 71. [CMR TS-106, 102]

35. (C) Ltr, 7AF/XP to numerous agencies, Subj: "Special Survey (U)," 5 Oct 71, with 1 atch: "Special Survey Excerpts (U)." [CMR TS-106, 102]

36. (TS) Intvw, Capt Thomas D. Des Brisay, Project CHECO, with Col James T. Nelson, Director of the Air Force Division, DAO, Saigon, 28 Oct 73. [CMR TS-232, 108]

37. (U) EOT Report, Col Cline, AFAT-6, 19 Jul 72. [CMR S-820, 8]

    (TS) Msg, AFGP to CSAF, Subj: "Reactivation of 981/982 (U)," 251055Z Apr 72. [CMR TS-192, 166]

38. (S) Review, MACV, "RVNAF Force Structure Review, FY 73 (U)," 12 Jan 72, Annex F, pp. 1 and 2. (Hereafter cited as FSR-73 (U).)[CMR TS-121,17]

39. Ibid., pp. 2, A-1.

40. (S) Briefing, AFGP/XP to Secretary Shedler, Asst Sec of AF for Financial Management, 12 Oct 72, p. 1. [CMR TS-192, 059]

    (S) Msg, AFGP to CINCPACAF, Subj: "VNAF FY 73 Objectives (U)," 020136Z Feb 72. [CMR S-820, 18]

41. (S) FSR-73 (U), Annex F, pp. 6-7.

42. (S) "VNAF FY 73 Objectives (U)," 020136Z Feb 72.

43. (S) FSR-73 (U), Annex F.

    (S) EOT Report by Col Raymond A. Boyd, USAF Director of Plans and Programs, AFGP, 14 Jul 72, p. 6.

    (TS) Msg, COMUSMACV, <u>Credible Chase Combat Evaluation (U)</u>, 011421Z Feb 72. [CMR TS-122,155]

44. (S) Ltr, Gen John D. Lavelle, Cmdr 7AF to COMUSMACV, Subj: "VNAF Manning Requirements (U)," 29 Nov 71. [CMR TS-191, 152]

   (S) Ltr, Maj Gen James H. Watkins, Chief AFGP, to MACJ-1, Subj: "Recruitment Authority for VNAF (U)," 29 Dec 71. [CMR S-820, 17]

   (S) Col Boyd EOT Report, p. 10.

45. (S) Col Boyd EOT Report, pp. 9-10.

46. Ibid.

   (S) Ltr, Director of Plans and Programs, AFGP to Hq VNAF, DCS Plans, Subj: "VNAF Force Structure Planning, FY 73 (U)," 28 May 72. [CMR S-820, 26]

47. (TS) Col Nelson Intvw.

48. (TS) "Reactivation of 981/982 (U)," 251055Z Apr 72.

49. (TS) Msg, CSAF to numerous agencies, Subj: "VNAF Combat Effectiveness (U)," 251246Z May 72. [CMR TS-192, 169]

50. (S) Msg, JCS to CINCPAC/COMUSMACV, Subj: "Military Assistance to the RVN (Project Enhance) (U)," 231923Z May 72. [CMR TS-192, 169]

51. (TS) Col Nelson Intvw.

52. (TS) Plan, USAF/LG, USAF Logistics Plan for Vietnam Air Force, Annex U, Project Enhance Directive (U), 30 May 72. (Hereafter cited as Annex U, V-Log.) [CMR TS-219, 200]

53. (S) Briefing to Secretary Shedler, p. 1.

   (S) Briefing, AFGP/XR to Gen Jumper, Cmdr AFGP, Subj: "VNAF Authorizations FY 72 and FY 73 (U)," 28 Jul 72. [CMR TS-192, 4]

54. (S) Talking Paper, AFGP/XR, Subj: "VNAF Force Structure (U)," 13 Jan 73. [CMR TS-191, 190]

55. (S) Msg, AFGP to COMUSMACV, et. al., Subj: "Revised VNAF FY 1973-74 Force Structure (U)," 130701Z Dec 72. [CMR S-890, 56]

56. (TS) Col Nelson Intvw, p. 29.

57. (S) Msg: Project Enhance Plus Policy and Guidance (U), CSAF 260323Z Oct 72. [CMR TS-169, 75]

58. (TS) Col Nelson Intvw, pp. 6-19.

59. Ibid., pp. 18-19.

   (U) Talking Paper, AFGP/XR, Air Logistics Command (U), 12 Jan 73. [CMR TS-191, 190]

   (TS) History: MACV History, January 1972-March 1973 (U), MACV, 15 Jul 73, Vol II, p. E-46.

60. (TS) Col Nelson Intvw, pp. 25, 26.

   (U) Air Logistics Command.

61. (S) Msg, 7AF, "VNAF Force Structure," 291030Z Nov 72.

62. (S) Report, Major General James J. Jumper, Chief AFGP, Project CORONA HARVEST End of Tour Report (U), 14 Jun 73, Tab A, pp. 1-2.

63. (TS) Col Nelson Intvw, pp. 25, 26.

64. (S) Msg, AFGP to CSAF, Subj: "Enhance Plus Additives and Revised VNAF Force Structure (U)," 011040Z Dec 72. [CMR S-833, 75]

65. Ibid.

66. Ibid.

67. (S) Ltr, Maj Gen J. J. Jumper, Chief, AFGP, to Lt Gen Tran Van Minh, Cmdr, VNAF, 9 Dec 72. [CMR S-833, 84]

68. (S) Paper, USAF, Evaluation of VNAF Force Structure (U), 22 Jan 73. (Hereafter cited as "USAF Paper (U).") [CMR TS-219, 181]

69. (S) Msg, AFGP to CINCPACAF, Subj: "Revised VNAF FY 73-74 Force Structure (U)," 280050Z Dec 72. [CMR S-833, 92]

70. (S) Msg, CINCPACAF to CSAF, Subj: "Revised VNAF FY 73-74 Force Structure (U)," 280050Z Dec 72. [CMR S-833, 92]

71. (S) USAF Paper (U).

72. (TS) Col Nelson Intvw.

　(S) Intvw, Capt Thomas D. Des Brisay, Project CHECO, with Mr. Paul L. Tollestrup, Dep Ch AF Div, DAO, Saigon, at ALC Bien Hoa AB RVN, 26 Nov 72. [CMR TS-232, 115]

　(S) Intvw, Capt Thomas D. Des Brisay, Project CHECO, with Col Ben H. Carnell, Commander ALC, Bien Hoa, at DAO, Saigon, 25 Nov 73. [CMR TS-232, 113]

73. (TS) Col Nelson Intvw, p. 30.

74. (S) Hist, First Quarter 1973 DAO Saigon Historical Report (U), 7 May 73. [CMR TS-213, 108]

　(TS) Col Nelson Intvw, p. 24.

75. (S) Background Paper, DAO (XOU), Vietnamization Program and Future Air Force Responsibilities (U), 27 Feb 73. [CMR TS-219, 181]

76. (U) Plan, USAF/LG, VNAF Logistics Guidance--Background, Status, Objectives (U), 6 Mar 73, pp. 1-2. [CMR S-897, 83]

77. (TS) Plan, USAF/LGXX, VNAF Maintenance Plan (U), 15 Dec 72, pp. 3, 5. [CMR TS-219, 179]

78. (U) Paper, DAO/AOSAF (Air Force Division), RVNAF Self-Sufficiency Progress, 1973. [CMR TS-220, 105]

79. (S) Report, DAO, Saigon, DAO Quarterly Assessment of Vietnamization of the VNAF, 1 Apr-1 Jul 73 (U), 24 Jul 73, p. 6-43. [CMR S-897, 53]

80. (TS) VNAF Maintenance Plan, p. 3.

81. (TS) Col Nelson Intvw.

82. (U) Ltr, Lt Gen Tran Vanh Minh, VNAF Cmdr, to Maj Gen Murray, Chief of the U.S. DAO, Saigon, 20 Aug 73. (Hereafter cited as Ltr, Gen Tran Vanh Minh, 20 Aug 73.) [CMR S-897, 177]

83. (TS) Col Nelson Intvw, p. 34.

84. (U) Plan, DAO, Saigon, United States Air Force Logistics Plans for the Vietnamese Air Force (Short Title, V-Log, Sep 73) (U), Sep 73, pp. 104. [CMR TS-220, 18]

85. (S/NFD) Report, DAO, Saigon, RVNAF Quarterly Assessment (U), Oct 73, pp. 12-1 through 12-14, and 12-28.

86. Ibid., pp. 12-10 through 12-12.

87. Ibid.

   (S) Report, Project CHECO, Hq PACAF, <u>Vietnamization of the TACS (U)</u>, 23 Sep 74.

88. (S/NFD) RVNAF Quarterly Assessment (U), Oct 73, p. 12-10.

89. Ibid.

90. Ibid., p. 12-12.

   (S) Vietnamization of the TACS (U).

91. (S/NFD) RVNAF Quarterly Assessment (U), Oct 73, p. 12-12.

92. (S) Vietnamization of the TACS (U).

93. (S) Col Boyd EOT Report, p. 7.

94. (S) Memo, JCSM-449-72, Aircraft for the Vietnamese Air Force (U), 11 Oct 72, Annex A. [CMR TS-180, 198]

95. (S) Msg, AFGP to CINCPACAF, Subj: "Progress of Vietnamization (U)," 200630Z Apr 72. [CMR TS-192, 129]

96. (TS) Msg, CINCPAC to JCS, Subj: "Logistics Requirements (U)," 230130Z Apr 72. [CMR TS-192, 164]

97. (S) Talking Paper, AFGP/XR, Subj: "Fighter Aircraft (U)," 9 Oct 72. [CMR TS-191, 156]

98. (TS) Memo, Brig Gen Richard G. Cross, Chief, Air Ops Div, MACV, Review of RVNAF Mid-Range Force Structure Plan (U), 5 Oct 72. [CMR TS-182, 21]

99. (S) JCSM-449-72, 11 Oct 72.

100. (S) Fact Sheet, DAO (AOSOP-O), Status of RVNAF at X Plus 90 (U), 1 May 73. [CMR TS-213, 117]

101. (TS) Report, EOT Report, Col John F. Nuding, Hq 7AF, 1972. [CMR TS-166, 116]

   (C) Plan, AF/LGF, VNAF F-5E Aircraft Logistics Support Plan (U), 27 Sep 73. [CMR TS-220, line 17]

102. (S) Ltr, AFGP/XP to MACDO-52, Subj: "Military Assistance to the RVN (U)," 26 May 72. [CMR TS-191, 107]

103. (S) Briefing to Secretary Shedler (U), 12 Oct 72.

104. (S) JSCM-449-72 (U), 11 Oct 72, Annex, p. 1.

105. (S) "Revised VNAF FY 1973-74 Force Structure (U)," 130701Z Dec 72.

106. (S) "DAO Quarterly Assessment (U)," 24 July 73, p. 6-1.

107. (C) Fact Sheet, DAO/AOSOP-OT, RVNAF Air Defense Capability (U), 9 Aug 73. [CMR TS-220, 61]

108. (S) Msg, DAO to CINCPACAF, Subj: "VNAF F-5 Augmentation (U)," 110945Z Oct 73. [CMR TS-219, 39]

109. (TS) Col Nelson Intvw, p. 42.

   (S) Report, 7AF/DOTACLO, SOFLO Activity Report #24-72 (16-30 Jun 72) (U), 27 Jun 72, p. 1.

   (S) Report, 7AF/DOTACLO, SOFLO Activity Report #29-72 (1-15 Sep 72) (U), 15 Sep 72, p. 3.

110. (S) DAO Quarterly Assessment (U), 24 Jul 73, pp. 6-43.

   (S) Fact Sheet, DAO/AOSOP-O, RVNAF Capability at X Plus 194 (U), 10 Aug 73. [CMR TS-220, 55]

111. (S) Fact Book, Assistant Secretary of the Air Force, Installation and Logistics--Alaska/Japan/Vietnam/Thailand (U), Mar 73, Item of Interest, Seek Point (U). [CMR S-901, 2]

112. Fact Sheet, USAF/DOOT, Seek Point (U), 2 Aug 73. [CMR S-897, 15]

113. (S) Report, USSAG/DOT, DAO Saigon Trip Report (19-24 Nov 73) (U), 3 Dec 73.

114. (S/NFD) RVNAF Quarterly Assessment (U), Oct 73.

115. (TS) Intvw, Capt Thomas D. Des Brisay, Project CHECO, with Lt Col James Alexander, USSAG/DOT, at Nakhon Phanom RTAFB, Thailand, 26 Apr 74.

(S) Report, DAO, Saigon, VNAF Operational Activities, Capabilities, Intentions (U), 18 Sep 73.

(S) DAO Saigon Trip Report (19-24 Nov 73)

(S) Assessment of Probable Outcome of Major Hostilities in Vietnam (U).

116. (S) DAO Saigon Trip Report (19-24 Nov 73) (U).

117. (S/NFD) Report, DCS/I, PACAF, VNAF Operational Activities, August 1973 (U), 7 Sep 73.

(S) VNAF Operational Activities, Capabilities, Intentions (U).

(S/NFD) RVNAF Quarterly Assessment (U), Oct 73, p. 12-10.

118. (S) DAO Saigon Trip Report (19-24 Nov 73) (U).

(S/NFD) Report, DCS/I, PACAF, PACAF Humint Collation Report 02-73 (U), 20 Sep 73.

119. Ibid.

(TS) Lt Col Alexander Interview (U).

(S) Report, USSAG/DOT, Report of the USSAG Assistance Team to DAO Saigon (U), 25 Mar 74.

120. (S/NFD) RVNAF Quarterly Assessment (U), Oct 73, pp. 2-15, 2-17.

(S) Report, USSAG/DOT, Report of the USSAG Assistance Team to DAO Saigon (U), 31 Dec 73.

121. (S/NFD) VNAF Operational Activities; August 1973 (U).

122. (S) Progress of Vietnamization (U), 200630Z Apr 72.

(S) Military Assistance to the RVN (U), 26 May 72.

123. (TS) Msg, CINCPACAF to CINCPAC, Subj: "A-1s and AC-119K's (U)," 092130Z Nov 72. [CMR TS-180, 206]

124. (S) Msg, Gen Vogt, Cmdr 7AF to Gen Clay, Cmdr PACAF, Subj: "A-1 and AC-119K (U)," 061153Z Nov 72. [CMR TS-180, 206]

125. (S) Revised VNAF FY 1973-74 Force Structure (U), 130701Z Dec 72.

   (S) Msg, 7AF, AC-119K Aircraft Transfer (U), 170045Z Jan 73.

   (C) Msg, CINCPACAF, Personal Congratulations (U), 132200Z Mar 73.

126. (S) VNAF Operational Activities, Capabilities, Intentions (U).

   (S) Report of the USSAG Assistance Team to DAO Saigon (U), 25 Mar 74.

   (TS) Msg, COMUSMACV to CINCPAC, Subj: "Progress of Vietnamization (U)," 171045Z Apr 72. [CMR TS-192, 127]

127. (TS) Military Assistance to the RVN (U), 231923Z May 72.

   (S) Msg, CINCPACAF to CINCPAC, Review of RVN Security Assistance Program Objective (U), 190331Z Sep 73.

128. (S) Msg, AFSSO, NKP, ["Proposed Enhancement of the RVNAF (U)"], 190950Z Dec 73.

129. (S) Report of the USSAG Assistance Team to DAO Saigon (U), 31 Dec 73.

   (S) Report of the USSAG Assistance Team to DAO Saigon (U), 25 Mar 74.

   (S) Msg, CINCPAC, Material Requirements of Republic of Vietnam Armed Forces (RVNAF) (U), CINCPAC, 032105Z Dec 73.

130. Ibid.

   (TS) Lt Col Alexander Interview (U).

131. (U) Talking Paper, AFGP/XR, GVN DOD Talking Paper for Westpac Visit (U), 30 Oct 71.

132. (S) Paper, Lt Gen Snavely, USAF DCS/System & Logistics, C-130 for the VNAF (U), Mar 73. [CMR TS-219, 177]

133. (S) Progress of Vietnamization (U), 200630Z Apr 72.

134. (S) C-130 for the VNAF (U), Mar 73.

135. (C) Proposal, AFGP/DO, Proposed CROC for Modernization of VNAF Transport Fleet (U), 24 Jun 72. [CMR S-821, 86]

137. (S) C-130 for the VNAF (U), Mar 73.

138. (TS) Review of RVNAF Mid-Range Force Structure Plan (U), 5 Oct 72.

139. (S) C-130 for the VNAF (U), Mar 73.

    (S) Briefing to Secretary Shedler (U), 12 Oct 72.

    (S) Memo, MACV, Meeting Between DEPCOMUS and Mr. E. J. Shafer (GAO) (U), 9 Oct 72.

    (S) C-130 for the VNAF (U), Mar 73.

140. Ibid.

    (S) Revised VNAF FY 1973-74 Force Structure (U), 130701Z Dec 72.

141. (S) Report, DAO, Saigon, Military Assistance Program, V-12 Report (U), July 1973. (Hereafter cited as MAP Report (U), with appropriate date.)

142. (C) Fact Sheet, DAO/AOSRD, Aerial Resupply (U), 9 Aug 73. [CMR TS-220, 50]

    (C) Fact Sheet, DAO/AOSAF, VNAF C-123K Aircraft Performance (U), 27 Sep 73. [CMR TS-220, 16]

143. (U) Fact Sheet, DAO/AOSAF, Status of VNAF C-130A Aircraft Program (U), 27 Sep 73. [CMR TS-220, 34]

144. (S) C-130 for the VNAF (U), Mar 73.

145. (U) Fact Sheet, RVNAF Logistics Fact Sheet #5, VNAF Equipment Modernization (U), Oct 73. [CMR TS-219, 125]

146. (U) Memo, DAO/AOSDA for Lt Gen Khuyen, RVNAF Logistics Fact Sheet #5, VNAF Equipment Modernization, October 1973 (U), 17 Oct 73. [CMR TS-219, 125]

147. (S) Col Nelson Intvw, p. 37.

148. (S) Mr. Tollestrup Intvw, p. 8.

149. (S) Status of RVNAF at X Plus 90 (U), 1 May 73.

    (S) RVNAF Capability at X Plus 194 (U), 10 Aug 73.

150. (C) Msg, DAO, Saigon to COMUSSAG, Subj: "DAO Status Report of Selected SEAsia Activities; Overview of RVNAF Logistics System (U), 310245Z May 73. [CMR S-901, 199]

151. (TS) Col Nelson Intvw, p. 37.

152. (S) Meeting Between DEPCOMUS and Mr. F. J. Shafer (GAO) (U), Tab B, 9 Oct 72.

   (C) Msg, AFGP to CSAF, Subj: "VNAF Employment (U)," 110300Z Nov 72. [CMR S-820, 13]

153. (TS) Col Nelson Intvw, p. 37.

   (S) Msg, Maj Gen Hardin, Vice Cmdr 7AF, to Gen Ryan, CSAF, and Gen Nazarro, CINCPACAF, 081130Z Apr 71. [CMR TS-101, 26]

   (TS) Msg, USAF to PACAF/7AF, Subj: "RVNAF Helicopter Force Structure (U)," 112100Z May 71. [CMR TS-121]

   (S) Memo, Gen Lavelle, Cmdr 7AF to MACV/CS, MACV VNAF Helicopter Project Group Report (U), 7 Sep 71. [CMR TS-104, 39]

154. (S) Meeting Between DEPCOMUS and Mr. F. J. Shafer (GAO) (U), Tab B, 9 Oct 72.

155. (S) Revised VNAF FY 1973-74 Force Structure (U), 130701Z Dec 72.

   (S) Report, AFGP, Enhance Plus After Action Report, 26 Oct 72-21 Dec 72 (U), Jan 73, pp. 32-33.

156. (TS) Col Nelson Intvw, p. 37.

157. (C) Study, AFGP/DOI, Study on VNAF O-1 Utilization (U), 8 Jul 72. [CMR S-827, 172]

158. (C) Memo, AFGP/DOI, "Field Trip I thru IV Corps (U)," undated, circa Jul 73. [CMR S-827, 172]

159. Ibid.

160. (C) Memo, AFGP/DOT, "Staff Visit to I Corps (U)," 12 Aug 72. [CMR S-827, 188]

161. (C) Msg, AFGP/AFAT-2 to AFGP/DO, Subj: "FAC Evaluation Report (U)," 190355Z Aug 72. [CMR S-827, 176]

162. (S/NFD) RVNAF Quarterly Assessment (U), Oct 73, p. 12-12.

   (S) Report of the USSAG Assistance Team to DAO Saigon (U), 31 Dec 73.

163. (S) Msg, AFGP, Transfer of 35 O-2 Aircraft to the VNAF, 091020Z Nov 72.

    (S) Enhance Plus After Action Report (U), p. 35.

164. (U) Ltr, Brig Gen James H. Watkins, Cmdr AFGP to 7AF/DO, Subj: "VNAF Reconnaissance (U)," 24 Aug 71. [CMR TS-193, 6]

165. (S) Fact Sheet, DAO/AOSOP, VNAF Air Reconnaissance Capability (U), 10 Aug 73. [CMR TS-220, 47]

    (S) Memo, 7AF/DO to 7AF/CS, Improved Camera System for MAP RF-5 Aircraft (U), 5 Aug 72. [CMR TS-161, 15]

166. (C) Report, DAO, Saigon, Air Reconnaissance and Aerial Photography Capabilities of the VNAF (U), 18 Sep 73.

    (S) Review, PACAF/XOOQ, Review of Improved VNAF Photo Recon Capability Actions (U), Jun 74.

167. (TS) Col Nelson Intvw, p. 28.

    (S) VNAF Air Reconnaissance Capability (U), 10 Aug 73.

    (C) Air Reconnaissance and Aerial Photography Photography Capabilities of the VNAF (U).

168. (S) VNAF Air Reconnaissance Capability (U), 10 Aug 73.

169. (S) Paper, AFGP/DOI, Status of the VNAF Sensor Program (U), with atch, 31 May 72. [CMR TS-193, 87]

170. (C) Ltr, AFGP/DOO to AFGP/XR, Reevaluation of Combat ROC's (U), 20 Nov 72. [CMR S-821, 62]

    (S) Status of the VNAF Sensor Program (U), with attachments.

171. (S) Msg, AFGP, Subj: "PAR/PART Cancellation (U)," 181015Z Dec 72. [CMR S-828, 187]

172. (TS) Col Nelson Intvw, pp. 28-29.

173. Ibid.

    (C) Fact Sheet, DAO/AOSAF, EC-47 Surveillance Aircraft (U), 27 Sep 73. [CMR TS-220, 34]

    (S/NFD) RVNAF Quarterly Assessment (U), Oct 73, pp. 3-14, 3-15.

174. (S) Memo, AFGP/XR, Aircraft for VNAF Market Time Operations (Ocean Surveillance Patrol) (U), 15 Nov 71. [CMR TS-191, 147]

175. (C) Staff Summary Sheet, AFGP/XR, Visual Aerial Reconnaissance & Surveillance (VARS) (U), 18 Sep 72, with attachments. [CMR TS-192, 78]

176. (S) Review, COMUSNAVFORCES, Vietnam, Market Time Review 1972 (U), 24 Jun 72. [CMR TS-193, 57]

(S) Msg, AFGP/CC to COMUSMACV, Subj: "VNAF Maritime Patrol Squadron (U)," 110301Z Jan 73. [CMR S-833, 134]

177. (S) "VNAF Maritime Patrol Squadron (U)," 110301Z Jan 73.

178. (S/NFD) Msg, COMNAVFORV, Saigon, "RVNAF Force Structure (U)," 190730Z Jan 73. [CMR S-833, 135]

179. (S) Talking Paper, AFGP/XP, RC-119C Program (U), 3 Aug 73. [CMR S-897]

180. Ibid.

181. (TS) Col Nelson Intvw, p. 26.

182. (S) DAO Saigon Trip Report (19-24 Nov 73) (U).

(S/NFD) DAO Quarterly Assessment (U), Oct 73, p. 12-10.

183. (S/NFD) VNAF Operational Activities, August 1973 (U).

184. (S) VNAF Operational Activities, Capabilities, Intentions (U), p. 5.

(S) Report of the USSAG Assistance Team to DAO Saigon (U), 31 Dec 73.

185. (S) Report of the USSAG Assistance Team to DAO Saigon (U), 25 Mar 74.

186. (C) Reevaluation of Combat ROCs (U), 20 Nov 72.

(C) Ltr, AFGP/DO/LG, Reevaluation of Combat ROCs (U), 9 Dec 72.

(S) Memo, PACAF/DOQ, Vietnamization (U), 22 Aug 73.

187. (S) <u>Vietnamization of the Air War 1970-1971 (U)</u>, p. 20.

188. (S) VNAF FY 73 Objectives (U), 020136Z Feb 72.

189. (S) Recruitment Authority for VNAF (U), 29 Dec 71.

190. (S) Col Boyd EOT Report.

191. (S) MAP Reports (U), 1st through 4th quarters, 1972.

192. (TS) Review of RVNAF Mid-Range Force Structure Plan (U), Oct 72.

193. (S) Briefing to Secretary Shedler (U), 12 Oct 72.

(TS) VNAF Maintenance Plan (U), 15 Dec 72.

194. (S) Report, U.S. Comptroller General, Report to the Congress, Logistics Aspects of Vietnamization--1969-72 (U), 31 Jan 73. (Hereafter cited as Logistics Aspects of Vietnamization (U).)

195. (U) Ltr, AFGP/TNI, On-the-Job Training (U), 26 Sep 72. [CMR TS-195, 135]

196. (S) Revised VNAF FY 1973-74 Force Structure (U), 130701Z Dec 72.

197. Ibid.

(U) Gen Tran Van Minh, 20 Aug 73 (U).

198. (S) Talking Paper, AFGP/TN/DO, Project Enhance Plus Training to 29 Dec 1972 (U), 28 Dec 72. [CMR TS-191, 186]

(C) Talking Paper, AFGP/TN/DO, Project Enhance Plus Training to 5 Jan 1972 (U), 4 Jan 73. [CMR TS-191, 187]

(C) Talking Paper, AFGP/TN/DO, Project Enhance Plus Training (U), 11 Jan 73. [CMR TS-191, 190]

199. (C) Report, AFGP/XR, Final Report-Transfer of U.S. Facilities to the VNAF (U), 10 Feb 73. [CMR S-900, 14]

200. (TS) Col Nelson Intvw, pp. 24, 39.

201. (S) First Quarter 1973 DAO Saigon Historical Report (U), 7 May 73.

(U) Talking Paper, DAO, VNAF Training (Off-shore) Talking Paper (U), 1973. [CMR S-897, 13]

(S) Point Paper, VNAF Aircrew Training (U), appears in (Installation and Logistics) Alaska/Japan/Vietnam/Thailand (U), Mar 73, already cited.

202. (U) Fact Sheet, DAO/AOSAF-LXT, Contractor OJT Training (U), 27 Sep 73. [CMR TS-220, 17]

    (S) Mr. Tollestrup Intvw (U), p. 11.

    (S/NFD) RVNAF Quarterly Assessment (U), 31 Oct 73, pp. 6-64.

    (TS) VNAF Maintenance Plan (U), 15 Dec 72, pp. 3-5.

    (S) Col Carnell Intvw (U), p. 5-7.

    (U) Fact Sheet, DAO/AOSSS-PM, Contract Support in RVN (U), 9 Aug 73. [CMR TS-220, 47]

    (U) Memo, GAO, Survey of U.S. Contract Activities in Support of the RVNAF--Interim Memorandum No. 1 (U), 5 Nov 73. (Hereafter cited as GAO Memo #1 (U).)

203. (S) Report, Major General James J. Jumper, Chief AFGP, Project CORONA HARVEST End-of-Tour Report (U), 14 Jun 73.

204. (S/NFD) RVNAF Quarterly Assessment (U), 31 Oct 73, pp. 6-1 through 6-5, and 6-53 through 6-56.

    (S) V-Log (U), Sep 73, pp. 2-3.

    (S) Memo, AFGP/XR, Visit by Mr. O'Dean, NSC (U), 6 Jul 73. [CMR S-820, 65]

    (U) GAO Memo #1 (U).

    (TS) Col Nelson Intvw (U), pp. 30-31.

    (S) Mr. Tollestrup Intvw (U), pp. 9, 11.

    (S) Col Carnell Intvw (U), pp. 5-9.

205. (C) Col Boyd EOT Report (U).

206. (U) Contract Support in RVN (U), 9 Aug 73.

207. (C) Col Nelson Intvw (U), pp. 30, 44.

208. (U) Fact Sheet, DAO/AOSAF, Overall VNAF Aircraft Maintenance Capability (U), 9 Aug 73.

    (U) Logistics Aspects of Vietnamization--1969-72 (U), pp. 94, 98.

209. (C) MAP Reports (U), 1st through 4th quarters, 1972.

(S) VNAF Measurement of Progress (U), 1st through 3rd quarters, 1972.

(C) Meeting Between DEPCOMUS and Mr. E. J. Shafer (GAO) (U), Tab 4.

210. (U) Audit, USAF Auditor General, Operational Review of the USAF Improvement and Modernization (I&M) of the Vietnamese Air Force (VNAF) Supply System (U), 27 Jul 71. [CMR TS-140]

(U) Audit, USAF Aud Gen, Report of Audit 4384-7, Common Item Support of VNAF Requirements, Tan Son Nhut AFB, RVN (U), 29 Jul 71. [CMR TS-140]

(U) Audit, USAF Aud Gen, Report of Audit 4320-2, Management of Aviation Fuels--Vietnamese Air Force, Bien Hoa AB, RVN (U), 31 Aug 71. [CMR TS-140]

(U) Audit, USAF Aud Gen, Audit Advice 4323-8, VNAF Improvement and Modernization (I&M) Program--Satellite Conversion of VNAF 1st Air Division (U), 27 Sep 71. [CMR TS-140, 19]

(U) Audit, USAF Aud Gen, Audit Advice 4320-615-2, Receipt of Selected USAF C-123 and AC-119G Assets Transferred to the Vietnamese Air Force Fifth Air Division (U), 17 Nov 71. [CMR TS-140, 20]

(U) Audit, USAF Aud Gen, Audit Advice 4320-615-1, Vietnamese Air Force Policies, Procedures, and Controls, Non-Operationally Ready--Supply (NORS) Requirements (U), 17 Nov 71. [CMR TS-140, 20]

(U) Audit, USAF Aud Gen, Audit Memorandum 4320-675-3, Repair Cycle Asset Control, VNAF 2nd Air Division, Nha Trang AB, RVN (U), 15 Jan 72. [CMR TS-140, 28]

(U) Audit, USAF Aud Gen, Memorandum 4320-675-3, Management and Control of Critical Supply Assets, Vietnamese Air Force (U), 2 Mar 72. [CMR TS-140]

(U) Audit, USAF Aud Gen, Audit Advice, 4320-675-5, Control of Reparable Assets, Air Logistics Command, Vietnamese Air Force (U), 28 Apr 72. [CMR TS-140, 31]

(U) Audit, USAF Aud Gen, Audit Advice 4320-675-6, Engine Management, Vietnamese Air Force (U), 28 Apr 72. [CMR TS-140]

(U) Summary, USAF Aud Gen, Summary Report of Audit, Operational Review of the USAF Improvement and Modernization of the Vietnamese Air Force Supply System (U), 29 Jul 72. [CMR TS-140, 4]

211. (S) Report, OASD, Deputy Assistance SECDEF Directorate for Military Assistance and Overseas Audits, Report on Review of the Maintenance of Equipment Furnished the Republic of Vietnam Armed Forces (U), 29 Oct 71, p. 2. [CMR TS-121, 52]

212. Ibid., p. 5.

213. (S) Memo, U.S. GAO, Saigon, GAO Review of the Adequacy of Accountability Controls Over Major End Items--Interim Memorandum No. 1 (U), 20 Nov 73. (Hereafter cited as GAO Review (U).)

214. (TS) Col Nelson Intvw (U), p. 14.

    (S) Msg, AFLC, Logistic Impact of Proposed Vietnam Air Force (VNAF) 66 Squadron Force Structure (S), 171735Z Jan 73.

215. Ibid.

    (U) VNAF Logistic Guidance-Background, Status, Objectives (U), 6 Mar 73, p. vi.

216. (U) Msg, AFAT-ALC/CC, Col Ben H. Carnell, to AFGP, and Hq PACAF/LG, Subj: "VNAF/ALC Master Planning Team (U)," 291000Z Jan 73. [CMR S-890, 7]

217. (U) VNAF Logistics Guidance--Background, Status, Objectives (U), 6 Mar 73.

218. Ibid.

219. Ibid.

220. (S) U.S. Comptroller General, Vietnamization: The Logistics Story (U), 1 Nov 72, Ch 1, p. 5.

221. Ibid., p. 6.

222. (TS) Col Nelson Intvw (U), pp. 32-33.

    (S) Vietnamization: The Logistics Story (U), 1 Nov 72.

223. (U) Memo, AFGP/LG, VNAF Air Logistic Computer System (U), 5 Oct 72. [CMR S-885, 127]

224. (TS) Col Nelson Intvw (U), pp. 19-21.

225. Ibid.

226. Ibid.

   (TS) Col Nelson Intvw (U), p. 13.

227. (U) Fact Sheet, DAO/AOSAF, Computer Downtime (U), 25 Sep 73. [CMR TS-220, 16]

228. (S) Mr. Tollestrup Intvw (U), p. 6.

229. (S) Col Carnell Intvw (U), pp. 13-14.

230. (U) Logistics Aspects of Vietnamization--1969-72 (U), p. 115.

231. (S) Logistic Impact of Proposed VNAF (U), 171735Z Jan 73.

232. (S) Msg, CSAF to AFLC Logistic Impacts of Proposed Vietnam Air Force (VNAF) 66 Squadron Force Structure (S), 292320Z Jan 73.

   (S) Fact Sheet, DAO/AOSAF, Status of Vietnamization at VNAF Air Logistics Command (U), 10 Aug 73.

   (S/NFD) RVNAF Quarterly Assessment (U), 31 Oct 73, p. 6-64.

   (U) Logistics Aspects of Vietnamization--1969-72 (U), p. 119.

233. (S) Fact Sheet, DAO/AOSAF, Overall Aircraft Maintenance Capability (U), 30 Sep 73. [CMR TS-220, 16]

234. (C) Msg, DAO to CINCPACAF, Logistical Support (U), 311001Z May 73.

235. (S) Mr. Tollestrup Intvw (U), p. 6.

236. (S) Overall Aircraft Maintenance Capability (U).

237. (S) DAO Quarterly Assessment (U), 24 Jul 73, pp. 6-43, 44.

238. (S/NFD) RVNAF Quarterly Assessment (U), Oct 73, pp. 6-35, 36, 6-44, 65.

239. (U) GAO Review (U), p. 3.

240. (S) Mr. Tollestrup Intvw (U), p. 10.

241. (C) Fact Sheet, DAO/AOSAF, Air Force Division Assessment (U), 10 Aug 73.

242. (S) Mr. Tollestrup Intvw (U), p. 12.

243. (U) Msg, 13AF, Maintenance Capability, 290500Z Dec 72.

244. (U) Ltr, Gen John D. Lavelle, Cmdr 7AF, VNAF I&M Program (U), circa Jan 73.

245. (C) Report, End-of-Tour Report, Lt Col Wilford C. Bain, USAF, Director C-E, 14 Jun 72. [CMR TS-195, 148]

   (S) Maj Gen Jumper EOT Report (U), p. 10.

246. (S) Rpt, Col Richard I. Skinner, DCS Plans, 7AF, Air Force Historical End-of-Tour Report Program (U), 6 Feb 73, p. 11.

247. (S) Maj Gen Jumper EOT Report (U), p. 11.

248. Ibid.

249. (S) Report, AFGP, COMUSMACV OPLAN J 215 Countdown After Action Report (U), 23 Mar 73, p. II-F-1.

250. Ibid., Tab 8.

   (S) Maj Gen Jumper EOT Report (U), P. 14.

251. (U) Msg, CINCPACAF to AFGP, Saigon, Subj: "VNAF Civil Engineering Supply Difficulties (U)," 282130Z Sep 73. [CMR S-897, 148]

252. Ibid.

253. (S) Maj Gen Jumper EOT Report (U), Tab D.

254. (U) Msg, CINCPACAF to DAO, Subj: "General Officer Review of VNAF, 20-25 Aug 73 (U)," 282130Z Sep 73. [CMR S-897, 148]

255. (U) Msg, DAO to CINCPACAF, Subj: "General Officer Review of VNAF, 20-25 Aug 73 (U)," 091007Z Oct 73. [CMR TS-219, 157]

256. Ibid.

257. Ibid.

258. (S/NFD) RVNAF Quarterly Assessment (U), Oct 73, p. 6-38.

259. Ibid., pp. 6-38 through 6-41.

260. (U) General Officer Review of VNAF, 20-25 Aug 73 (U), 091007Z Oct 73.

261. (C) Brochure, Lt Col Greene, USAF, Director, C-E, VNAF Communications and Electronics Brochure (U), Feb 73. [CMR S-897, 18]

262. (C) Lt Col Bain EOT Report (U).

263. Ibid.

(U) Staff Summary Sheet, AFGP/DC, Effect of Acquisition of Phu Cat and Phan Rang ABs and MR-1 Navigational Aids on VNAF C&E I&M Program (U), 25 Jan 72. [CMR TS-195, 116]

264. (S) Maj Gen Jumper EOT Report (U).

265. (U) Talking Paper, DAO/AOSAF-C, No title, 15 Aug 73. [CMR S-897, 38]

266. (U) Memo, DAO/AOSAF-CM, VNAF NAVAIDs and AC&W Radar Problems (U), 11 Aug 73. [CMR S-897, 35]

267. Ibid.

268. Ibid.

269. Ibid.

270. Ibid.

271. (S/NFD) RVNAF Quarterly Assessment, Oct 73, pp. 6-41 through 6-43.

272. (S) Ltr, AFGP/CC to MACJ3-031, U.S. Advisors in the RVN (U), 9 Oct 71, with attachment, Question/Answer Sheets (U). [CMR TS-121, 36]

273. (U) Report, 7AF Auditor General, Preparation of Summary Report--Audit Evaluation of the VNAF I&M Program (U), 15 May 72. [CMR S-885, 119]

274. (U) Survey, USAF Aud Gen, "Survey of Opinions--The Preparation of USAF Personnel for the VNAF Advisory Role (U)," 16 Dec 71. [CMR TS-140, 5]

275. Ibid.

276. Ibid.

277. Memo: The American Military Advisor and His Foreign Counterpart: The Case of Vietnam (U), G. C. Hickey, Mar 65. (C)

278. (TS) Col Nelson Intvw, pp. 24-25.

(S) Mr. Tollestrup Intvw, p. 4.

(S) Col Carnell Intvw, p. 1.

279. Ibid.

280. (U) Plan, AFGP/DO, Withdrawal Plan (U), 26 Jan 73. [CMR S-827, 160]

281. (TS) Col Nelson Intvw, p. 24.

282. (S) Col Carnell Intvw, pp. 3, 4, 15.

283. (S) Msg, AMEMBASSY Saigon, VNAF F5As (U), 120350Z Oct 73.

284. (S) Msg, JCS, Organization Changes in Southeast Asia (U), 270055Z Oct 73.

285. (C) Ltr, Maj Gen Jumper, AFGP/CC to Maj Gen Bray, Hq USAF/XOV, VNAF Standard of Living (U), 20 May 72. [CMR S-820, 108]

286. (S) Visit by Mr. O'Dean, NSC (U).

287. Ibid.

288. (S/NFD) RVNAF Quarterly Assessment (U), Oct 73, pp. 11-26 through 11-29.

289. (U) Fact Sheet, DAO/AOSSS-EA, Inflation, RVNAF Pay and Corruption (U), 10 Aug 73. [CMR TS-220, 47]

290. (U) Fact Sheet, DAO/AOSSS-EA, DOD Economic Support Programs (U), 10 Aug 73. [CMR TS-220, 47]

291. (S/NFD) RVNAF Quarterly Assessment (U), Oct 73, pp. 11-33, 34.

292. Ibid.

293. (TS) Col Nelson Intvw (U), pp. 38-40.

294. (S) Col Carnell Intvw (U), pp. 9, 11.

295. (TS) Col Nelson Intvw (U), p. 40.

296. (C) Fact Sheet, DAO/AOSOP-OR, RVNAF Capability (U), 9 Aug 73. [CMR TS-220, 48]

    (S/NFD) RVNAF Quarterly Assessment (U), Oct 73, foreword.

297. (S/NFD) RVNAF Quarterly Assessment (U), Oct 73, p. 13-1.

298. Ibid., p. 1-1.

299. (TS) Col Nelson Intvw (U), p. 35.

300. (S/NFD) RVNAF Quarterly Assessment (U), Oct 73, pp. 1-1 and 1-2.

301. Ibid.

302. Ibid.

303. Ibid.

304. (S) RVNAF Capability at X plus 194 (U).

    (S/NFD) RVNAF Quarterly Assessment (U), Oct 73, foreword and pp. 13-1, 2.

305. Ibid.

306. Ibid.

    (S) DAO Saigon Trip Report (10-24 Nov 73) (U).

    (TS) Lt Col Alexander Intvw (U).

307. (S) Msg, CSAF, Revised V-Log Tasking (U), 131947Z Mar 74.

308. (S) Col Carnell Intvw (U).

GLOSSARY (U)

AA	Antiaircraft
AAA	Antiaircraft Artillery
AB	Air Base
AC&W	Aircraft Control and Warning
AD	Air Defense, Air Division
AFGP	Air Force Advisory Group
AFLC	Air Force Logistics Command
AGE	Aerospace Ground Equipment
ALC	Air Logistics Command
ALO	Air Liaison Officer
AOB	Air Order of Battle
ARVN	Army of the Republic of Vietnam
ATC	Air Training Command
AWOL	Absent Without Leave
BCE	Base Civil Engineering
BOBS	Beacon Only Bombing System
CAS	Close Air Support
CE	Civil Engineering
C-E	Communications-Electronics
CHECO	Contemporary Historical Examination of Current Operations
CINCPAC	Commander-in-Chief, Pacific Command
CINCPACAF	Commander-in-Chief, Pacific Air Forces
COL	Colonel
COMUSMACV	Commander, U.S. Military Assistance Command, Vietnam
CONUS	Continental United States
CRIMP	Consolidated Republic of Vietnam Improvement and Modernization Program
CROC	Combat Required Operational Capability
CSAF	Chief of Staff, USAF
CY	Calendar Year
DAO	Defense Attache Office
DASC	Direct Air Support Center
DOD	Department of Defense
DRVN	Democratic Republic of Vietnam (North Vietnam)
ECM	Electronic Countermeasures
ELINT	Electronic Intelligence
FAC	Forward Air Controller
FFAR	Folding Fin Aircraft Rockets
FSR	Force Structure Review
FY	Fiscal Year

GCA	Ground Controlled Approach
GCI	Ground Controlled Intercept
GVN	Government of Vietnam
HUMINT	Human Resource Intelligence
I&M	Improvement and Modernization
INT	Interdiction
IR	Infrared
IRAN	Inspect and Repair as Necessary
IRCM	Infrared Counter Measures
JCS	Joint Chiefs of Staff
JGS	Joint General Staff
LOC	Lines of Communication
LTC	Lieutenant Colonel
LTL	Interprovincial Road
MACV	Military Assistance Command, Vietnam
MAP	Military Assistance Program
MEDEVAC	Medical Evacuation
MERS	Multiple Ejection Rack System
mm	milimeter
MR	Military Region
NAVAIDS	Navigational Aids
NCO	Non-commissioned Officer
NM	Nautical Mile
NOA	Not Operationally Aircraft
NORM	Not Operationally Ready, Maintenance
NORS	Not Operationally Ready, Supply
NSC	National Security Council
NSDM	National Security Council Decision Memorandum
NVA	North Vietnamese Army
NVAF	North Vietnamese Air Force
NVN	North Vietnam(ese)
O&I	Operations and Inspection
OJT	On-the-Job Training
OR	Operationally Ready
OSD	Office of the Secretary of Defense
PACAF	Pacific Air Forces
PAR	Palletized Airborne Relay
PARS	Palletized Airborne Relay System
PART	Palletized Airborne Relay Terminal
PCS	Permanent Change of Station
PDM	Periodic Depot Maintenance
PHOTINT	Photographic Intelligence
PMEL	Precision Measuring Equipment Laboratory

POL	Petroleum, Oil, and Lubricants
POW	Prisoner of War
RAM	Rapid Area Maintenance
RAS	Rapid Area Supply
Recce	Reconnaissance
RF	Regional Forces
RHAW	Radar Homing and Warning
ROC	Required Operational Capability
ROKAF	Republic of Korea Air Force
RVN	Republic of Vietnam
RVNAF	Republic of Vietnam Armed Forces
SA-7	Strella (Grail) Surface-to-Air Missile
SAM	Surface-to-Air Missile
SAR	Search and Rescue, Search and Recovery
SEA	Southeast Asia
SECDEF	Secretary ofDefense
SIGINT	Signal Intelligence
STOL	Short Take-off and Landing
SVN	South Vietnam
TACAIR	Tactical Aircraft
TACAN	Tactical Air Navigation
TACC	Tactical Air Control Center
TACS	Tactical Air Control System
TDY	Temporary Duty
TERS	Triple Ejection Rack System
TIC	Troops-In-Contact
TOC	Tactical Operations Center
TO&E	Table of Organization and Equipment
TSN	Tan Son Nhut
UDL	Unit Detail Listing
UE	Unit Equipment
UHT	Undergraduate Helicopter Training
UPT	Undergraduate Pilot Training
USA	U.S. Army
USARV	U.S. Army, Vietnam
USN	U.S. Navy
USSAG	U.S. Support Activities Group
VARS	Visual Aerial Reconnaissance and Surveillance
VC	Viet Cong
VFR	Visual Flight Rules
V-LOG	Vietnamization-Logistics
VMC	Visual Meteorological Conditions
VNAF	(South) Vietnamese Air Force
VNN	(South) Vietnamese Navy
VR	Visual Reconnaissance

www.ingramcontent.com/pod-product-compliance
Lightning Source LLC
Chambersburg PA
CBHW082117230426
43671CB00015B/2724